Freedom's Promise

Freedom's Promise

Ex-Slave Families and Citizenship
in the Age of Emancipation

ELIZABETH REGOSIN

UNIVERSITY PRESS OF VIRGINIA
CHARLOTTESVILLE AND LONDON

THE UNIVERSITY PRESS OF VIRGINIA
© 2002 by the Rector and Visitors of the University of Virginia
Printed in the United States of America on acid-free paper

First published 2002

9 8 7 6 5 4 3 2 1

LIBRARY OF CONGRESS CATALOGING-IN-PUBLICATION DATA
Regosin, Elizabeth Ann.
    Freedom's promise : ex-slave families and citizenship in the Age of
Emancipation/Elizabeth Regosin
        p.   cm.
    Includes bibliographical references and index
    ISBN 0-8139-2095-7 (cloth : alk. paper)—ISBN 0-8139-2096-5 (pbk : alk.
paper)
        1. Slaves—Emancipation—United States. 2. Liberty—Social aspects—
United States—History—19th century. 3. African American families—
History—19th century. 4. Freedmen—United States—Social conditions.
5. Freedmen—Legal status, laws, etc.—United States. 6. Citizenship—
United States—History—19th century.   I. Title.

E185.2 .R44 2002
973.7'14—dc21

                                            2001045573

For My Parents

Contents

Preface

*I*N 1897, after eight frustrating years of pursuing a Civil War pension, former slaves William and Alice Timmons wrote an impassioned plea to the commissioner of pensions: "We from our birth was called Wm and Alice Timmons . . . please allow us a chance to Identify ourselves." William and Alice, brother and sister, claimed a pension on behalf of their father's service in the United States Colored Troops. The success of their claim rested upon their ability to prove that they were their father's legitimate children, as the pension system required of all minors who claimed pensions.

William and Alice's case was complicated; as slaves, their familial relationships had been neither sanctioned nor protected by the law. Because they could not establish the existence of their parents' marriage under slavery, they failed to establish their own legitimacy. Their plea to the commissioner of pensions requesting confirmation of their very identity betrays their fear of the imminent rejection of their claim. As they so poignantly illustrated, a rejection meant not only a loss of financial compensation but the perpetuation of their illegitimacy and the denial of their identity.

William and Alice's plea on behalf of personal and familial identity reflects broad social and historical issues that frame this study of family in the transition from slavery to freedom in the United States. Emancipation and the citizenship that followed conferred upon former slaves the right to family. Family rela-

tionships were sanctioned, recognized, and regulated by the law
of domestic relations that governed the families of all citizens
of the country. What did the acquisition of legal familial status mean to former slaves, personally and socially? How actively
did former slaves pursue legal status? Were their lives changed
as individuals, as members of families, and within a broader social context? Among the many rights that citizenship conferred, did former slaves also envision the right to family?

Because the Civil War pension system presents the family at
the intersection of the personal and the political, it offers a fascinating source of documentation bearing on these questions.
The provisions made for Civil War pensions in 1862 and beyond created a vast social welfare system that compensated not
only eligible Union veterans but also the families who suffered
the loss of a husband, father, son, or brother who had served in
the war. In considering pension applications of soldiers' relatives, pension officials paid particular attention to how people
were related. By asking claimants to prove their affiliation, the
pension system obliged former slaves to reproduce and represent the inner workings of their familial relationships.

There is not a single answer to any of my questions, obviously, but a wide range that represents the expanse of former
slaves' family experiences in the years after emancipation. The
answers lie within the vibrant patchwork of lives and stories
that burst out of the pension records. They demonstrate the
pertinence of asking questions about the relationship between
citizenship and the families of former slaves.

I OWE A deep debt of gratitude to several people who have
helped this project come to fruition. During the dissertation
period Michael P. Johnson read and commented on everything
I ever asked him to look at and offered professional guidance
and his generosity of spirit. I must thank Michael Meier at the
National Archives for leading me to the Civil War pension
records and helping me to find my way through them. My gratitude goes also to my friend and colleague Donald Shaffer, who

shares my fascination with the pension records and who was a great help with the dissertation.

Joseph Reidy and Noralee Frankel helped to move this project from a dissertation to a book and have offered their support in the later stages. Reidy's comments on the dissertation and suggestions about making the transition to a book proved invaluable.

At a moment when I needed encouragement the most, my colleague Len Moore's thoughtful reading of the manuscript helped immensely. Never once did he object when I knocked on his door and interrupted his work so that he could read the latest paragraph I had written. I must also thank Rita Hewlett, Joan Larsen, and Sondra Smith, all of whom helped me pull the final pieces together with patience and good humor.

My debt to Peter Bardaglio is immeasurable. As the final reader for the University Press of Virginia, he went far beyond the call of duty, reading and commenting extensively on the entire manuscript three times and making the revision process a pleasure. I am grateful to have worked so closely with him, particularly in the final stages of the project.

My heartfelt thanks to Richard Holway at the University Press of Virginia for all his help and encouragement in the past several years.

My love and gratitude to my family, Tom, Anna, and Brittany. They have suffered and celebrated with me every step of the way.

Finally, and most importantly, I must thank my father for all he has done for me since I first began this project. He has read and commented upon nearly every word I have ever written and has treated my work with the respect of a colleague and the love of a parent.

Freedom's Promise

Introduction

I N 1777 Samuel Adams argued that the American experiment "shall succeed if we are virtuous. . . . I am infinitely
more apprehensive of the contagion of Vice than the Power of
all other Enemies."[1] From the Republic's inception Americans
believed that its survival depended upon a citizenry who were
virtuous. They defined this virtue both in the traditional republican sense of a willingness to sacrifice individual wants for
the good of the community and especially in a more personal
or private sense of individual piety, responsibility, and morality, the very antithesis of European monarchical corruption.[2]
How did a nation produce such citizens? What would be the
source of this virtue? As Linda Kerber has argued, American
republicanism relied upon institutions outside of government—churches, schools, and most notably families—to instill
virtue in its citizens. Typical of the age, Americans believed
that the qualities necessary to virtue were instilled in the home
during childhood and reinforced there during adulthood.
Throughout the nineteenth century Americans remained
steadfastly convinced that the family was the "seedbed of
virtue," the place where virtuous citizens were nurtured.[3]

Excluded from this constitutive role were slave families,
which, according to the laws that governed the slave South,
were not really families at all. To consider the slave a member
of a family was to accord a legal, social, and moral status that
could challenge or undermine the master's economic and so-

cial interests. How could a slave owner demand the full fruits of his slave's labor if that slave was obligated to provide for his own family? How could a slave owner command absolute obedience from a slave child if that child was under the rightful protection of his or her parents? How could a slave owner govern his slave's reproductive capacity and thus fulfill his need for manpower if she controlled it herself? These issues led southern lawmakers to ignore the existence of the slave family, to exclude slaves from the laws that governed other families, and to argue that slaves were not citizens and thus were not entitled to the right to civil marriage and its benefits.[4] For many in the South, denying family rights to slaves did not threaten the stability of the Republic.

More was at stake in the denial of family rights to slaves than the master's best interests, perhaps because the existence of slavery in America underscored the rights of those who were free. In his discussion of the enthusiasm of proslavery Virginians for the republican ideals of freedom and equality, Edmund Morgan has suggested that the immediate presence of slavery shaped the meaning of freedom: "Virginians may have had a special appreciation of the freedom dear to republicans, because they saw every day what life without it could be like."[5] And as Judith Shklar and others have contended, citizenship itself depended upon principles of exclusion and denial. Shklar has argued that American citizenship was constructed in contradistinction to slavery, in direct relation to what it was not; a person's citizenship was defined and affirmed by the constant presence of its antithesis in American society, the institution of slavery. The value of citizenship was measured by its denial to significant portions of the population, especially slaves. Tangible privileges of citizenship—those of suffrage and remuneration for one's labor—"marked" citizens precisely because slaves (as well as white women and many free African Americans, among others) did not possess them.[6] Extending this logic makes it proper to consider the right to family as a defining badge of citizenship.[7] When slaves were barred from formal marriage and other domestic relationships and denied the legal means to protect the sanctity of the family, they were relegated to a status unlike, and outside of, any other portion of American society.

How ironic it seems, then, that in 1866 former slave Louisa Caldwell was awarded a Civil War widow's pension, a return upon the death of the "husband" to whom she could not have been "married" under slavery. Louisa's case is striking in part because she exercised the right to compensation for military service, the government's reciprocal responsibility to the soldier who had risked his life for the Union. Although formerly a slave, her husband apparently was treated as a citizen because he joined the army. In fact, the government did extend this right of citizenship to former slaves and free blacks who had served in the United States Colored Troops (USCT) during the war, precisely because they served the Union as any citizen would have. What is more significant is that Louisa received the pension as an inheritance of sorts, a direct benefit of civil family relations to which she was entitled.[8] And Louisa's case was not an aberration; many former slave widows, children, parents, and siblings made successful claims for pensions predicated upon the very family relationships that slavery had attempted to deny.

African-American Citizenship

THE OPERATION of the pension system can serve as a dramatic and poignant example of the ambiguity that plagued the post-bellum era concerning the place of former slaves in American society. Pension claims initiated by former slaves invariably raised complicated questions about which rights newly freed African Americans would possess and about the relationship between their former status and their citizenship. Between 1862 and 1865 approximately 180,000 black soldiers served in the Union army, and of those, some 36,000 to 37,000 lost their lives.[9] When the war was over, and for many years after, black

Civil War veterans and the relatives of their deceased comrades exercised their newly won rights by applying for pensions from the government.

When the Thirteenth Amendment abolished slavery in 1865, it led Americans to ponder the meaning of citizenship anew. If slaves were slaves no more, no longer the defining polar opposite of the citizen's status, what did it mean to be a citizen? Debates over the Civil Rights Act of 1866 and the Fourteenth Amendment centered around highly controversial questions about what rights—civil, political, natural—citizenship entailed and under whose jurisdiction—state or federal—citizenship rights would be protected.[10] In those contentious discussions congressmen also debated the terms of citizenship for African Americans. Where would the former slave fit into this new society? Were former slaves to be on an equal plane with white citizens, offered the same rights of citizenship and the same protection? "What shall we do with the Negro?" politicians and abolitionists alike asked themselves. Would it be better to emancipate slaves as full citizens or to guide them gradually through the transition from slavery to citizenship? As Eric Foner has pointed out, the establishment of the Freedmen's Bureau, a temporary arm of the War Department created to assist slaves in the transition to freedom, suggested that the government was leaning toward the latter position, yet disagreement was rife among members of Congress and between Congress and the president about the citizenship rights to which newly freed slaves would be entitled.[11]

In the aftermath of the war and emancipation, President Andrew Johnson, southern legislators, and Democrats and moderate and radical Republicans in Congress battled over the extent to which African Americans would possess civil rights and political equality. In 1865 and 1866 lawmakers in Mississippi and South Carolina drafted the first, and most blatantly discriminatory, Black Codes. Theoretically designed to outline former slaves' new privileges and responsibilities, these state laws gave African Americans, among other rights, those of owning property, making contracts, and having access to the legal system. Overshadowing the gains of these basic rights of citizenship, however, were very restrictive measures, including the limitation of former slaves' mobility and labor options and the imposition of unequally harsh punishment for crimes. If the determination of their citizenship was left in the hands of the southern states, African Americans would possess neither full civil rights nor true political equality.[12]

In response to the harshness of the Black Codes and the belief that only the federal government could guarantee African Americans' civil rights in southern states, Republicans in Congress passed a civil rights act in 1866, overturning a presidential veto in the process. In an unprecedented expansion of the scope and power of the federal government, the Civil Rights Act of 1866 provided federal protection of African-American citizenship. The act guaranteed that "the inhabitants of every race" would possess the same basic rights of contract, property, and access to courts and that all would be treated equally under the laws, including equal punishment for violations of the law. State infringement on such rights or a state's failure to enforce civil rights would be prosecuted in federal courts, reversing the American tradition of making the individual states the guardians of citizenship.[13]

The Fourteenth Amendment provided constitutional backing for the Civil Rights Act of 1866. In part an effort to protect the act from repeal in the future, the amendment also represented an attempt to clean up the detritus left by the war: issues of war debts, the configuration of representation in a postslavery society, and the political fate of Confederate leaders.[14] In debate on the amendment, framers raised the oft-asked question of African-American suffrage: should this fundamental political privilege automatically follow emancipation? Both moderate and radical Republicans also were concerned about African-American suffrage because the Thirteenth Amendment nullified the prewar system of apportioning representation. With the demise of the three-fifths compromise, the provision in the Constitution that apportioned congressional representation by counting three-fifths of each state's total slave population, the South would have more representatives than it had in the past. Republicans saw African-American suffrage as a way to counter this potential rise in southern Democratic power because the new citizens were sure to vote with the party that had freed them.[15] In the end, despite the attention given the suffrage issue, congressmen put it on hold in favor of more general and relatively less problematic questions about guaranteeing basic civil rights.

Some lawmakers acknowledged that the Dred Scott decision, which had denied African-American citizenship, made it necessary to extend citizenship itself to African Americans by constitutional amendment.[16] Section 1 of the Fourteenth Amendment offered the first constitutional definition of a citizen: "All persons born or naturalized in the United States, and subject to the jurisdiction thereof, are citizens of the United States and of the State wherein they reside." A final repudiation of *Scott v. Sanford*, the amendment gave priority to national citizenship over state citizenship and extended both to African Americans.[17] Section 1 also guaranteed that every citizen's natural rights to "life, liberty, [and] property" would be protected from violation by individual states and that all citizens had "equal protection of the laws." With the ratification of the Fourteenth Amendment in 1868, African Americans' citizenship became constitutional fact, but the granting of voting rights was left to the discretion of individual states, reflecting the persistence of the long tradition of allowing states to control their own affairs in spite of newly expanded federal power. Though the amendment gave constitutional support to the guarantees of the 1866 act, it did not specify the rights of citizenship, nor did it explicitly extend equal political rights to African Americans.[18]

African-American males finally won the right to vote in 1870 when the states ratified the Fifteenth Amendment; African Americans now possessed what many perceived as the key to political equality and the surest sign of full citizenship. The Civil Rights Act and the Fourteenth and Fifteenth Amendments vested African Americans with many rights and protections of citizenship, yet discrimination in the labor market, unfair practices on the part of white landowners in the South, southern states' continued violation of their civil rights, and increasing violence against them served to remind African Americans that they were still not considered ordinary citizens. Procuring a constitutional promise of citizenship rights and their federal protection could not necessarily guarantee that African Americans would have access to the full fruits of citizenship.

Looking only at how Congress constructed a formal African-American citizenship and how states and individuals attempted to infringe upon it, however, obscures African Americans' informal assertion of their own citizenship in the actions they took in their daily lives. Citizenship was not only to be granted, to be given through statute or constitutional amendment, but was to be claimed, taken by those who so desired it. Fighting for the Union can be seen as a manifestation of the former slaves' hunger for citizenship, just as their demand for political rights both during and after the war indicated their aspiration to join "the people," to become full members of American society. In both cases former slaves acted like citizens, fulfilling the obligations of citizenship with the expectation that the action itself would produce the rewards or benefits of citizenship. The creation of a special branch of the armed forces in which African Americans could fight for the Union, the distribution of military pensions, the extension of suffrage and access to political office to African-American males, in part the results of their actions, suggest that former slaves contributed to the construction of their own citizenship.[19]

Former slaves' efforts to formalize family ties or to order their domestic affairs were also manifestations of the creation of their own citizenship. From the time the first tenacious slaves ran away to the Union army to well into the postwar era, former slaves were legalizing existing marriages or ending unsuitable relationships into which they had been forced under slavery.[20] They could have had many reasons to do so: to exercise their freedom, to be in compliance with the laws, to reap such benefits of formal family relations as access to an inheritance or a pension, and/or to reaffirm relationships that had been perpetually jeopardized in slavery. As they had done with military service, many former slaves took the right to family for themselves. The uniforms African American veterans wore were tangible, visible signs of their new status, marking them not as slaves, as their skin color had done for over two hundred years, but as soldiers, as citizens. So too were formalized family relations signs of their status because their legality stood in striking contrast to all that had been denied to African Americans in slavery. As Peter Bardaglio has argued, "Most African Americans viewed the ability to solemnize their customary ties as a badge of freedom, a powerful symbol of their newfound status as citizens."[21]

Reconstructing Former Slaves' Families

IN THE CONTEXT of this newly emergent citizenship and the ambiguous place former slaves held in American society, Louisa Caldwell's successful widow's pension claim is perhaps not as ironic as it initially appeared. Once slaves were free, whites became concerned about the state of the slave family in a way that they never had been before. The Freedmen's Inquiry Commission, a group of men who went to the South during the war to assess the condition of refugee slaves there, reported to Congress that, particularly for the deeper South, "the disintegration of the family relation is one of the most striking and most melancholy indications of this progress of barbarism. The slave was not permitted to own a family name; instances occurred in which he was flogged for presuming to use one. He did not eat with his children or with their mother. . . . The entire day, until after sunset, was spent in the field; the night in huts of a single room, where all ages and both sexes herded promiscuously." The members of the commission, like most white Americans, assumed that because the law did not guide or protect them and because the circumstances of slavery were not conducive to the kind of family life free people were accustomed to, slave families could not properly exist. Leon Litwack has argued that whites commonly believed the former slaves were "a race of moral cripples who placed little value on marital and familial ties." He has pointed out that "even some of the most dedicated abolitionists subscribed to these theories, attributing the blacks' moral insensibility, 'licentiousness,' and 'false ideas touching chastity' to the evil influences of bondage."[22]

The prevailing belief in Western culture and ideology was that a family's existence was contingent upon legal sanction. As Michael Grossberg has pointed out about the opinions of whites in the nineteenth century concerning the prohibition of slave marriage, "Without such legitimacy, a sexual union was considered only a casual connection between a man and a woman."[23] The implications of a nonlegal union extended beyond a couple to affect their children: the child born out of legal wedlock was illegitimate, without family ties. Of the many ills of slavery that needed to be corrected, the denial of the right to family was one the commission held up as especially vital.

Beyond the correction of slavery's ills, many believed that reconstructing African-American families was crucial to the survival of the postslavery Republic. If the institution of family was a fundamental element of American society, a crucial source of virtue, it was imperative that former slaves formalize their family relationships. William McFeely has explained that this kind of encouragement was an integral part of the Freedmen's Bureau's mission: "It would not be an overstatement to say that the bureau men in the field saw marriage and the formation of stable family groups as the most important thing they should accomplish for the freedmen in their charge. Belonging themselves to a culture in which families were of enormous importance, the encouragement of that institution among the freedmen was the natural thing to do."[24] The success of emancipation, of finding a place for former slaves in American society, rested in part upon the existence of viable African-American families.[25]

The federal government began addressing former slaves' right to family and the construction of "proper" families by allowing army chaplains to perform marriage ceremonies for slaves during the war, a practice taken up later by missionaries and Freedmen's Bureau agents.[26] Under their new Black Codes, southern states either automatically legalized existing marriages or ordered former slaves to formalize their marriage relations. In Florida, for example, the law compelled couples to "appear before some person legally authorized to perform the marriage ceremony, and be regularly joined in the holy bonds of matrimony." Couples found living as husband and wife without having formalized their marriage within nine months after the passage of the law would be considered guilty of a misdemeanor and "upon conviction shall be subjected to the pains and penalties prescribed by the statute for the punishment of fornication and adultery." In North Carolina former slaves risked punishment for failing to have their marriages recorded by a government official.[27]

But clearly most whites believed that legal sanction alone would not be sufficient to guarantee that former slaves would form moral, stable families. Freedmen's Bureau agents not only encouraged and enforced these provisions, they also instructed former slaves about "proper" family structure, roles, and responsibilities. In 1865 the assistant commissioner of the Freedmen's Bureau for South Carolina, Georgia, and Florida published a list of "Marriage Rules" designed to "aid the freedmen in properly appreciating and religiously observing the sacred obligations of the marriage state." These rules explained in great detail how marriages were made and dissolved and outlined the duties and rights of husbands, wives, and children.[28]

Politicians' and reformers' sense that they could indeed promote former slave families suitable to free society was rooted in the widespread belief that the state had the power to intervene in families that were not functioning effectively. As Grossberg has argued, the nineteenth century saw the consolidation of domestic relations law, a trend in lawmaking that marked the shift from the consideration of the family as a private institution governed by the paterfamilias to its consideration as a civil institution, a unit of equal members subject to control by the state in matters of marital relations, contraception and abortion, bastardy, and child custody.[29] That individual states and the federal government would become interested in ordering the domestic affairs of former slaves seemed natural in a society that sanctioned state interference in family life.

The extension to former slaves of the right to family and the accompanying right to inherit a pension therefore must be seen not only as an offering of citizenship but as a manifestation of white society's desire to mold former slaves into proper citizens, to find a specific place for them in American society. Though freedom offered former slaves the privileges of marriage and control over family life, it would be circumscribed by the state's prerogative to intervene in family life. Perhaps the most striking example, and thus the most compelling reminder of the state's awesome power, was the creation of laws preventing marriages between people of different races and promoting the practice of apprenticing the children of former slaves. After the war southern states passed legislation that outlawed marriages between whites and blacks, demonstrating that the state possessed the power to determine who could marry whom. The Black Codes endowed southern judges with the power to bind out African-American children who had no parents or whose parents were deemed incapable of supporting them.[30]

But the state interfered in family life in less overtly invasive ways as well. The very fact that former slaves had to register their marriages, that couples living together outside of formal matrimony after a certain date were to be punished, suggests as much. Ira Berlin, Steven F. Miller, and Leslie Rowland have argued that emancipation both "strengthened and transformed" former slave families. They pointed out that legal sanction transformed these families by redefining relationships between family members and by assigning new responsibilities, including providing for the members and caring for the young, the sick, and the elderly.[31] In a sense one might argue that former slaves traded one master for another, albeit a more benign and protective one. As citizens, former slaves were now subject to new laws, new constraints and restrictions that redefined the family and familial relationships.

Former slaves' child custody contests, inheritance disputes, and divorce and bigamy cases that found their way to southern courts after emancipation demonstrate that acquiring the right to family required some adjustment by the judiciary as well as by former slaves. Southern judges found themselves grappling with the thorny issues of slave marriage that had never come up under the laws of slavery. Though they found ways to make decisions in such instances, the very existence of cases in which two sets of children argued over their father's estate or in which two women claimed to be married to the same man indicated the need to sort out relationships begun in slavery that did not meet the new criteria under the laws of free society.[32]

This same process of adjustment is evident in the pension claims of former slave widows, children, parents, and siblings. Reminiscent of the cases adjudicated in southern courts, such pension claims brought to light the identical question of the status of slave marriage and its effect on other family relationships. Within the pension system these questions were handled in a more uniform manner; rather than being adjudicated within the many southern state courts, the cases came under the single control of the federal Pension Office, the government office that processed claims. Congress enacted legislation that set down the general requirements for a pension, what one had to do to prove he or she was indeed the soldier's widow, child,

parent, or sibling. In cases in which former slave family relationships did not fit neatly into the legislated categories, pension officials ruled on them, sometimes according to precedent
set in state or federal courts and sometimes according to their
own conception of domestic relations law. In some instances
specific problems cropped up consistently enough to compel
Congress to enact special legislation altering the requirements
for pensions.

The pension system also played a role in the process of socializing former slaves to take up "proper" family relationships.
Familial relationships between soldiers and their relatives were
a central focus of the pension process. In order to gain a pension, a soldier's family member had to prove that he or she was
the relative in question by meeting the government's standards
for what constituted a widow, child, mother, father, or sibling.
Because pension requirements were rooted in the same notions
of family that informed domestic relations law, the pension system introduced and reinforced the same set of social expectations about how family members should behave. Just as others
have done with statutes, I am suggesting that we look at the
pension legislation enacted by Congress to determine how
Americans defined family and family relationships.[33] Meeting
the requirements for a pension meant adjusting to the definition of family relationships set down in pension legislation, because most of the legislation that constituted the Civil War pension system treated former slaves as citizens like any others.
Although some pension legislation made distinctions between
black and white citizens in order to deal with such issues as
slaves' lack of legal marriage, for the most part the government
expected former slaves to apply for pensions through the same
channels and according to the same requirements as freeborn
citizens. Suggesting that the pension process could be complicated is not to say that slave family relationships were totally
incompatible with the prescribed norm or, more specifically,
that former slaves could not meet any of the requirements for

a pension. The context of slavery and the extralegal nature of slave family relationships made the two incongruous but not irreconcilably different.

The pension claims suggest that former slaves' socialization into families deemed worthy of nurturing good citizens was not simply a matter of fitting into the government's mold or of casting aside their own conception of family and family relationships. Louisa Caldwell won her pension claim by meeting the legal standards of proper family relations. But what might have been identical in form was not necessarily so in content; though Louisa's slave family might have looked just like families governed by the laws of free society, it was not in fact so. For example, the claim application demanded that Louisa furnish a maiden name, implying that the applicant had taken her husband's name in marriage, a practice that in free society signified a wife's entrance into her husband's family and the merging of her legal status into his. Louisa offered a maiden name on her application, but the application cannot tell us what the significance of having taken her husband's name was under the customs of slavery. We know it could not have been the same as under the laws of freedom; by law or, to be more precise, by exclusion from the law, Louisa's marriage did not make her a member of her husband's family, nor did it offer her any of the legal privileges enjoyed by free women. How can we determine Louisa's motivation or intention in taking her husband's name? Did she indeed possess this name during slavery? If she took it afterwards, did she do so to simulate the practices of free society or to assert her freedom and her right to do so? Could this be an example of the guile and guise that survival had earlier required of many slaves, a matter in this new situation of giving the Pension Office what it wanted so that she could get a pension? Louisa received her pension by meeting the guidelines laid out by the government, but whether this altered the nature of her family relationships in any meaningful way remains problematical.

Considering the Source

FOR THOSE who seek definitive answers to the questions about the inner dynamics of family life during slavery, Civil War pension claims are both rewarding and frustrating because they yield tantalizingly little hard evidence about earlier slave families. Former slaves' Civil War pension claims represent the moment in which the claim itself was constructed, the moment at which pressure was being put on slave families to transform themselves, to re-create themselves in a new image and with new significance. The pension claims are invaluable nonetheless precisely because they allow us to turn our attention toward public family roles, toward a legal and political status of former slaves' families that changed or had never existed before emancipation. No longer ignored, no longer denied protection from arbitrary interference by the master, the former slave family was now a recognized civil entity, subject to the same protection and regulation as the white family. As many historians have demonstrated, slave family ties were much stronger than whites ever imagined, and those ties endured when slavery ended.[34] Yet if this social element of the family remained constant, the legal and political terrain upon which former slave families rested shifted dramatically. The pension claims provide the means for thinking about the family as a legal institution, considering the kinds of changes that take place when what the law and society previously ignored becomes subject to both. Finally, the pension claims make it possible to address the broader question of the legal, political, cultural, and social transformations that occurred in the process by which slaves became citizens.

Rather than constituting dry, static, official documentation, the affidavits, the correspondence, even the seemingly standard forms within any USCT pension file tell powerful stories about the pension process and about claimants' lives. Much of the evidence within each case consists of the recorded testimony of claimants and witnesses who responded to queries seeking to confirm their familial relationships, employment, economic circumstances, previous ownership, and other issues related to the pension process. Although the official questions asked of these claimants shaped the subject matter of former slaves' responses, the testimony itself remains in their own words. In this sense the pension records are as much oral history as the Works Progress Administration (WPA) interviews with former slaves, as much autobiography as traditional slave narratives. Yet in some ways the pension records have unique value. Unlike the WPA interviews or slave narratives, the pension records are contemporary to the events described within; they were not constructed after the fact but represent the lived experience of the pension process itself.[35]

This book is about the two stories that unfold in the pension records. The first follows the pension process: the pursuit of a pension from first application to final decision. This process reveals, on the one hand, the guidelines of family structure that free society imposed upon former slaves and, on the other hand, former slaves' own efforts to negotiate within and around those guidelines. The claimants, the witnesses, the government agents who collected information and determined the success or failure of the cases all play significant roles in this particular drama. The outcome of the case, why that decision was made, and where slave customs either coincided or conflicted with the laws of freedom all speak to the kinds of challenges former slaves faced in organizing familial relationships after emancipation. This study is narrowly focused on the pension process because it demonstrates the agency of seemingly powerless historical actors. Rather than portraying victims, the pension records depict individual former slaves as they wielded power in the more traditional sense by striving toward full citizenship and grappling with their government and in less acknowledged ways while mediating between government regulation and their own experiences to define their lives and relationships.

There is a second story that the pension records tell, the stories former slaves recount of their lives. I refer to former slaves' personal narratives as stories not to suggest that they are fictitious but rather to direct attention to the role that narratives play in the construction of identity. To a certain degree we are the stories we tell about ourselves. In their own claims for pensions and as witnesses for others, former slaves created, envisioned, and imagined relationships and lives, reconstructing communities and families. Analyzing the terms of their discourse can reveal how former slaves pieced together their personal and familial histories, how they attempted to mold their experiences to fit within the narrow confines of the government's concept of family. Whether accurate or not, whether the exact account of lived experiences or created for the benefit of pension officials, the stories former slaves recounted in the pension claims have historical import because they represent not only the lives lived outside and before the pension process but also the complex moment of the telling: how former slaves saw their lives and how they wanted their lives to be seen, how they understood the pension system and the demands it placed on them, and what they thought government officials wanted to hear. These stories both reflected on the lives lived and helped to give them shape and meaning, and may even have changed the way some would live their lives in the future. By juxtaposing these stories and the stories of other participants in the pension process—government agents, former slave owners, other former slaves—I have attempted to draw out many of the complexities of the transition of individuals and families from slavery to freedom.

In many respects those who applied for pensions were representative of former slaves in general, and their stories shed light on the experiences of others. Except for the very young, who learned from the memories of the older generations, the claimants in this study lived with slavery in their immediate past. They shared the experiences of surviving the war and, as Leslie Schwalm has put it, "surviving the peace," getting through challenges of financial and material want and other formidable obstacles in the first days of freedom.[36] These former slaves battled against southern whites' resistance to their efforts to be independent and government interference in their lives. They attempted in their own ways to create a life in freedom, to make it distinct from slavery, and to define what being free meant. Like many of their generation, they changed their names, moved around, reconnected with family members lost to them in slavery, and went to work. They strove to acquire some land for their own use and, failing that, to shape the nature of their labor and their labor relations. To read the pension records is to open a perspective on the collective experience, what "typical" former slaves were doing on a day-to-day basis.

The textured nature of the pension records also offers the rare opportunity to get to know individual former slaves in some depth. Each story represents the unique experiences, character, and imagination of the storyteller. The files contain the details of their lives: how they met their spouses; what their marriage ceremonies were like; when their children were born; who were the members of their families and communities. This information often emerges from short answers to questions posed by agents and from application forms. Frequently these specific details come to life in narrative form; here they are more than just the facts of a person's life because that person's voice rings through, telling the story in his or her own words rather than having an observer summarize them, which is often the case in other contemporary sources. The personality of the storyteller has been preserved, how he or she crafted responses to questions about past and present relationships, the kinds of questions he or she encouraged or evaded, how he or she engaged with other former slaves and with government agents. Getting to know the individual storytellers makes it possible to better understand the full range of African Americans' experiences in the transition from slavery to freedom.

Where the documentation could not speak for itself, I have attempted to fill in what was left out, to recover all that is implicit in the stories the former slaves told, and to connect them

to the broad cultural, social, economic, and political forces that
shaped these narratives. I have sought to fill in the blanks, when
possible, with other sources: slave narratives, the accounts of
missionaries and government agents who were in the South in
the first decade of emancipation, pension legislation, Pension
Office documents, and domestic relations law. I have also considered these narratives within the context of what historians
have learned about slavery, emancipation, and nineteenth-century
white society. But all along, and most importantly, I have situated
the narratives at the forefront of my analysis and have sought
to allow them to speak for themselves as much as possible.

Although it is difficult to determine how many black soldiers
and relatives applied for or received pensions, the number of
potential applicants was quite large, for approximately 180,000
black soldiers served in the Union army. A random sample of
542 Union pension applicants showed that USCT soldiers or
their family members represented approximately 6 percent of
all claimants. Considering that African Americans made up
nearly 10 percent of the Union forces, it seems reasonable to
conclude that African-American veterans and their families
were making good use of the pension system.[37] Similar to
Theda Skocpol's findings about the "take-up" rate of all Union
soldiers—meaning those who signed up for pensions—the
sample demonstrates a significant increase in applications by
African Americans after 1890, when Congress passed legislation making pensions more readily available to Civil War veterans and their survivors.[38] Within the sample approximately
87.5 percent of applications on behalf of white soldiers were
successful, while the success rate of pensions on behalf of black
soldiers was approximately 65.7 percent.[39] We can surmise that
African-American applicants, particularly southerners plagued
by poverty, illiteracy, misinformation about the pension system,
a dearth of personal documentation, and white hostility, generally found the application process more difficult than white
applicants.[40]

Considering the Selected Sample

BECAUSE I have chosen to focus on the distinct nature of each pension claim and on the narratives of claimants and witnesses, the scope of this study is not intended to be all-inclusive or conclusive. Although the pension records are vast enough to create a large sample, I have chosen to examine a limited number of claims in order to explore individual cases in their totality, to exploit their depth and the richness of the evidence within. The sample of one hundred cases in this study consists of the pension claims of widows, children, mothers, fathers, and soldiers.[41] The vast majority of claimants were former slaves, but I have included a few cases belonging to free persons of color to make points of comparison. I focus on pension legislation passed between 1862, when provision for the Civil War pension system was first made, and 1890, when a new law broadened eligibility for pensions.

I came to the pension records almost by accident, finding the first few cases by following a paper trail from the records of the Freedmen's Bureau, where I was looking for information about the formalization of former slaves' marriages. Most historians attributed that process to the eagerness of former slaves; I wondered if it had not been more complicated.[42] Freedmen's Bureau agents helping former slaves apply for pensions wrote to headquarters of their frustration at searching for elusive evidence of slave marriages. Many letters contained reference to Proof of Cohabitation or Proof of Marriage forms, but those forms were not in the Freedmen's Bureau records.[43] When a thoughtful archivist at the National Archives pointed me in the direction of the pension records, it seemed as if I had unearthed a whole treasure chest of source material. After finding the pension claims of those widows mentioned in the Freedmen's Bureau records, I randomly searched the Civil War General Pension Index, arranged alphabetically, for more cases. I looked for claims on behalf of soldiers who had served in southern units of the USCT, because the vast majority of those had been slaves. I chose cases filed as near 1865 as possible to stay close to the era of emancipation, though I soon learned that numerous cases filed before 1890, when the requirements for a pension became more liberal, shared the questions and the complications of the earlier cases. When I learned that pension claims were also indexed by regiment, I looked for cases in at least one, and often several, regiments from every state in the South, including the border states.

The claims featured in this study are not geographically representative because my main concern was to choose both well-documented cases to permit as full an analysis as possible and the most involved cases to explore the complexity and the intricacy of the transition from slave to free families. Rather than weight the study in favor of soldiers' records, which represent the largest number of cases, I use only a few soldiers' claims, preferring instead to rely upon the claims of widows, children, and parents because they offer a better opportunity to examine and analyze the questions of familial relationships at their core.

Instead of geography or numbers then, my interest was to identify the range of problems that former slaves encountered within the pension process. These problems centered around the kinds of evidence given and the differences between slave and free familial relationships that arose as claimants sought to meet government requirements for proving one's identity as a soldier's widow, child, parent, or sibling. If my sample of cases is unique in that each individual story is unique, what is typical about them is the questions they raise about making the transition from slave to free familial status. How did a person who had no documented surname in slavery establish his or her own identity or that of a family member in a society that held surnames as a key determinant of identity? How did a widow prove she had been married to a soldier if the marriage had no legal sanction and thus she had no material evidence of its existence? How did a child of slave parents prove he or she was legitimate? The cases in this sample represent a wide array of responses to the problem of establishing personal and familial identity in free society.

To some degree the nature of the documentation has shaped my approach to the family. Because the government offered pensions to three groups of relatives—widows, children, and other dependent relatives (parents and siblings)—I have addressed broader questions about the family within the context of the relationships of husband and wife, parent and child, and older parents and their adult children. The various claims of mothers and fathers, widows, and children all speak to the same issues of the transformation of emancipated families.

ONE

The Pension Process

A View from Both Sides

SHORTLY AFTER they were married in June 1863, Harriet Berry and her husband Joseph escaped from slavery, running to freedom behind Union army lines. The young couple made it to Norfolk, Virginia, where Joseph soon enlisted in the United States Colored Troops. After a year in the service of the Union, Joseph contracted pneumonia and died, a common fate among Civil War soldiers. In 1878, alone in the world, scraping out a living as a servant, Harriet applied to the government for a widow's pension.

To illustrate the pension process, this chapter traces Harriet Berry's pension claim from her first application to the Pension Office's final decision. I have chosen to use Harriet's claim because her general experience, the problematic areas of her claim, and her concerns about the pension process are representative of those found in other former slaves' pension claims. To capture the broader implications of the pension process for former slaves and to uncover the traces of slaves' transition to citizenship that lay just beneath its surface, one must pry the case apart to expose its two different dimensions. Examining the pension process from the point of view of the government as well as from that of former slaves allows an assessment of what the government demanded from former slaves and of the ways in which former slaves, armed with limited resources and a different cultural perspective, attempted to meet such demands. This view of the pension process also reveals the experiences of former slaves as they crossed over from slavery to citizenship, as they became subject to the forces that governed the lives of all American citizens.

Harriet Berry: From Slavery to Freedom

HARRIET AND Joseph were married in the midst of America's bloodiest war, yet Harriet's account of the event suggests that to some extent the rhythm of daily life went uninterrupted. Harriet and Joseph, nineteen and twenty years old, respectively, belonged to different masters in Camden County in northeastern North Carolina. They married as many slaves had, by procuring the consent of their owners. Though there was no ceremony, "no minister of the gospel present," the slaves of both masters celebrated the marriage at a party given by a relative of Harriet's owner.[1] Harriet made no mention of it in her pension claim, but one wonders how the presence of the Union army fifty miles north at Fort Monroe in Virginia and on the islands just off the coast might have touched the celebration of her marriage. Perhaps it added to the jubilant atmosphere of the occasion as the celebrants contemplated the promise of freedom. Or the occasion might have been tinged by apprehension as slaves and masters alike questioned what the future might bring.

Both jubilation and apprehension must have characterized Harriet and Joseph's feelings shortly after their marriage as they fled their masters. During the course of the war, throughout the South wherever Union army forces had penetrated Confederate territory, many thousands of slaves ran away, determined to find freedom behind Union lines. They made perilous journeys, sometimes hundreds of miles, hiding out during the day in woods, swamps, or under brush and traveling by night under the cover of darkness by land, by water.[2] Harriet and Joseph were among the thousands from their own area who made the fifty-mile trek toward Fort Monroe, an outpost under Union control in a Union-occupied area of southeastern Virginia.[3]

The timing of their escape indicates that Harriet and Joseph must have heard about the Emancipation Proclamation and desired to test its validity. As Captain C. B. Wilder, superintendent of contrabands at Fort Monroe, explained, "Some men who came here from North Carolina, knew all about the Proclammation and they started on the belief in it; but they had heard these stories and they wanted to know how it was."[4] The news that Federal forces were near bolstered the courage of many who ran away during the early years of the war. Others were encouraged by the return of runaways who had made it safely to freedom and had come back for their families. In North Carolina slave men learned that they could join the Union army from recruiters stationed at Fort Monroe who traveled into North Carolina to enlist the services of slaves there. Though many were forcibly impressed into service, others joined willingly with the hope of fighting for their freedom.[5]

Harriet and Joseph arrived in Norfolk where they boarded with a woman named Polly Wilson and her husband. Unlike her boarders, Polly had lived in Virginia before the war began. The fact that Polly and her husband owned a house suggests that they were among Virginia's 58,000 free people of color at the time of the war.[6] In her deposition Polly explained that she had not known Harriet and Joseph before they boarded with her. She described their living situation: "When they came here they lived in my house. I rented them rooms, they lived up stairs and I lived down stairs."[7] Harriet and Joseph appear to have lived in a community that included people they knew from North Carolina. Several witnesses in Harriet's claim testified that they had known her during slavery; Prince Hughes and Mariah Wiggins had even attended her marriage celebration. Because slaves often ran away in groups of families, it is possible that they had all come to Virginia together.

Harriet's claim offers no information as to how the young couple survived in those first months. Boarding in a private home in Norfolk, they managed to avoid the wretched conditions of refugee camps where starvation and disease often ran rampant. Like many other slave men and women who fled across Union lines, Harriet and Joseph probably survived by working for the army. Men worked as laborers at Fort Monroe or at "contraband camps, army installations, and government-supervised farms." When work was available, women found employment as servants, cooks, or laundresses for Union troops. A few months after they arrived in Norfolk, Joseph became one of the 8,000 men enlisted in black regiments in the region of tidewater Virginia and North Carolina.[8]

After Joseph enlisted, daily survival must have been difficult for Harriet, who was either pregnant or had just given birth to a son. Joseph was stationed near Norfolk at first and might have helped Harriet with food or money. Harriet's claim makes no mention of help from the Union; she said nothing of the aid promised to families of enlisted men by Union general Benjamin Butler in December 1863 on the premise that "the labor of the able-bodied would pay for the army's maintenance of the dependent."[9] But as Ira Berlin and others have argued, "The integrity of black family life seldom ranked among the military's highest priorities, and promises often went unfulfilled"; it appears that like many other wives and children of enlisted men, Harriet was left to care for herself.[10] Jacqueline Jones has suggested that former slaves' family and community relations continued to be characterized by the "ethos of mutuality" developed in slavery, the offering of ready assistance to family members and neighbors in need.[11] No doubt Harriet persevered with the help of Polly Wilson, Prince Hughes, Mariah Wiggins, and other people she had known in North Carolina or had come to know in her short time in Norfolk.

Not long after the war ended, Harriet received a letter from the captain of Joseph's regiment in the USCT. Presumably news of the war's imminent end had prompted Harriet to send a letter to Joseph. She had probably asked where he was, when he would be coming home. Because Harriet had moved from Norfolk to Portsmouth during the war, she might have sent the letter to inform Joseph of her whereabouts. Perhaps she had sent him the heartbreaking news that Andrew, their only child, had died in infancy. Harriet could not read or write, but she must have sensed the importance of the letter she received that day in April, a letter written in a stranger's hand. Had Joseph found someone to write a letter for him? Was this news of his fate? She must have exhausted all the possible reasons that the letter had come long before she found someone to read it to her. Harriet probably did not want to believe what was foremost in her mind, what the letter confirmed about her husband.

> Madam,
> It is my painful duty to inform you that your husband to whom you directed a letter . . . which came into my hands yesterday is no more: he died July 19 1864 of Pneumonia. . . . He had been sick only a few days and did not suffer much. . . . Console yourself with the conviction that he died for a glorious cause and that god has willed it so that he should give his life as a sacrifice towards it.
>
> There will be a handsome amount of back pay due to your late husband which you have a right to collect but you must take the greatest care that you are not swindled out of it by some unprincipled person. . . . I have sent your husbands final statements to the Adjutant General's office soon after his death so there can be no delay on that account. Inquire if you are also entitled to a pension. I am not certain about it.
>
> > Yours respectfully,
> > Constantine Nitzsche
> > Capt. 37 US Col. Inft.[12]

The Claimant: Filing a Pension Claim

WITHIN A year Harriet found a lawyer and applied for and received her husband's bounty of $300, money promised to him by the government for enlisting in the army. Harriet's right to apply for her husband's bounty came from the July 1864 act that offered bounties to black volunteers at the same rate as those offered to whites. One of its provisions gave the right to claim bounties to the widows, children, and mothers of soldiers who had died in the service.[13] Harriet first applied for a widow's pension in 1868 but did not follow through with a full application until 1878. Her explanation for the delay was that the lawyer who prosecuted her bounty claim had cheated her. As she testified, "When I drew my Bounty, Lawyer Cooper tried to get all my money, and I did not know who else to make application through."[14] Harriet's problem with her lawyer was not unusual.

Surely Harriet's financial situation impelled her to pursue a pension after so many years. Widowed and childless, Harriet relied upon her own labor to survive. Like most southern black women living in urban areas after the war, Harriet's employment opportunities were limited to some form of domestic labor in a white person's home. She listed her occupation as that of a servant. Harriet probably spent long hours washing dishes, cleaning floors, changing linens, dusting, polishing, and performing other domestic chores. Employers hired separate cooks and washerwomen, but the flexible nature of such occupations suggests that Harriet might have worked in any or all of these jobs throughout the 1870s. Making a living as a domestic laborer generally meant grueling work, harsh treatment by one's employer, and minimal pay.[15] After a decade of such work, the monthly stipend of $8 promised by a pension, undoubtedly more than she made as a servant, offered a powerful incentive for Harriet to overcome her wariness of lawyers and pension agents.[16]

Finally locating a reliable person to help her with the application process prompted Harriet to file her pension claim in 1878. Sometime around 1866 she had made the acquaintance of Henry Knight, a literate black merchant, who appears to have become a trusted friend. Harriet probably met Henry through her active association with Deep Creek Baptist Church in Portsmouth. She boarded with Henry and his wife for a short time and then moved to a place near their home. That Henry was literate and a merchant by profession suggests that he had elevated status within his community and contact with whites outside, both of which made him a likely person for Harriet to turn to with the problem of her pension. It was Henry who recommended that she consult John L. Desendorff, a man Henry felt Harriet could trust with the process of applying for her pension. Though the claim is silent as to Desendorff's exact identity, he appears to have been a white lawyer or claim agent who helped Harriet file her claim in 1878. She described him as one of the "persons instrumental in the prosecution of [her] claim for pension."[17]

In its basic outline Harriet's case followed the course of any other pension claim, whether the claimant was black or white, freeborn or former slave. A claimant applied for a pension through an agent or a lawyer, attempted to present pertinent documentation such as birth or marriage records, and/or brought forth witnesses who would testify in the claimant's behalf. A soldier also underwent a physical examination by a government-appointed surgeon who assessed the nature and extent of his disability. After the relevant evidence and testimony had been gathered and the papers had been filled out, the claimant's agent or lawyer sent the claim to the appropriate division of the Pension Office.[18] If and when the Pension Office approved the claim, the pensioner received payment through a government-appointed pension agency.[19]

However, Harriet's case differed from those of freeborn whites by virtue of the fact that she had been a slave. Some of the circumstances of her case that could be attributed to her former status—the difficulties caused by her inability to read and write, the lack of family records, the lengthy gap between the soldier's death and the filing of an application, prejudice toward Harriet or her witnesses—might also have appeared in cases of other illiterate, poor Americans, black or white. Like all widows, black or white, Harriet's access to the pension system was not as ready as it was for surviving veterans who had other veterans and government officials on hand to guide them through the process. But other factors that played a significant role in Harriet's case were unique to former slaves' claims. Whites' notions about the effects of slavery upon the slave, the lack of legal sanction for slave families, the presence of a white owner in slaves' lives, and the development of a distinctive slave community and culture together shaped the complex pension experience for former slaves.

From the outset Harriet's claim indicated such complexity. The letter from Joseph Berry's army captain provided the catalyst for the initiation of Harriet's pension claim. Many former slaves' cases made no mention of how claimants discovered the death of the soldier or how the claimant came to apply for a pension. Harriet's case provided a clue as to how one might have acquired such knowledge. Harriet learned of her husband's death nine months after it occurred, and only after the captain had come into possession of a letter she had sent to Joseph. Harriet's letter alerted the captain to the fact that Joseph Berry had a wife and enabled the officer to find her.

One wonders how Harriet might have heard about her husband's death had she not sent that fateful letter. She might have attempted to contact the government, but she would have to know the name Joseph enlisted under, where he enlisted, and with which regiment or company. Though Harriet may have possessed such information, many other former slaves did not. Slaves often ran away to places unknown to enlist or changed their names when they enlisted. Like countless other former slaves, Harriet had moved several times after Joseph had enlisted; she might have been impossible to contact if the army did not know who to look for or where to find her. Perhaps, as other cases suggest, Harriet would have heard from surviving soldiers from her husband's regiment or company. Or perhaps she would have heard from acquaintances. Former slave Hagar Washington recalled that she had learned of her husband George's death "shortly after its occurrence from Emily

Cragget . . . and Milly Roach, who . . . saw my husband before
he died, and knowing us told me the news."[20]

Though her husband's captain had been unsure, Harriet was
indeed eligible for a pension. We cannot be certain just how
Harriet received confirmation of her right to a pension. Other
former slaves learned they were entitled to a pension from such
sources as an agent of the Freedmen's Bureau, another pensioner, or solicitation by a pension agent. The act of July 14,
1862, the basis of the Civil War pension system, allowed pensions for soldiers who had been disabled by wounds or injuries
received as a result of military service or by disease incurred
during military service. If a soldier died from any of these
causes, the act provided pensions for his widow and children
or his "other dependent relatives." The Civil War pension system evolved through a series of subsequent acts that refined the
rates for different disabilities and the qualifications for proving
eligibility; increased the rates of pension for widows, children,
and other relatives; and provided other specific details on such
things as the order of succession of eligible relatives, the
method of payment, and arrears of pension.[21]

Harriet's description of applying for her pension reveals the
extent to which she was at the mercy of those who helped her:
"I went first to see Mr. Dezendorf and he was not in, then his
wife, she wrote a note, and I think she filled up a paper—and
told me to go to some body at the Court House, I went there
then and the gentleman made out some papers."[22] Clearly Harriet needed some kind of intermediary, not simply to negotiate the bureaucratic maze that was the pension process but also
because she could not read or write. The importance of being
able to trust this intermediary was evident in the fact that Harriet had no idea what Mrs. Desendorff had written on the paper
she "filled up" or what the "gentleman" at the court did with
the papers he made out. Harriet could only hope that each person performed his or her task properly.

Filling out the application papers would prove the least com-

plicated aspect of the pension process. Problems associated
with the fact that Harriet had been a slave soon would begin
to take their toll as she attempted to meet the government's requirements for evidence about her identity. The Civil War pension system required that Harriet prove that she was the widow
of the soldier and that the soldier had died while in the service of
the USCT or from disease or wounds incurred while in the service. The latter was easy for Harriet to establish because her husband's captain had sent information of his death to the adjutant
general's office, where the Pension Office would first check for
the soldier's service history. However, proving her identity as
the widow in question would be difficult. Harriet and Joseph
were slaves when they married, and because the law in the
South did not permit legal marriage between slaves, Harriet
possessed no formal document with which to prove that she and
Joseph had indeed been husband and wife. As Harriet reiterated,
"There was no licence issued to celebrate my marriage and no
record evidence of said marriage can be had there being none."[23]

As Harriet's case suggests, applying for a pension might have
been among a former slave's first acts as a citizen. Before taking such action, he or she might not have been processed into
public records as a citizen with an official public identity. For
the most part slaves had no birth records (unless their owners
kept them), no marriage records or contracts, no photographs,
no material evidence with which to prove their identity. Yet in
order to gain a pension, a person was required to present sufficient hard evidence to prove that he or she was the relative in
question. Producing such proof was less problematic for soldiers than for their relatives because their public identity was
established in the documents created in the enlistment process.
The soldier's name, personal description, and service history
became part of the permanent public record and could be called
up whenever necessary.

In lieu of material evidence, Harriet offered the testimony of
"reliable" witnesses who had been present when her owner
gave permission for Harriet to marry or who knew her to be the

widow of Joseph Berry. Her own account could not constitute the truth of the matter, for there exists in Western legal tradition the ancient maxim "No one can be a witness on his or her own behalf."[24] Although a person might testify within his or her own case, he or she would not be a witness, an objective observer. The testimony of a person speaking on his or her own behalf is discounted or devalued as the expression of self-interest. Traditionally judges, arbiters, and courts have turned to neutral observers with little or no apparent stake in the case for a disconnected and therefore reliable account. Because Harriet, as the object of scrutiny, could not be trusted to tell the truth, the Pension Office could not simply take her word that she was who she claimed to be. Proof of Harriet's identity would lie in the testimony of witnesses, in the voices of parties who stood neither to lose nor to gain by their participation and who thus could speak truthfully of her claim. Harriet tried to produce as many witnesses as possible, for it seemed that the more people who could identify her as who she said she was, the more that identity was valid.

Although there was nothing unusual about the fact that Harriet's testimony alone was not sufficient to prove her identity, its implications were of serious proportions because of the fact that she had no fixed legal or public identity. What was at stake was not simply proving that she was Joseph's wife for the sake of a pension but her very existence within the realm of citizenship. In the absence of proper documentation to establish her public identity, Harriet's existence was not self-contained, not something that she alone could substantiate, but depended upon recognition and affirmation from people around her.

The question of Harriet's identity resurfaced as her claim was renewed after several years of inactivity on the part of the Pension Office. The record reveals little about what happened to Harriet's claim between 1879, when her lawyer sent it to the Pension Office in Washington, D.C., and 1884, when Harriet began asking questions about it.[25] The claim might have gotten lost in the shuffle of papers that made their way through the

Pension Office, or it might simply have taken that long for Harriet's claim to come up. Either scenario seems plausible: in the year that Harriet made her claim, for army widows and dependents alone 6,661 new pension applications made their way through the Pension Office, as well as 516 applications for pension increases, and 33,876 pending claims were left over from the year before.[26]

Whatever the cause for the delay, in 1884 Harriet traveled to Washington, D.C., with Henry Knight to look into the status of her case. J. W. Bostick, an examiner with whom Harriet spoke, noted that Harriet herself initiated further action on her application: "This case was referred to me to take the claimant's statement, she having come from Portsmouth, Va. and called up the case."[27] At this urging, Bostick began a "special examination," a course of action undertaken when a claim appeared suspicious or incomplete.

Bostick took statements from Harriet and Henry and recommended further investigation, suggesting that although he felt Harriet's case was "meritorious," it would be up to an examiner to "procure [Harriet and Henry's] credibility." In other words, though he personally judged Harriet and Henry to be truthful, their statements needed corroboration by additional evidence. Bostick recommended that the case be investigated in Portsmouth, Virginia, where Harriet lived, and in Elizabeth City, North Carolina, where Harriet's former owner lived. He specifically requested the testimony of Harriet's owner to establish the "legality" of Harriet's marriage and her identity as Joseph Berry's widow.

During his examination of Harriet's case, Bostick called attention to the fact that Harriet's name had been recorded as "Harriet Bell" in the initial application for a pension, and he suggested that the investigation include the procurement of proof of her identity, an explanation for her two surnames. In the ensuing special examination, John G. Greenwalt, the examiner in the field, determined that an honest mistake had been made, one that Harriet herself would not have noticed because she could not read: "When she came to the Clerk of the Court, however, he understands her name to be 'Bell,' and so fills it in, she of course, knew nothing about it, not being able to read."[28]

But if such a mistake justified Harriet's concern about trusting those who helped her, it also cast a suspicious pall over her claim. Because the surname is a key determinant of a person's identity, especially the identity of a woman as a particular man's wife, Harriet's dual naming had to be investigated before it could be written off as a simple clerical error. If she had in fact remarried, Harriet would be ineligible for a pension. According to the Civil War pension system, when a widow, mother, or sister remarried, she lost her pension eligibility.[29] Was Harriet who she claimed to be? That the introduction of a second surname would call her identity and her credibility further into question reveals the instability of Harriet's existence within the realm of citizenship. Without proper means of identification, one might become unrecognizable in the eyes of the government in an instant.

Greenwalt interviewed Harriet's neighbors and the members of her church, all former slaves or persons of color. Only one had known her during slavery, but he had been a young boy then and had been reacquainted with her accidentally when he moved to Virginia in 1879. Some of the other witnesses had met Joseph before he enlisted and could confirm that Harriet was the widow in question and that she had remained a widow since her husband's death. Greenwalt asked the witnesses again and again if they knew a woman named Harriet Berry or Bell, as if she may not have been one and the same person. All replied that they knew only Harriet Berry, the claimant.[30]

Although other witnesses corroborated Harriet's claim to be Harriet Berry, her former mistress, Martha Burgess, gave potentially damaging testimony. When Greenwalt questioned Burgess as to Harriet's identity, she responded with bitterness, as a former slave owner might. "She used to belong to me, and run off and left me during the war," Burgess testified; "she went away after the Federals came in here." Burgess denied knowing that Harriet had ever been married or knowing of the existence of a slave named Joseph Berry. When Greenwalt asked her to sign her statement, Burgess refused: "I don't know why I should sign anything for her to get money from the government in, she run away from me and I never got anything for her."[31]

Harriet's case might have been greatly damaged by her former mistress's testimony, especially because Bostick had expressly recommended that it be sought out to clear up the question of Harriet's widowhood. However, other witnesses who had been slave owners and who had known Harriet during slavery corroborated Harriet's story. Greenwalt interviewed both Robert Berry, the son of Joseph's former owner, and Mary Burgess (who might have been related to Martha Burgess), a white woman who had hired Harriet from her mistress before the war. Both testified that Harriet and Joseph had been married and that they had obtained their owners' permission to do so, as was customary during slavery.[32] Their testimony not only confirmed Harriet's identity as Joseph's widow but also called Martha Burgess's testimony into question. Because reliable and disinterested witnesses claimed that Harriet had received her mistress's permission to marry, Martha Burgess's own testimony became suspect. She had to have known who Joseph Berry was and that Harriet had married him. Coupled with her bitter attitude, the suspicious nature of Martha Burgess's testimony revealed her as having a clear interest in the outcome of Harriet's claim, thus minimizing the damage her testimony might have inflicted upon it.

Greenwalt submitted Harriet's completed claim to the Pension Office on April 16, 1884. Six days later the claim was approved. Harriet would receive $8 per month, dating back to the time of her husband's death, as long as she remained a widow.

The Pension Office: Prosecuting a Pension Claim

IF THE question of Harriet's two names had been problematic for the claimant herself, it had taken on nightmarish proportions from the point of view of the Pension Office. Harriet's lack of some concrete documentation that she could offer to verify her identity was antithetical to the nature of the Pension Office, which shared with other bureaucratic institutions its emphasis on efficiency and accuracy and its concern that recorded information be verifiable. Suspended over a fraudulent case, one claim agent pleaded his innocence with an excuse that revealed the deeply disturbing problem related to the lack of documentation in the cases of countless black claimants: "Of course it must be granted that that accuracy and uniformity which can be adhered to in the preparation of the claims of *Whites* cannot be adhered to in those of *Colored* who have no record evidence of anything."[33] Without the only kind of evidence it believed could assure "accuracy and uniformity," the Pension Office could not be sure that Harriet was not lying or that her lawyer or agent had not submitted a case under false pretenses.

In 1883 the Southern Division of the Pension Office reported that insufficient documentation was a problem endemic to the South where records of southern regiments and of the USCT were "very meager." In addition, the upheaval of the South after the war made it difficult to locate pertinent witnesses or to obtain evidence. The Southern Division singled out the claims of former slaves and other persons of color as especially difficult to prosecute, stating simply that "the obstacles met in endeavoring to obtain evidence in claims on account of service in the colored troops will be appreciated."[34] Apparently the unparalleled complications associated with such claims were so well understood that no further explanation was necessary.

To see Harriet's claim as representative requires addressing questions about the trustworthiness of Harriet and her lawyer or agent within the broader context of the Pension Office's concern with fraudulent claims and accurate evidence. In 1881 the Pension Office created the Division of Special Examinations in hopes that it would alleviate the problem of the

ex parte system of gathering evidence for claims.[35] Throughout the late 1860s and 1870s, the various commissioners of pensions complained that a system in which the claimant's representative was solely responsible for gathering evidence and
procuring witnesses' testimony was open to the perpetration of
fraudulent claims. Commissioners often used the word *secret* to
describe this system, suggesting that the absence of any Pension Office representative in this process made the agent's activities suspicious.[36] In addition to allowing the claimant to be
present at the time testimony against him or her was taken, the
process of special examination would allow a representative of
the Pension Office to cross-examine witnesses and to inquire
into the nature of the evidence presented. If special examination could not solve the problem of a system conducive to
fraud, it at least could offer the Pension Office more involvement in the application process.

In the eyes of the Pension Office, such measures were necessary especially to guard against the "unprincipled" claim
agents who were, it believed, at the root of most fraudulent
claims. Not to be confused with clerks or regular employees of
the Pension Office who were civil service men appointed by the
government, claim agents primarily operated independently of
the government. The government regulated their activities to
some extent through legislation that set a standard fee for ini-
tiating the pension process and by keeping track of good and
bad agents. As Commissioner Chris C. Cox reported in 1868,
"Many of the attorneys prosecuting claims before this office
have, by courtesy of deportment and evident honesty of purpose, commended themselves to favorable consideration; while
others have been suspended from practice for cause, and in
some cases convicted and punished for flagrant violations of
law."[37] Agents caught charging exorbitant fees or filing false evidence or false claims were either suspended or prosecuted.
However, the Pension Office was vulnerable to agents precisely
because they played a key role in the pension process in their
preparation of claims, a part of the process to which the Pen-

sion Office had no access. Further, because claim agents made their living from the number of claimants they solicited, they stood to gain from increasing those numbers. The inducement to file fraudulent claims was a powerful one.

The Pension Office expressed some worry that black claimants would become the unwitting victims or pawns of such unprincipled claim agents. In 1870 Commissioner H. Van Aernam pointed out the necessity for special rules and regulations that would protect "ignorant" black pensioners and claimants from pension agents in Alabama, Mississippi, and Tennessee, implying that blacks were unable to detect fraud for themselves.[38] It is noteworthy that the commissioner pointed to southern states, in which the majority of claimants were most likely former slaves. Five years later Commissioner H. M. Atkinson noted in his annual report that "in numerous instances what is called 'manufactured evidence' has been filed by unscrupulous claim agents, particularly in cases of colored claimants."[39] Whether Atkinson believed that such claimants were duped out of ignorance or were willing accomplices is unclear. However, the result would be the same: the Pension Office would keep a watchful eye on the claims of former slaves and other persons of color.

As the bias toward material evidence expressed in the claim agent's excuse suggested, the Pension Office's concern with accurate evidence arose in reaction to the use of oral testimony. J. A. Bentley, commissioner of pensions between 1876 and 1881, argued that fraud would continue "until some measure shall be adopted by which the truth of the parol testimony which is offered can be tested."[40] Theda Skocpol has pointed out that parole, or oral, testimony might include "the supportive testimony of kinspeople, neighbors, and former comrades in arms."[41] Commissioner J. H. Baker (1871–74) exempted material evidence from his argument against the ex parte system, explaining that "so long as pensions are to be granted upon evidence which (except record evidence) is purely *ex-parte,* so long frauds will continue to exist."[42] The devaluation of oral

testimony as one-sided and involving secrecy suggests that the
Pension Office believed that the historically valuable element
of oral testimony—the ability to cross-examine or question witnesses' responses—was missing in the pension process because
no one from the other side was present at the time such testimony was taken. By virtue of its seemingly objective nature,
only "record evidence" was free from this one-sidedness.

Oral testimony appears to have been considered especially
suspect in former slaves' claims, where witnesses were often
other former slaves or persons of color. That the Pension Office
seemed implicitly less willing to accept the reliability of former
slaves' testimony than that of whites is evident in its preference
for former owners' testimony. A booklet of instructions to special examiners advised that whenever possible they should procure testimony from former owners and former fellow slaves.[43]
Yet the cases themselves suggest the Pension Office viewed former owners' testimony as the more credible of the two. The
government turned to former owners to validate a claimant's
identity, his or her relationship with the soldier, and/or pertinent dates such as date of marriage or date of birth. In Harriet's
case the Pension Office expected the mistress's testimony to
verify that Harriet and Joseph had indeed been properly married. Yet the use of owners' testimony appears not simply to
have been the product of overt racism. Rather, it stemmed from
a combination of whites' cultural differences with slaves, preconceived notions about slaves, and the general quest for accuracy within the Pension Office. Skocpol has reached a similar conclusion from her study of Pension Office annual reports
and other published material. She argued that the Pension
Office was not formally racist but that "both its universalistic
procedures and its informal presumptions could create difficulties for former slaves, illiterates, and others with disadvan-
taged personal histories."[44]

Officials' Attitudes toward Former Slaves

IT IS NOT clear where the practice of searching out the former owner originated. Although it may have been initiated by claim agents, who perhaps presumed that a white owner's testimony would be more valuable, the Pension Office appears to have been of the same mind. If the former owner's testimony was not part of the original application, the Pension Office might send a letter to the claimant requesting it, or in the course of a special examination the examiner himself might search out the former owner, as occurred in Harriet's case.[45] When no material evidence existed, the white master's testimony met the standard for reliability and accuracy.

Clearly the Pension Office relied upon former owners to establish dates because they shared a common sense of time and because masters often kept records about their slaves. The Pension Office instructed examiners: "On some plantations negroes were married by a regular ceremony, and marriages and births were recorded by the planter. The Examiner should learn if such was the case in any claim in his hands."[46]

Because slaves were members of an oral culture, as were many whites in the rural South, they marked time and significant events differently from those who could read and write. Dates that could prove a child was a minor at the time of the soldier's death or that a widow had married the soldier before a certain time were difficult to determine accurately. Most of the former slaves within this sample could offer only an approximation of their ages. Consistent with dating practices in oral cultures, many slaves remembered events by associating them with other significant events that served as "markers of time."[47] An oft-quoted example is former slaves' reference to the North's capture of Port Royal as "when the first gun shoot."[48] Events were recalled as having occurred before or after this time. In their pension claims former slaves attempted to provide dates by referring to events that occurred during the war. Nancy White explained that she was separated from her husband when her master took some of his slaves to Texas during the war: "Mr. Connor sent us all to Texas when the war [came near]. Natchez had not then been taken by the Yankees."[49]

The Pension Office did not automatically discredit former slaves' testimony regarding dates, however. Officials used former slaves' own methods of marking time to devise a technique for procuring dates from former slaves and other persons of color. Examiners were advised to "call attention of the witnesses to some important event, holiday, &c., to enable them to testify with any approach to accuracy in regard to dates." If they could fix upon a particular year, examiners might determine the month and day by "reference in a similar manner to holidays, the seasons of the year, &c." Pension officials accepted this method as a means of establishing dates "pretty accurately."[50]

A few cases offer the sense that the Pension Office might have believed that whites had a better sense of time than former slaves did. Although many former owners may have kept records of dates, some appear to have remembered dates in a fashion similar to that of their slaves. Yet the accuracy of the owners' testimony was not called into question. Harriet Berry's mistress estimated that Harriet left the plantation "after the Federals came in here." Starkey White could only approximate the birth dates of the children belonging to his former slave Isabella Cherry: "His knowledge . . . in part derived from a comparison with the dates of birth of some of his own children born near the same time."[51] In spite of its speculative nature, White's testimony was recorded as fact.

Beyond establishing dates, the Pension Office sought former owners over former slave witnesses to verify other pertinent facts within a claim. For the most part former owners' testimony was not questioned but cited as proof positive. For example, the examiner in Tennessee Lissia's widow's claim concluded that "this case depends" upon her former mistress's testimony; "her evidence may be regarded as conclusive as to the marriage of the claimant and soldier, and of their recognition as husband and wife" in spite of the fact that he had spoken to several other witnesses. In the case of the children of Richard Martin, the master's testimony was taken as "sufficient to establish the soldier's first marriage, legitimacy and date of birth of the first three children," even though the examiner had taken the testimony of numerous witnesses.[52] Interestingly, in this case even one of the claimants pointed to the master as the best source of information about her family.

For the most part former owners supported their former slaves' claims and corroborated their testimony. Among the forty-seven cases in which an owner's testimony was included, Harriet's mistress appears to be the only one who refused to testify. Perhaps the reasons that owners' testimony did not appear in other cases included their refusal to testify, but no mention was made of that fact. Other reasons given included the claimant's or the Pension Office representative's inability to locate the owner or the fact that the owner had died. A few former owners offered testimony that proved damaging because it contradicted the claimant's own story.[53] However, many former owners appeared more than willing to testify in their former slaves' behalf. Some went so far as to testify numerous times or even to help their former slaves with the pension process, as in Rena Eason's case. William Beaman, Rena's former owner, not only testified in Rena's claim four times, but he also "looked after all her pension papers during the time she was working for her pension" and was instrumental in the success of her claim.[54] Beaman's willingness to testify and to help Rena suggests that he was not vindictive or jealous, as Harriet Berry's case might lead us to believe about her former owner. Furthermore, owners' corroboration of their former slaves' testimony suggests that ex-slaves were indeed telling the truth, that they were honest even if the Pension Office was not so sure. In these cases the owners appear to have been a kind of patron for their former slaves, boosting the former slave's credibility by offering him or her the backing of an established white citizen.

Why did former owners offer supportive testimony in their former slaves' pension claims? The range of reasons is probably as broad as the spectrum of human relationships and as complex as the relationship between master and slave. One obvious answer is the expectation of direct or indirect financial gain. Laney Jane Joiner's claim contains a rare but suggestive instance. When asked if she had any interest in the claim, Laney Jane's former mistress replied, "I have no interest in the said claim only I was promised by the claimant that I would be paid for my trouble to testify."[55] Rena Eason bought land from William Beaman with her bounty money; his willingness to testify in her pension claim might have been rooted in the assumption that Rena would use her pension money to purchase more land or perhaps farming implements or supplies from him. There were other ways former owners might have benefited from testifying. For planters seeking to control black labor, a small pension from the government might well have pacified laborers who were inclined to move in search of better circumstances. Other former owners might have offered supportive testimony because they were compelled by the prospect of making former slaves beholden to them. Elusive though concrete evidence might be within the pension records, such motivation is easy to imagine in view of the desire of planters to find alternative ways to maintain power over the formerly enslaved population. Beyond personal gain, some former owners might have been moved by a sense of responsibility or obligation toward former slaves, or perhaps even by genuine concern. Former slaveholder Thomas Harris had been a constant presence in the lives of Richard Martin's children in the many years after their parents died and offered supportive testimony in their pension claim numerous times over the course of five years. Reporting on Harris's reputation in his community, a pension official stated, "He is . . . apparently a friend to his colored people."[56] Whatever former owners' own personal motives, the ultimate result often worked to the benefit of former slaves in the success of their pension claims.

Beyond its preference for former owners' testimony, the Pension Office appears to have been generally suspicious of former slaves and other persons of color. In a section about "Colored Claimants," the 1882 special examiners' instruction booklet warned that some "colored claimants (widows) adopt for the time being . . . children not their own . . . in order to obtain the increase allowed for minor children." The Pension Office gave no such warning in its general section on widows. Moreover, the booklet cautioned, examination in some cases might reveal "that the claimant was in no way related to the soldier, but has been picked up by interested parties to represent the widow or some other relative." Again, the Pension Office made no reference to such attempts at fraud on the part of white claimants.[57]

Perhaps the pervasive belief in white society that slavery corrupted slaves' morality, including their sense of honesty, played a key role in the priority given to owners' testimony and the suspicion of black claimants. Frederick Douglass told the story of a slave who was sold away from his family and friends after having spoken honestly with the master. Douglass explained to his white readers that the moral to his story was that the slave paid a penalty for telling the truth.[58] In its report about the condition of newly freed slaves, the American Freedmen's Inquiry Commission informed Congress that dishonesty was one of the chief vices learned in slavery, because "men who are subjected to despotic rule acquire the habit of shielding themselves from arbitrary punishment by subterfuges or by a direct departure from the truth."[59] Several advice tracts published and distributed or read to slaves exhorted them to be honest. One such tract was *Plain Counsels for Freedmen,* by Clinton B. Fisk, assistant commissioner of the Freedmen's Bureau. "All agree that slavery fosters lying and stealing," Fisk wrote. "But as slavery has been for ever abolished in this country, that cause has been removed, although the effects have not ceased." In other words, slavery taught the slave to lie, and though the slave had been freed, in white eyes he had not necessarily begun to tell the truth.[60]

Such attitudes can be seen at play within the pension records. Though examiner E. M. Clarke judged former slave Nancy White to possess a good moral character, he believed that she was unique among her peers: "She is an aged—and from the testimony of all her neighbors, both white and black—of the most upright moral character, exceptionally so, for her race and condition."[61] It was not unusual for an examiner to hold up a good former slave witness as exemplary within his or her race, as an exception to the norm.

In the case of William and Alice Timmons, the examiner's suspicion of former slaves' honesty led him to reject the material evidence so highly regarded within his profession. William and Alice produced a written record to establish their identity, an "age book" in which their mother's owner had recorded the births and deaths of her siblings and children. William, Alice, and their half sister Priscilla continually deferred to the authority of the age book in matters of family history. "I do not know my age," Priscilla claimed; "when I want to know my age I go to my 'age book' and find out. . . . If that book says I was born on Aug 7/48—the book is right—the book knows better than I do."[62] Yet examiner Walter Ayres questioned "how much faith and credit should be accorded the book." Ironically, Ayres had lamented that the case had been difficult to examine in part because of the witnesses' "poor memories." Rather than accepting the only written evidence in the claim, however, he reported that the document's reliability could be determined only after an examiner had interviewed the "white families . . . to whom these claimants and their relatives formerly belonged."[63] Ayres's suspicion of the former slaves' honesty led him to question the source of this written family record. Though he would not dismiss the evidence altogether, Ayres would accept its validity only if whites had confirmed it.

Pension officials' attitudes appear to have been similar to those of other northerners—Union army officials, missionaries, Freedmen's Bureau agents—working with former slaves in the South. The paternalistic nature of these occupations fueled feelings of ambivalence toward former slaves. The genuine desire or the responsibility to offer assistance to former slaves was often colored by the belief that blacks possessed inferior moral capacities which might affect their work ethic, family life, and general character, though many whites differed over whether this inferiority was an innate condition, an effect of slavery, or some combination of both. In her work on northern missionaries in Georgia during Reconstruction, Jones referred to expression of this attitude as "racialism," distinguishing it from racism but arguing that "it often manifested itself in an arrogance that was akin to racial prejudice."[64] Many questioned whether former slaves could ever overcome the devastation of slavery. Willie Lee Rose has described the attitude of missionaries on the island of Port Royal, off the coast of South Carolina, during the early years of the war: "In most of their observances on the effects of slavery upon the Negro, the missionaries stated that the institution had 'degraded' him, had reduced him from his original state of independence to a childish reliance upon others. . . . The destructive aspects of slavery had always been emphasized by abolitionists. Now one had to ask: Could slavery as an institution have been so degrading to its victims as to make them *incapable* of the immediate assumption of the responsibilities of free men?"[65] Pension officials clearly entertained the same doubts.

Special Examination: Scrutinizing Questionable Claims

YET IN SPITE of any wariness with which the Pension Office might have viewed former slaves, it did not automatically discredit them as witnesses. Rather, it assessed their reputations in order to judge the validity of their testimony, just as it did for white witnesses. The process of special examination demonstrates how a clerk of the Pension Office might have determined a former slave's credibility. Examiners asked others within the community about a claimant or a witness's reputation for honesty. Many examiners requested a statement of the claimant's identity from the postmaster or postmistress, who would know many of the local residents and was in the government's employ.

Examiners also relied upon their own judgment to determine a witness's character. In the case of Toney Sharp, after having been assured of the reliability of two witnesses by Toney's former owner, Special Examiner L. Turner reported that his own impressions of them were favorable. He judged their character by what he observed of their behavior: "The witness Harriet Sharp stands good. In giving her testimony she was much impressed by the fact that she was under oath, being a strong church woman. . . . While the witness is not intelligent, she is not as ignorant as the class common to this locality, having as it is termed here a great deal of 'mother wit.'"[66] Turner's sense that Harriet understood the notion of being under oath and was "much impressed" by it was key to his assessment of her character. All testimony recorded by a notary public, an authorized examiner, or a clerk of the court was given under oath. Within the administration of the oath lay the assumption that a person's belief in God would lead him or her to honor that oath by speaking the truth. The prevailing belief that former slaves were heathens, that they had not received proper religious instruction during slavery, might have undermined the government's belief in the effectiveness of placing former slaves under oath. That Harriet was a "strong church woman," in other words, that she exhibited a strong sense of religious devotion, made her oath more valid.

Turner's assessment was based on the belief that the more intelligent or clear-thinking a person was, the more capable he or she was of telling the truth. In part, examiners associated a person's ability to supply accurate evidence with his or her level of literacy. It is telling that the Southern Division of the Pension Office blamed the illiteracy of its claimants and witnesses for augmenting the problem of insufficient evidence: "The proportion of illiterate claimants and witnesses in the cases before this division is large, obviously increasing the difficulty of obtaining from them satisfactory evidence."[67] The report did not specify whether the problem was specific to the disproportionate number of former slaves within its jurisdiction or if it believed illiteracy was characteristic of the South in general. In either case, a person's level of literacy played a prominent role in an examiner's assessment of his or her character.

However, the question of Harriet's intelligence was not limited to her ability (or inability) to read and write. Whites viewed slaves as ignorant in the many senses of the word: illiterate, naive, unschooled in the ways of white society, and ready to believe what they were told. Though she was illiterate, Harriet was not as "ignorant" as the others within her class, according to Turner, because she possessed "mother wit," a kind of common sense. Yet Turner considered Harriet an exception to the norm. Some examiners believed that former slaves were not dishonest but that their ignorance made them incapable of distinguishing between fact and fiction. The Pension Office's fear that claim agents would dupe black claimants suggested as much.

In Hagar Washington's case examiner Julius Lemkowitz's familiarity with the people living within his jurisdiction helped him to assess all but one witness as possessing "fair reputations for veracity." The one exception was a man named William Jefferson who testified "so much and so often that he frequently becomes lost in the mazes of the multifarious evidence sworn by him." Lemkowitz reported that Jefferson had testified in practically every other case that he had examined in the area and that Jefferson's testimony was usually erroneous. However, the examiner admitted that in Hagar Washington's case, Jefferson "unintentionally" told the truth, though how Lemkowitz knew this, he did not say. This case suggests that after the creation of the special examination division of the Pension Office, it might have been difficult to falsify evidence or to produce false witnesses in an area where a single examiner investigated numerous claims.

Cases that lacked sufficient evidence were not written off but investigated further through special examination. Because I purposely searched for the more complicated cases, many from this sample are cases that underwent special examinations for reasons ranging from suspected fraud to concern that sufficient evidence had not been uncovered to give the claimant a fair hearing. Several cases offer examples of the warning flags that often led the Pension Office to take such action. Charles Anderson, who had been receiving a pension for his disability for twenty-five years, was put under special examination when he happened to run into an examiner who was looking into another case. In the course of a conversation, the examiner learned that although Charles had received his pension under the name Anderson, his master's name, he went by the name Cobb, his father's name. As in Harriet Berry's case, Anderson's two names cast doubt upon his true identity. The Pension Office wanted to be certain that Charles Anderson and Charles Cobb were one and the same person. Rena Eason's case was called into question when her husband, presumed dead for over twenty-four years, showed up in town one day, alive and well. Had Rena known he was alive all along? The Pension Office needed to be sure that Rena had not been profiting from a fraudulent claim. Rachel Walters's case was under a routine special examination to assess the "merits of her claim," a typical practice. When the examiner reexamined her former master and mistress, they told him that Rachel had remarried, and he had to determine if this was indeed the case. Finally, Catherine Camphor's mother's pension was called into question when her son's widow applied for a pension. Catherine had claimed that her son had never married; had she lied? The Pension Office investigated to find the truth in these and other cases.[68]

In addition to Catherine Camphor, five other claimants in this sample were discovered to have been lying to win their pensions. Suspended claim agent M. M. Cloon had been responsible for the claim of Tanya Butler, a former slave who had applied for a mother's pension. A year after Tanya's claim had been approved, Cloon reported that Tanya had "practiced fraud in the prosecution of her pension by furnishing the testimony of persons who have known nothing of her or her family." How the agent discovered this deception and how long his suspension lasted are not revealed, but the use of false witnesses cost Tanya her pension.[69]

In one case full of complicated twists of plot, an investigation by the U.S. attorney for Maryland revealed two separate false claims and a third legitimate claim. In 1868 Spriggs Barney applied for and received the pension of his son, Thomas, who Barney claimed left no wife or minor children. A year later a woman claiming to be Thomas Barney's widow filed a pension claim. In 1870 an investigation revealed that Spriggs Barney was not Thomas's biological father and that Barney was not his surname. Spriggs (his true surname) admitted that Thomas "was the son of his wife before marriage to her and [Thomas] must have been 15 years old at the time of the marriage." Spriggs may have been a "fraud undoubtedly" as the investigator believed, or he may have been trying to circumvent pension laws that did not recognize a stepfather as a legitimate candidate for a pension. In the course of this investigation, investigators discovered that a woman had received Thomas Barney's bounty by claiming to be his sister. The U.S. attorney's office was able to prove that "she was an impostor and that the soldier had no sister living at the time of his death." Only the widow's claim appeared to be valid.[70]

In another case Milly Martin admitted that she had lied within her widow's claim. In her 1868 application for a pension, Milly testified that she had not remarried after her husband's death. Five years later Milly changed her mind and confessed to her agent that she had remarried in 1866, shortly after her husband died. She asked her agent to withdraw her claim and to initiate a new application for a pension that corresponded with her shortened term of widowhood. No doubt Milly lied because she knew that if she had remarried so soon after her husband's death, she would be ineligible for a pension or would only receive a small amount of money.[71]

Tracing the Transition from Slavery to Citizenship

MILLY MARTIN's lie probably would not have been discovered
had she not confessed because she presented a credible case to
the Pension Office, offering evidence that the Pension Office
would accept as the truth. Milly successfully manipulated the
pension process, claiming she had not remarried and providing
witnesses who would corroborate her story. Yet more important than the issue of Milly's dishonesty is the fact that her
identity and rights as the soldier's widow were contingent upon
not being someone else's wife and that Milly caught on to this,
either through her own experience or with the help of a claim
agent, and responded accordingly. No doubt others lied and did
not confess. But the question of truth is less important than
what the claims reveal about the government's criteria for good
citizens and proper familial relations and the widespread responses to such standards. The extent to which former slaves
had to conform to meet these standards, how they measured up
to preconceived notions of citizenship, and how they negoti-
ated within the parameters of the government's requirements
reveal much about the slaves' transition to citizenship.

The general complications that arose within Harriet Berry's
claim—the problems with documentation, evidence, names, relationships, and identity—show a typical former slave woman
in the midst of a transition. Harriet was at once an insider and
an outsider in free white society, no longer a slave but not quite
a full citizen. In one instant Harriet was a new citizen, hiring a
lawyer, going to the courthouse, demanding from the government that which was rightfully hers. In the next, Harriet was
a nonperson, lacking a public identity, a former piece of property, and the object of scrutiny and suspicion. Examination of
the pension process exposes the transition as former slaves adjusted, as they situated themselves in an alien social, cultural,
political, economic, and legal milieu.

In the chapters that follow, the focus is narrowed to address
the specific questions and problematic areas concerning famil-

ial roles and relationships that arose in former slaves' pension claims. A claimant's attempt to remedy the question of his or her two names, a widow's efforts to prove the existence of a relationship not recognized by law, and a child's attempt to establish his or her parentage without the aid of birth records reveal the moments at which freedom could offer no point of reference for the experience of slavery, the moments at which former slaves were forced to conform to fit the profile of a widow, a legitimate child, or a dependent relative. Such cases uncover the government's definition of particular familial relationships—their boundaries, their place in a hierarchy of relationships, and the roles inscribed within them—and how former slaves maneuvered within the parameters of these definitions.

Some problematic areas are similar in all cases. Others that I have chosen as representative are often the most complex of their type, cases in which the demand for evidence could not be met, in which the claim had been contested by one or more parties, or in which the government's standards did not apply. Yet they serve to underscore the complexity and confusion that occurred as ex-slaves entered the world of citizens.

TWO

"We All Have Two Names"

Surnames and Familial Identity

*H*ARRIET BERRY'S identity as the widow of Joseph Berry
was called into question when pension officials discovered
that her surname might have been Bell. In free white society
surnames operated according to traditional assumptions about
the nature of family and familial roles and relationships. A surname was the outward sign of familial identity. Signifying the
descent of the family through the male line, the family name
passed from father to son, who kept it permanently. A daughter also inherited the family name from her father but used it
only until she married. According to the principles of coverture, when a woman married, she took her husband's name.
Thus Harriet should have possessed the same surname as her
husband. That she did not suggested to pension officials that
Harriet may not have been Joseph Berry's widow.

In free white society every citizen had a permanent family
name by which he or she could be identified. Within the pension process, as within any large bureaucratic organization, a
surname provided officials with an efficient means to locate a
particular soldier's records. A surname also served as a cursory
method of identifying a claimant's relationship to a soldier, as
Harriet's case suggests. Harriet's predicament—that her surname actually complicated rather than clarified family relationships—leads to the question of what role naming practices
played in the transition from slavery to freedom.

Naming Practices among Slaves and Ex-Slaves

THOUGH WHITE southerners may have been generally interested in monitoring the size of the slave population, only masters were concerned with keeping track of individual slaves.
Once the slaves were freed, they had to be accounted for like all
members of free society. When former slaves enlisted in the
army, enrolled in school, applied for aid, registered their marriages, or applied for pensions, officials asked them for their full
names. Because many former slaves had not possessed a surname in slavery, whites encouraged them to adopt one. The
Freedmen's Bureau instructed former slaves: "Every freedman
having only one name is required to assume a 'title' or family
name. It may be the name of a former owner, or any other person. When once assumed it must always thereafter be used, and
no other."[1] Bureau officials did not appear concerned about
what particular surname a former slave chose, as long as the
name was permanent.

Some whites advised former slaves to choose surnames more
carefully. Helen E. Brown, a northern white woman, wrote ed-
ucational tracts designed to guide former slaves through the
transition from slavery to freedom. In 1864 she published *John
Freeman and His Family* with the American Tract Society, an
association that published books of "practical advice" for newly
freed slaves. Brown's chapter on John Freeman's surname is
suggestive of how many whites conceived of a surname's function and expected former slaves to choose their surnames
accordingly.

In Brown's story a surname was crucial to self-definition.
When a lieutenant in the Union army asked the character of the
former slave for his name, the former slave could only respond
with his given name.

"John what?"
     "I'm Colchester Lenox's John," was the reply, "I've no other
name."

"John Lenox, then, I shall call you from this time forward for ever. Remember, will you?"

"Oh, no, master lieutenant, please don't put that down . . . I've objections to that. . . . It will always make me think of the old ways, sir, and I'm a free man now, sir. . . ."

"Suppose we call you John Freeman, then."[2]

When asked to elaborate upon his identity, the former slave referred to himself as the property of his former master, calling himself "Colchester Lenox's John." According to Brown, the problem with John's name was not simply that he lacked a surname but that this lack left him unable to define himself independently of his slave past. Further, the story suggests, just as it would not do for John to refer to himself as Colchester Lenox's John, it was not proper for him to take his former master's surname. John's adamant rejection of his master's surname as one that would remind him of slavery underscored this need to rid the name of the past. Instead, he received a totally new name, which was in Brown's words, "clean of slavery," affirming his new identity as a free man.

According to Brown, a person's surname was an outward or public sign of his or her familial identity as well. Once John agreed to the surname Freeman, the lieutenant gave him further instructions: "You must give your wife the same name, then, mind, and all your children. Then we shall know you all belong together. You'll be *the Freeman family;* and so the names were recorded on the books."[3] As the male head of the Freeman family, John passed his surname to his wife and children, marking them as a discrete family unit. As the lieutenant said, once the members of the Freeman family all had the same surname, outsiders would know they belonged to the same family. That their name was then "recorded on the books" implied a surname's broader public role as well as its permanence. In this case the lieutenant took John's name to register him for employment with the government. John and his family were now accounted for, written into the public record.

Yet the expectation that former slaves' surnames would automatically operate upon the principles of surnames in free society did not take into consideration the fact that former slaves had their own naming practices. When northern missionary Elizabeth Hyde Botume took down the names of the ex-slave children in her South Carolina Sea Island freedmen's school, she did not get the classroom "regulated," as she imagined she would. Instead, Botume grew ever more "puzzled." Some students appeared to have surnames, others did not. Some gave her their old master's surname as their own; others took the name of someone else's master. Many children invented new names with "much ingenuity" and then changed them daily.[4] The children's choices of surnames seemed "indiscriminate" to Botume, and she deemed it "hopeless" to understand them. Botume offered an example of a single family in which each member had a different surname: "In one family there were nine brothers and half-brothers, and each took a different title. One took Hamilton, and another Singleton, and another Baker, and others Smith, Simmons, etc. Their father was 'Jimmy of the Battery,' or 'Jimmy Black.' I asked why his title was Black. 'Oh, him *look* so. Him one very black man,' they said."[5] It appeared to Botume that former slaves did not share her sense that a surname came from one's father or that family members shared a single, stable surname.

In stark contrast to this notion of a surname's source and function, there were numerous potential reasons why the members of Jimmy Black's family possessed different surnames. Perhaps, as occurred in use of first names in slavery, the sons' surnames reflected ties to other relatives such as grandparents or aunts and uncles.[6] Or, because some were half brothers, Jimmy's sons may have belonged to different owners, and each may have taken the surname of his mother's owner. Each might have been compelled to choose a name when the others were not around, perhaps when he enrolled in school, enlisted in the army, or signed a labor contract. It is also possible that each son simply adopted a name that he liked or a name that he felt defined him, as the names Black and Jimmy of the Battery defined his father. Botume's example may have been rare—most former slaves may have chosen common family names—but it suggests that the reasons former slaves chose names varied beyond the uniform practices of whites' naming conventions.

Yet if no single practice characterized former slaves' adoption of surnames, it is clear that their choices were not necessarily indiscriminate, or taken without much thought, as Botume had assumed. Certainly some former slaves were assigned surnames from a host of outside forces including Freedmen's Bureau agents and missionaries. Others, like Doc Edwards, went by the names they had used during slavery. Edwards explained, "My Pappy was Murphy McCullers. . . . Dat would make me a McCullers, but I was always knowed as Doc Edwards an' dat is what I am called to dis day."[7]

Whether it meant casting off a master's name or choosing a surname for the first time, most slaves adopted surnames to assert their free status and mark a new beginning in their lives.[8] Bill Simms, a former slave living in Kansas in the 1930s, had assumed his master's surname. In his eyes, though, the act clearly signified his transition from chattel to free man. "My master's name was Simms and I was known as Simm's Bill, just like horses. When I came out here I just changed my name from Simm's Bill, to Bill Simms."[9] Harrison Beckett's new surname reflected the discovery of vital family connections lost during slavery. Under slavery his parents went by the name Thomas, having been owned by a man named Thomas. "But after freedom [daddy] goes back to Florida and find out he people and git he real name, and dat am Beckett."[10]

Ex-slaves who chose names for the first time often took common family names, particularly their father's surname. Jack Aldredge, a former slave from Mississippi, offers one such example. "Marsa, he sho wuz'nt good to my mammy and pappy and when de war wuz over we never took his name. No sir, us took my pappy's old name."[11] USCT soldier Charles Cobb enlisted under Anderson, his owner's name. Whether that had been his surname in slavery, was the name he chose when he enlisted, or was assigned to him by a military official because he offered none of his own is unclear. What is clear is that after he was discharged, Charles changed his surname to Cobb, his father's name.[12] Thomas Cole argued that he went against convention by refusing his father's name: "I was sposed to take my father's name, but he was sech a bad, ornery, nocount sech a human, I jes' taken my old massa's name."[13]

Some freed people took the name of an original owner or an owner from their distant past to recognize ties to family members also owned by them.[14] In a 1937 interview former slave Isaac Adams explained how he came to choose his surname: "When my Pappy was born his parents belonged to a Mr. Adams, so he took Adams for his last name, and I did too, because I was his son."[15] W. L. Bost of Asheville, North Carolina, made a connection to his maternal line through his former owner's name. "My massa's name was Jonas Bost," he told interviewers; "my mother and grandmother both belonged to the Bost family."[16]

Complications within the pension process often arose because pension officials treated former slaves' surnames as if they operated according to free society's assumptions about family, familial relationships, and family names. These complications reveal that slaves and ex-slaves made choices about their surnames according to personal perceptions about family and what a surname stood for and that these choices were affected by circumstance as well. Thus, that a woman and her husband possessed different surnames did not necessarily mean they were not married. Further, these complications illustrate that the relationship between a family name and familial identity was not so absolute as imagined in white society. If people did not believe that a couple was married because their surnames differed, then a surname actually disturbed family relationships, calling them into question rather than substantiating them. Questions about surnames provide a good starting point to explore the relationship between slave and ex-slave custom and the governing forces of free society that not only would dictate this outward expression of familial identity but would attempt to shape the inner workings of family as well.

Surnames in the Gap between Orality and Literacy

LUCINDA TWINE nearly lost her claim to a mother's pension in the rough passage from an oral to a literate society. Her son Anderson had enlisted in the USCC at Fort Monroe in 1863 and died of disease just over a year later. In 1873 Lucinda received his bounty and applied for a pension, though nothing seems to have come of that claim. When Lucinda reapplied under the less stringent 1890 law, which required only that parents prove a general state of dependence, she seemed an obvious candidate for a pension. Then living in North Carolina, Lucinda was in her sixties with no husband and no other children to provide for her needs as she grew older and less capable of taking care of herself. One of her neighbors described Lucinda's financial situation: "She gets surport by her labors and what other people choose to give to her. She is very old and nearly past labor."[17] Lucinda owned no property; one witness described her possessions as "a few things in the house—and not many of them—all of them would not sell for more than twenty dollars."[18] Yet in spite of Lucinda's obvious state of poverty and the fact that she had successfully acquired Anderson's bounty, the Pension Office rejected her claim because no Anderson Twine existed in their records.

The physical death of Anderson Twine had been preceded by the demise of his identity in the written world. Through the pension process Lucinda learned that when her son enlisted in the army, the agent taking down the information recorded his name as Anderson Toyan instead of Anderson Twine.[19] In his autobiographical work *Black Boy*, Richard Wright related a similar story about his grandfather. Wright offered several reasons of how such a mistake could have occurred, including his grandfather's mispronunciation of his own name, the poor

English skills of the white officer, or the deliberate act of a cruel southerner. Whatever the specific reason in Anderson's case, in the gap between the oral and the written, between what was said and what was recorded, Anderson Twine was literally written out of existence.[20]

Anderson's case illustrates some of the complexity of becoming a member of a literate society, in which information was preserved through written records. Within free white society a surname was both oral and visual; its permanence was assured in the act of recording it. In slavery a surname was primarily an oral thing. Among slaves it was both spoken and heard, but rarely written down. Because most slaves were illiterate, they would not have ever written their names or have known how to spell them.[21]

Rather than marking Anderson's identity as a distinct free person and allowing his mother to locate him, Anderson's surname became the source of much confusion. Pension officials searched through records for him that appeared under the surnames Loyan, Loyon, Logan, and Togan, before they found some more under the name Anderson Toyan. The case demonstrates that a surname did not automatically or conveniently identify Lucinda and Anderson as members of the same family. The difference in surnames confused the situation and made it difficult for Lucinda to demonstrate clearly to pension officials her relationship to her son. Moreover, in her attempts to procure Anderson's pension, Lucinda used different surnames, trying to match her son's enlisted name, demonstrating as well that the surname was not necessarily an accurate means of determining familial relationships if it could be manipulated so easily.

The problem of Anderson Twine's documentary nonidentity was exacerbated by the fallibility of the very thing that promised reliability, the written word. During the Civil War era, agents of the government and army personnel recorded all information by hand. At some point someone mistook Toyan for Loyan, then Loyan for Logan, and so on. Even if the first agent had recorded Anderson's name correctly, the written word offered no guarantee that mistakes would not occur later. It took the pension office eight years to clear up the confusion. Finally in 1898 it approved Lucinda's claim. In the end, however, it did not altogether accept her version of the family name. Lucinda Twine received the pension for her son, the soldier "Anderson Twine, alias, Toyan."

Military and pension officials recorded Huldah Gordon's surname just as she dictated it, which was just as she had heard it spoken during slavery, but the pension process revealed that her surname failed to mark the familial association she believed it had. During slavery Huldah belonged to John C. Cahoon, a prosperous planter in Nansemond County, Virginia, whose Cedar Vale plantation lay just south of Suffolk. Herbert Gutman featured Cahoon in his seminal work on slave families. Using Cahoon's plantation records, which contained slaves' proper names, Gutman traced generations of family lines among Cahoon's slaves. Gutman's study offers details of Huldah's family life under slavery that are absent in her pension claim: who her parents were, for whom her children were named, the broader contours of her family and community life. Conversely, Huldah's pension claim reveals what Cahoon's records do not: her surname, how she came by it, and what it meant to her.[22]

Huldah was raised on Cahoon's plantation, which had over forty slaves, one of the ten largest groups of slaves in the county. Through Cahoon's records we learn that Huldah's parents, Jenny and Bob, were among the first generation of Cahoon's slaves, some twenty-eight slaves purchased from twelve different sources. According to Gutman, Cahoon "never bought either a completed slave family or a young married couple," which meant that his entry into the business of large-scale agriculture was predicated upon the destruction of numerous slave families.[23] By the time Huldah's generation came of age in the 1830s and 1840s, Gutman argued, family life at Cedar Vale was relatively stable. Cahoon had allowed his slaves to live in settled families because it suited his economic needs. Gutman pointed out, however, that family life was always subject to disruption by sale, gift-transfer, and death.[24]

Huldah married Robert, another of Cahoon's slaves, with their master's consent around 1840, "before the Yellow Fever," in a ceremony presided over by a black preacher. They had eight children, three of whom died in childhood. Cahoon's records show that Huldah and Robert named five of their children—Jenny, Edward, Elijah, Adeline, and Sylvia—after their own parents and siblings, making connections to both sides of the family. Gutman suggested that such naming practices reflect the self-conscious creation of strong family and community ties among slaves.[25] Huldah's own painful experience of being separated from her oldest son, Miles, underscores the importance of customs that reinforced family and community ties. She explained to pension officials that Miles, for whose service she claimed a pension, had been hired out to other people as a young boy. "Miles staid with us till he was so high (4 ft.)(about 14) when he was hired out to an old colored woman . . . for 2 years and then to Mr. Cox . . . for 4 years till the war broke out. . . . After he, Miles, went to Cox's he came home every Christmas till the war broke out."[26]

The war years proved tumultuous for Huldah's family. Robert Gordon died in 1862, just a short time before Federal forces evacuated Suffolk and Huldah and her children left their master's plantation. Miles appears to have run away from Cox's place and made his way up to Norfolk, where he enlisted in the USCC. Two years later Miles was killed when a soldier in his regiment accidentally shot him while cleaning his gun.

After the war Huldah worked as a farm laborer and lived with two of her sons, Edward, age twenty, who labored in a sawmill, and Elijah, age nineteen, who worked in the oyster business. Among her neighbors were her daughter Jenny Smith; Robert's mother, Margaret Gordon; Robert's sister, Huldah Orton; and Lucy Ann Smith, who was Huldah Orton's daughter. After Miles died Huldah had received his bounty, which had been deposited for her in the Freedman's Bank, an institution designed by the federal government during Reconstruction to aid and encourage former slaves to save their money.[27] Huldah was not sure just how much money she had gotten, but she drew upon the account until she was told it was empty. In 1870, probably just as the bounty money ran out, Huldah filed a mother's claim for a pension.

Identifying Huldah Gordon, the pension applicant, as Huldah Jr., the slave on Cahoon's plantation addressed in Gutman's work, happened purely accidentally. A deliberate search for Miles Gordon's military records would have been difficult to initiate because Cahoon's records do not include most of his slaves' surnames. Complicating matters further, the family name Gordon appears to have surfaced in the gap between orality and literacy, when what was recorded differed from what was heard.

Though the name Gordon spanned three generations, Huldah and her family had not acquired it automatically through birth or marriage, as whites would have. According to Huldah, Robert's father had been owned by a man named George Gordon and had taken his master's surname as his own, though she did not offer his reasons for doing so. In her claim Huldah reported that Robert had deliberately chosen the name Gordon, his father's surname, and that she and their children had not inherited the surname Gordon from Robert but made a conscious decision to take it after he died.

Huldah revealed that as a slave her husband had gone by two different names. Robert "called his name Gordon after his father, but . . . the white people called him Calhoun after his master."[28] If Robert's case shows that a master's power to name his slaves was not so total, it also demonstrates the limits of a slave's ability to forge his own identity. Many slaves shared Robert's predicament. Although the white community recognized him as Cahoon, his master's name, Robert called himself Gordon, his father's name. On the one hand, Robert refused to be named exclusively by others. He was his own man, establishing his own persona by naming himself. On the other hand, the whites tried to determine his identity, naming him for his master. Possessing the same surname as his master did not make Robert a blood relative but marked him as his master's property, as a slave, someone else's man.

Yet freedom offered no guarantee that one could effectively escape this sort of predicament. When Huldah's former young master, William Cahoon, testified on her behalf, he stated that he did not "know about the negroes taking the name of Godwin. Robert's father was sometimes called Thomas Godwin."[29] Huldah did not know that Cahoon's father bought Robert's father from a man named George Godwin rather than George Gordon. Apparently, Robert took the wrong name. Because Godwin and Gordon could be considered as homophonic and because it is likely that Robert could not read or write to verify his name, it is probable that he never realized the mistake. By mistaking the name Godwin for Gordon, Robert further complicated the question of his own identity.

Though Robert was still a slave when he took the name Gordon, his experience underscores the precariousness of stepping from the oral to the written world. Robert took the name in trying to identify with his father. But his inability to read or write led him to take the wrong name. Much like the slaves who chose different surnames from their masters, Robert's misnaming distanced him from his father, differentiating rather than connecting them. Robert's legacy would be that his wife and children would also mistakenly assume the name Gordon and carry it with them into freedom.

Surnames and Public Identity

REGARDLESS OF the effect upon his personal identity, within the relatively small world of the slave quarters Robert Gordon's two surnames would not have obscured his public identity in any way. Once he entered free society and became one of its vast numbers of inhabitants, however, he would need one fixed title if he ever hoped to be officially recognized. For the same reason people without surnames as slaves were quick to select them in freedom. Quite often they chose a surname on the spur of the moment when the necessity arose.

Precisely because the surname became the key determinant of a person's public identity, it could also become the source of a person's public nonidentity, as Anderson Twine's case suggests. When the war was over, former slaves began to search for their relatives and apply for their pensions. Because no single convention characterized former slaves' choices of surnames, many could not begin to imagine what names their relatives had chosen or, to put it another way, who they had become. Lack of such knowledge within a system that yoked the surname and familial identity together so tightly made it difficult, if not impossible, for some former slaves to reconstruct their families after the war.

In 1867 a former slave owner wrote a letter to the secretary of war on behalf of a woman who had been his slave. The woman's son Albert had run off in 1864 to join General Sherman's army in Savannah and had died shortly thereafter. "His mother with a heavy family of eight children—down to the cradle," the man wrote, "after a year and a half absence struggling to maintain her family in hard times has returned to me for help." The former owner had written the letter in hopes that Albert's mother could get her son's pension. However, he knew he faced one problem: "by what name he enlisted Albert __ who? I do not know—we cannot find out."[30] Perhaps they did not know Albert's surname because he did not possess one in slavery. Or Albert might have had a surname but might have changed it to express his freedom or to avoid being captured by his master.

Though Benjamin B. Manson had successfully applied for his son's bounty at the war's end, when he made an application for a pension in the early 1900s, he could not remember under which name his son had enlisted. "John was our first child. As was the costom in that day and time, John went by the name of his owner and grew up and was known by the name of John

White."[31] Despite the fact that his son had grown up with the surname White, Benjamin thought that he had enlisted under the name Manson. "I never knew under what name my son John enlisted," he claimed, "but supposed it was under the name of John Manson, but may have been John White or some other name."[32] Benjamin explained that his confusion grew out of the fact that "after the colored people were set free many of them selected names by which they wished to be called and went by such names."[33]

Benjamin's statement contrasted the absoluteness of the "costom in that day and time" with his uncertainty about his son's new name. His pairing of order with slavery and chaos with freedom reversed whites' expectations of the surname. Rather than allowing a father to pass on information about his son, the naming act thwarted Benjamin's ability to identify his son. Freedom's new conventions left Benjamin uncertain about what his son called himself. Would John have kept his master's name because he had been known by it for so long? Would he have adopted the custom of free society and taken his father's name? Benjamin could not be sure.

Taking the Master's Name

In *John Freeman and His Family*, Helen Brown urged former slaves to take names that were "clean of slavery." Did this mean former slaves should take a name that would not evoke painful reminders of slavery each time it was uttered? Did it mean that former slaves should take names of their own that signified their own family line? Sometimes neither was possible because no matter how painful, slavery was a part of their past and thus a part of their identity. Noralee Frankel has shown how a slave's ownership served as a locus of identity in her description of a conversation between two USCT soldiers. The two strangers were getting acquainted and began broadly by "referring to their respective masters. In a more personally meaningful way, they also placed themselves by making connections with other slaves, particularly family members."[34] African Americans forged kinship and community ties in the context of slavery that could not simply be ignored or forgotten in freedom.

Despite historians' tendency to point toward the opposite, many former slaves assumed the surname of their last master. The WPA narratives are full of examples like that of Clayton Holbert, who explained: "We didn't have a name. The slaves were always known by the master's last name, and after we were freed we just took the last name of our masters and used it."[35] Rather than interpret such action as nostalgic yearning for the days of slavery, we might see it as former slaves' assumption of names they had long recognized as their own or to which they felt entitled. Lizzie Fant Brown evidenced such entitlement in her statement about her maiden name: "My mother was Nancy Fant, my father George Fant and my grandfather was Charlie Fant. Marse Jeemes Fant and Miss Liza wus my master and mistress. Our plantation (I always calls it 'ours' 'cause being a Fant nigger makes me a Fant too) wus a great big one."[36]

Robert Gordon's family took the name Gordon because they associated it with Robert's father, even if they heard the name wrong. It is not clear if Huldah had a surname before emancipation, or what it might have been. According to William Cahoon, Huldah and her children went by the name Cahoon. But if whites called Robert by the name Cahoon and he called himself Gordon, then perhaps Huldah went by another name as well. It is clear that upon her emancipation, she chose Gordon as her new name. Choosing this name may have been an act of establishing her free identity. Huldah's rejection of the name Cahoon, one by which whites already knew her, suggests a symbolic casting off of slavery's yoke.

Yet the name Huldah chose was not new, nor did it make a radical break with her slave past. Instead, Huldah chose a name intimately connected to that past. Like many of her contemporaries, although she rejected the name of her owner, she did take the name thought to be that of a past owner. Most likely Huldah did not do this to recognize the owner but to connect to her husband. Thus, by taking the name of Robert's father, Huldah and her children were not embracing their slave past but recognizing it as inextricably linked to their identity. As Leon Litwack has argued, "No matter how harsh a bondage they had endured, few freed slaves revealed any desire to obliterate their entire past or family heritage, and those whose given names or surnames reflected kinship ties tended to guard them zealously."[37] In many cases to take the master's surname was not to associate with his family or with slavery but to acknowledge family history. Erasing the memory of slavery would have meant erasing this family history as well.

At the same time it is impossible to ignore the fact that they thought Gordon was the name of the man who owned Robert's father. The name indicated more than a bloodline; it signified a family history shaped by the institution of slavery and the personal decisions of a slave owner. Consider Huldah's description of how she met Robert: "Capt Cahoon bought Robert's father from Geo. Gordon, and he Robert's father married a slave belonging to him Cahoon by the name of Margaret, and Robert was born to them, on the same farm. We were brought up as children on the same farm although he was a little older than I was."[38] Her family history included not only who married whom and who gave birth to whom but also who bought and sold whom. Many of the circumstances of slaves' lives—who they met, where they lived, whether they remained with their families—were intertwined with their masters' lives. The master, as part of the past, became part of their identity, so much so that over time their master's surnames had become their own.[39]

Benjamin B. Manson took the name of his last master. When he applied for his son's pension, he supplied his family history. Benjamin's story reveals his sense of the interconnectedness of his life with that of his owners:

> I was born in the state of Va as the property of Mrs. Nancy
> Manson of said state. When I was about 11 years of age
> my owner, Mrs. Nancy Manson, moved to the state of

Tennessee, bringing her slaves with her. When she died her slaves were divided among her children. In this division I fell to her son Joseph Manson. When I was about 18 or 19 years of age I married Sarah who was the property of Dr L. B. White.

Joseph Manson, to whom I belonged, married a daughter of my wifes owner. . . . Several years before the civil war my said owner became financially involved in some way and I became the property of Dr White. After the death of Dr. White . . . in some sort of family settlement, I again became the property of my former owner Joseph Manson.[40]

Within the pension system, which operated upon the assumption that a surname marked off discrete family groups, adoption of a master's surname could have adverse effects. After drawing a pension for eight years, former slave Rena Eason reported to her pension agency in 1888 that her husband, presumed dead for twenty-four years, was actually alive. It happened that Miles Eason had not joined the Union army as his parents, wife, and children believed he would when he left Gates County, North Carolina, in 1862 and "with many others repaired to the Federal Post at Suffolk, Va."[41] Instead, Miles ran off and worked as a servant for an officer in the Union army. When he left his position, Miles did not return home but moved to Washington, D.C., where he met and married another woman. Miles did not go back to Gates County until 1888, and only then did his family learn he was still alive.[42]

In the years after the war, Rena, her five children, Miles's parents, and other slaves who had lived on the Beaman place stayed on in Gates County. Though many former slaves left the site of their enslavement, others chose to remain either on the same farms and plantations or in areas nearby. They did so for varied reasons: for the short term out of apprehension of the unknown, the promise of employment, or the desire to locate family members. More permanently, former slaves settled where they had lived under slavery for the same reasons that one historian has argued drove them to attempt to acquire the land they had worked as slaves: "a profound attachment to place" and strong ties to the families and communities forged there.[43] Using $150 of the bounty money she had procured after Miles had been reported dead, Rena purchased thirty acres of land from her former owner, William Beaman, and made a living by farming the land with her children. Beaman's sale of land to one of his former slaves seems surprising in light of most planters' strong resistance to blacks' desire to own land. Landownership translated into independence and political and economic power in the predominantly agricultural postbellum South, and planters generally refrained from offering former slaves access to any means of independence or power.[44] Reports of Beaman's character suggest that he genuinely cared about his former slaves, that he represented the kind of planters Joseph Reidy has described as "old-line Whig paternalists . . . [who] tended to be of middle-age or older; they cultivated paternalistic ties with their black tenants and customers; and they felt a certain degree of civic responsibility for their social inferiors within what they believed to be a modified version of the old organic society." Yet the quality of the land Beaman sold to Rena—described as "swampy . . . and therefore undesirable"— might also explain his actions.[45]

Compared to many former slaves, Rena and her children lived quite well. They had achieved landownership, a goal long sought after but infrequently realized and a prerequisite in most freed people's eyes for living independently of whites.[46] In 1889 Rena's entire estate was valued at $286 in the Gates County tax list. In addition to the land itself, the Easons had acquired five head of cattle, two hogs, farming implements valued at $27, and other property including cotton and seeds worth $25. On the land stood a small two-story house and "one or two very poor outbuildings."[47] In her work on nearby Granville County, Laura Edwards cautioned that even landownership did not guarantee independence to blacks, particularly if their holdings were meager.[48] For the Easons daily survival must have required hard work, considering the swampy land and the unpredictable nature of the weather, insects, and the market. No doubt they welcomed the monthly income Rena's pension provided.

As soon as she learned that Miles was still alive, Rena wrote to her local pension agency and returned her most recent payment. Fearing she might be prosecuted for filing a fraudulent pension claim, Rena explained that she truly believed Miles had been killed in the army. Miles's family assumed he had joined the USCT, and they had not heard from him. Therefore, when Rena and her family learned that a Miles Eason from their area had been killed, they concluded that it was their Miles Eason, though they knew of at least two other men with the same name. One man was Miles's father, and the other was a man they knew of who lived nearby. As it turned out, the man who was killed in the service of the 37th U.S. Colored Volunteers was not Rena's husband but the third Miles Eason. In what Rena called "a mistake of identity," she had made a successful claim for the pension of a man with her husband's name.[49]

Rena explained the existence of so many Miles Easons by pointing out that "there were many slaves of the Eason family," suggesting these slaves shared the surname Eason with their masters and with each other.[50] Rena's husband may have been named after his father, who may have been owned by a member of the Eason family. Perhaps there were dense kinship networks among the Easons' slaves, and these slaves took the name to acknowledge these family ties. Or perhaps they took it to identify themselves with a large community of slaves to whom they felt connected. They may have carried the surname Eason because it was the custom to identify slaves with the name of the family who owned them.

Clearly Rena's "mistake of identity" arose from the fact that her husband and the other man shared both their first and last names. But this was not simple coincidence as it might have been for free whites who had the same name; the root of the problem lay in their common slave surname. The fact that Eason was the masters' name meant that relationships between Easons within the slave community had implications beyond consanguineous groups. For even if they had taken the name only to recognize their own family ties, these slaves were connected in another sense, beyond the familial, because of their common master. When slaves were freed and became part of the world beyond the plantation or the individual slave community, though outsiders may not have recognized this connection, it remained. That former slaves' notions of what bound people together and how those relationships were identified differed from those of free society in general also led Rena to mistake another man's name for her husband's.

Naming Practices among Married Women

Pension claims made by widows of USCT soldiers further illustrate the gap between slave and free family relationships, in this case a gap widened by the difference between the legal and extralegal status of the marriages in question. A vast majority of the widows making claims for pensions had the same surname as their husbands. In light of the fact that many former slaves were changing their surnames or adopting surnames for the first time, one wonders whether all the women took the surnames of their fathers and husbands, or if any of them chose names for themselves. Did female former slaves take their husbands' names because they were compelled to do so by law? Did they do so out of choice? Was this practice carried over from slavery? Did they do it to strengthen their pension claims? In other words, how freely did female slaves choose their names?

These questions become all the more intriguing when one considers that in white society naming was a male act. Former slave William Wells Brown took a surname upon the urging of his white benefactor who suggested that the surname represented one's freedom and thus the achievement of one's full manhood: "Since thee has got out of slavery, thee has become a man, and men always have two names."[51] In *John Freeman and His Family*, the lieutenant gave John a surname and told him, "You must give your wife the same name, then, mind, all your children." The naming practices of free society reflected the hierarchical relations of men and women in that society; when a woman married, she took her husband's name. This practice assured that the husband's identity remained intact, while it simultaneously rendered invisible the wife's identity outside of the marriage relation.[52] Taking the husband's name was symbolic of a woman's legal, social, political, and sexual subordination within a male-dominated society.

The pension application required that a widow provide a maiden name, the family name she possessed as a young, unmarried woman. The multiple meanings of a maiden name, signifying at once a girl, a virgin, a first, all suggest the temporary nature of a young woman's original name or family tie. The expectation was that a young woman would come of age, marry, and become a member of her husband's family. Taking her husband's surname signified her entrance into his family, but it also marked her coverture, the submersion of her legal and civil identity into his. When she married, a woman relinquished her property rights to her husband.[53] Without her husband's consent or intervention, a married woman could not sue or be sued, make a contract, or execute a will. Any wages a wife might earn belonged to her husband. A married woman's legal dependence was reinforced by limited economic opportunity; jobs for men were much more plentiful and lucrative than jobs for women.[54] Though the status of the *feme covert* had already begun to unravel by the 1860s with the creation of married women's property rights in some states and the loosening of the father's absolute authority over the children in domestic relations law, a married woman's subordination to her husband was still a matter of fact in the postbellum era.[55] In the specifications for applying for a pension, the request for a maiden name signified the notion that the applicant's material dependence had shifted at the time of her marriage from her father to her husband and that the loss of her husband thus necessitated aid from the government.

Although we know relatively little about slaves' surnames, we know even less about the gendered nature of the naming process in slavery. Because Huldah Gordon took her husband's name after her emancipation, her case indicates that some slave women did not take their husband's surname. Some examples from WPA interviews suggest the same. Several former slaves whose parents belonged to different owners testified as John Smith had: "My mother was named Charlotte Smith and father was named Richmond Sanders. . . . My mother belonged to John Smith and father belonged to Richmond Sanders." Tabby Abbey explained, "My husband wuz name Tom Mango, but us niggers always went by our Marster's name, so my name is Tabby Abbey."[56]

Yet other examples suggest that slave women did assume their husbands' surnames. Amsy O. Alexander reported: "My father's name was John Alexander and my mother was Esther McColley. That was her maiden name of course."[57] Ellen Trell, a former slave living in North Carolina, told interviewers that although she and her mother were owned by Needham Price, "My father belonged to Tom Bodie . . . and mother and I went by the name of Bodie."[58] In Nancy White's pension claim, a witness testified that Nancy had married John White while they were slaves: "I did not see [John and Nancy] married. . . . I heard of them getting married and when I saw her again she was called Nancy White instead of Nancy Haley. . . . I know she was always called Nancy White after this."[59] The witness knew that Nancy and John had been married, even if she had not been present at their marriage, because Nancy had changed her name.

If not legally bound to do so, why would a slave woman take her husband's surname? Perhaps, as Nancy White's witnesses suggested, doing so was one way of marking a significant change or rite of passage in a woman's life. A pension official asked one man when he had become acquainted with Nancy.

He replied that he knew her "all my life . . . when I first knew her she was called Nancy Haley."[60] Most slaves did not mark time according to the Christian calendar but by significant events in their lifetime. In this sense, a name change provided a means of charting the passage of time. Perhaps a woman took her husband's name to signify her entrance into his family, just as women did in free society.

Whatever the social or cultural implications taking a husband's name may have had in slavery, it did not have the same effect of marking a woman's inferior legal and social status as it did for free white women. Some historians have argued that slave women had more autonomy in their marriages than free white women, in part because many slave couples lived on different plantations and also because slave men did not control property or material resources the way that the laws of free society allowed free white men to do.[61] Another historian has countered that whether a slave woman had a better position in her marriage is a moot point because slave marriage occurred in a profoundly different setting, one in which neither slave men nor slave women had any property to control and both were in an inferior position to the master.[62] In either case, certainly, the law did not determine the power dynamic within slave marriage as it did for free white marriage. If slavery made slave women subordinate to white men and women, it did not necessarily subordinate them to slave men as well. The legalization of their marriages and the rights of freedom, however, would provide former slave men with access to the kinds of resources that gave husbands power over their wives.

Did the names that former slaves took reflect an acknowledgment of this new power dynamic? Frankel has argued that freedwomen and children accepted the father's paternal surname in symbolic recognition of his assumption of family power. She was careful to point out, however, that although freedmen plainly had a stronger position in the public realm in relation to freedwomen and acted as the legal heads of households, the term *patriarchy* is misapplied in the case of freedmen because African-American men "held much less power than white men did over white women, African American males, and African American female laborers."[63] Further, as both Edwards and Leslie Schwalm have illustrated, many freedwomen frequently challenged the new boundaries of male authority by taking their husbands to court or making appeals to the Freedmen's Bureau when they felt their husbands had overstepped these bounds or failed to live up to their new responsibilities. Edwards noted that in their daily lives freedmen and freedwomen "clashed regularly over the relative distribution of power and the substance of their responsibilities as husbands and wives."[64] Rather than acknowledge or consent to the authority of their husbands, then, did freedwomen take their husband's surnames simply to adapt to the norms of free society?

Raising such questions about surnames and former slave women's surnames in particular demonstrates the significant relationship between naming and public identity. Whether a surname had important personal meaning in terms of one's self-identity or represented family or kin ties, or whether it had little meaning beyond expediency, beyond the need simply to have one in order to join the army, to get married, or to receive aid from the government, it mattered differently in the broader context of postemancipation society. Regardless of a person's intentions in choosing his or her surname, surnames took on unexpected meaning and yielded unintended consequences when interpreted according to the norms of free society. The confusion that resulted revealed to former slaves that a person's familial identity, his or her connection to a particular family, was not taken for granted in free society but had to be substantiated, especially in order to reap the benefits that stemmed from family relationships such as a pension or an inheritance. What also became clear was that each citizen had a public identity, one that was inextricably bound to his or her familial identity. When one's familial identity was called into question, so too was one's public identity.

It seems that much of the confusion about identity that sur-

names created was rooted in the fact that in free society surnames reflected norms of family structure and relationships,
norms that also shaped and were shaped by domestic relations
laws as well as the laws that determined pension eligibility. An
examination of surnames, then, leads to the question of family
relationships and roles. Answering it reveals how those who had
not previously been granted the right to legal familial relationships fared when the pension system called their family relationships into question.

THREE

"According to the Custom of Slaves"

Widows' Pension Claims and the Bounds of Marriage

*I*N 1866 Freedmen's Bureau agent J. M. Tracy appealed to bureau headquarters for guidance in collecting evidence for the pension claims of former slave widows. "Where slaves were *given* in marriage and married by colored ministers, no licens were used, and no records kept, and seldom witnessed by white persons what rule will I be governed by in such cases? Will the testimony of colored persons be taken in such cases? And where *no* evidence of any kind can be produced, aside from the widows own affidavit, will that be sufficient?"[1] What is significant about Tracy's appeal is less the formal problem of the lack of documentation than the reason for its absence. The obstacles Tracy encountered in compiling former slave widows' pension claims proved not to be insurmountable. That claimants lacked documentation establishing their marriages was not unusual. America was only beginning to develop its bureaucratic apparatus, and at this point there existed no regular system to keep track of marriages. The practice of issuing or requiring marriage licenses did not occur in any uniform, widespread manner until the latter part of the nineteenth century. The combination of poor record keeping and the acceptance of informal marriage meant that the problem of lack of documentation was not unfamiliar to the state. As Megan McClintock has noted, many white widows applying for pensions had similar problems furnishing proof of their marriages.[2] In most cases the Pension Office handled the problem much the way that judges dealt with informal marriages, by presuming marriage "from the acknowledgments, cohabitation, and reputation of a couple."[3] In time, pension laws sorted out what evidence would be sufficient to make a successful claim.

Yet in striking contrast to the reasons white widows lacked marriage licenses, the absence of a formal bureaucratic apparatus was not the reason that most former slaves could not document the existence of their marriages. Even if the practice of issuing licenses had been formalized, they still would not have possessed the requisite papers because the state did not accord legal recognition to their familial relationships. Former slaves would not have had any papers because according to the laws that governed the family in free society, slave marriages did not exist. Slaves' marriages possessed none of the protection, benefits, or obligations of marriage under the laws of freedom. Instead, their masters ultimately controlled their familial relations, as Tracy implied when he stated that slaves were "given" in marriage.

Legitimate Marriages: Legality and Morality

WHAT CONSTITUTED proper marital relations for American society? How did Americans distinguish valid marriages from illicit sexual relations? For the most part colonial legislatures had assured that couples took formal steps—either civil or religious—to create valid unions. In the post-Revolutionary period, however, the question of formal procedure stood at the center of the debate about the extent to which marriage was a private act. Influenced by republican concepts of the private nature of contracts, individualism, and self-regulation, nineteenth-century America saw a growing acceptance of marriages that occurred without formal sanction, what were known as common-law marriages. Though there were dissenting opinions on the subject, most judges tended to presume a marriage rather than a case of "immoral cohabitation" when a couple had lived together as husband and wife.[4] Yet there was room for debate about what constituted a valid marriage. Whether a couple cohabited with "matrimonial intent" was left for individual judges to ascertain on a case-by-case basis.[5]

Regardless of what criteria were used to determine matrimonial intent, civil sanction itself distinguished a valid marriage from illicit and immoral cohabitation. Only recognition by the state, either at the inauguration of the marriage or at some point afterward, removed the question of moral wrongdoing on the part of the cohabiting couple. To marry, or to live in licit cohabitation, was a right, contingent upon a person's civil identity. Slaves did not possess this right because they were not citizens. In this context slaves found themselves in an impossible bind. Though many slave couples might have been able to meet the requirements for common-law marriage (mutual and public recognition of their relationship as husband and wife), common-law status did not apply to them precisely because southern law did not consider slaves to be citizens.

Not surprisingly, in this conception of marriage, legality and morality so overlapped that each became indistinguishable from the other. Slave marriages were thus not only illicit but immoral as well. This conflation is evident in the instruction given to former slaves about legalizing their marriages and behaving properly within the bounds of that relationship. Freedmen's Bureau assistant commissioner Clinton B. Fisk counseled former slaves: "When you were slaves you 'took up' with each other, and were not taught what a bad thing it was to break God's law of marriage. But now you can only be sorry for the past and begin life anew, and on a pure foundation."[6] Fisk's advice assumed that the purity found in the institution of marriage under the law was lacking in slave marriage. Pointing to slavery's worst ills—robbing slave women of their chastity—the American Freedmen's Inquiry Commission argued similarly that because slave women were not regularly married, "the natural result is that the instinct of chastity remains underdeveloped or becomes obscured."[7] Clearly morality developed under the proper condition of lawful marriage, and not outside of it.

It could be argued that American virtue—the fusion of republican sacrifice and morality—found its truest expression in the institution of marriage in nineteenth-century society. Echoing the sentiment of his time, a Freedmen's Bureau agent working in Virginia wrote to headquarters, "I think it would add much to the stability as well as morality of . . . this community [of former slaves] if the parties now living together as man and wife, were compelled in every case to appear before the clerk of the court . . . [to] acknowledge their present relations, receive marriage certificates, [and have their children] legitimated and entitled to right of inheritance."[8] State-sanctioned marriage promoted both moral behavior and societal stability by providing a proper context for sexuality and assuring the systematic conveyance of property and proper morals from one generation to the next. If former slaves were to make the crucial transition from slaves to citizens, it was incumbent upon them to engage in lawful, documented marital relations both to assure their integration into American society and to demonstrate their worthiness as citizens. Americans prescribed legal marriage as a means of civilizing former slaves and used the status of former slaves' marital relationships to measure their progress.[9]

Requirements for a Widow's Pension

INTERESTINGLY, the view that slaves had not been properly married conflicted with the state's decision to offer pensions to the families of slaves who fought for the Union.[10] The desire to accord ex-slaves the pensions that were now rightly theirs as new citizens apparently overrode any doubts about the sanctity of slave marriages and even explicitly acknowledged their validity. Arguing before Congress for the need to amend pension legislation to address the unusual circumstances of slave marriage, Senator Lafayette S. Foster of Connecticut stated: "The blacks who came from the slave States, and who probably were slaves before they entered the service, although they had wives and children, were not, according to the laws of the States within which they lived, legally married, and of course if [the soldier] were killed . . . they could not by law be recognized as the wives or widows and children of [the soldier]. We thought that this was unjust."[11]

The soldier's death eradicated any opportunity for the wife or child to forge legal family relationships with him, an opportunity that would have existed if the soldier had lived. By pointing to the injustice of denying pensions to slave wives and children simply because southern laws did not sanction slave familial relationships, Foster allowed for an ex post facto affirmation of slave marriage as a valid institution. With such views in mind, Congress enacted legislation that enabled pension officials to treat slave marriage as a form of common-law marriage, to give them legal status after the fact.

The congressional act of July 4, 1864, was the first to address slave marriages. It provided that the widows of "colored soldiers" who lived in states where slaves could not marry needed only to prove, by the testimony of "credible" witnesses, that they had lived as man and wife for no less than two years before the soldier's enlistment.[12] This provision followed the principle of common-law marriage that to live as man and wife was to be man and wife. This piece of legislation provided a means by which pension officials could determine legitimate slave marriages.[13]

In 1866 this act was amended in consideration of emancipation and the complications that slave marriages often encountered during these years of upheaval. Questions raised in the congressional debate about the act of 1864 centered on several key issues: the involuntary separation of husband and wife who then could not have cohabited for two years before the soldier's enlistment; marriages contracted during the rebellion that could not meet the requirement that they precede enlistment by two years; soldiers who had more than one wife; and former slaves who were driven into free states but were unable to solemnize their marriages.[14] Addressing these many issues, the amendment left the determination of the legitimacy of a slave marriage in large part to the discretion of the commissioner of pensions. The act now read: "The widows and children of colored soldiers and sailors . . . shall be entitled to receive the pensions, bounty, and back pay provided by law, without other evidence of marriage than proof, satisfactory to the Commissioner of Pensions, that the parties had habitually recognized each other as man and wife, and lived together as such; and the children born of any marriage so proved shall be deemed and taken to be the children of the soldier or sailor."[15]

On March 3, 1873, this legislation was revised again to redefine the bounds of legitimate slave marriages. In addition to proof of mutual recognition as husband and wife, a widow had to offer evidence that others in her community recognized them as such. This act also acknowledged slaves' marriage ceremonies as binding, in spite of the inability of such ceremonies to provide legal sanction. A widow also could establish a marriage by proving that she had been married "by some ceremony deemed by them obligatory" and that she and her husband lived together as husband and wife up to the date of the soldier's enlistment or death in the service.[16]

Although this special pension legislation formally recognized slave marriages, such recognition did not change the fact that slave marriages had not occurred within the context of southern domestic relations law or according to the same norms that shaped formal or common-law marriages. Nor did offering slave marriages ex post facto validity erase the stigma of immorality that whites attached to them. At the root of the pension legislation was the notion that marriage was a civil contract, a legal relationship that legitimated what would otherwise be immoral cohabitation. Though such legislation suggested a certain sensitivity to the intricacy of dealing with slave marriages on the part of the state and the necessity for flexibility on the part of the law, the standard of marriage remained the traditional legal union that was initiated by formal ceremony and dissolved by death or divorce. Slave marriages complicated that institution as pension officials understood it; as they prosecuted former slave widows' claims, pension officials constantly grappled with these complexities and found themselves forced to redefine their conceptions.

The cases that follow in this chapter offer a wide range of responses by both former slaves and pension officials to the complicated procedure of applying pension system requirements to slave marriages and vice versa. They evidence the continuous and often subtle negotiation of the differences between slave and free marriage and the terms of the laws themselves. These cases dramatically represent a two-sided process taking place within the arena of the pension system. As white society sought to transform slaves into citizens by imposing the traditional marriage relationship, former slaves boldly claimed their citizenship for themselves by exercising their familial right to a pension. By either path the road to citizenship passed through this most contested relationship.

Marriage: When the Customs of Slaves and the Laws of Freedom Collide

SARAH B. PITTS applied for a widow's pension in 1867. A single woman in her late thirties or perhaps early forties, Sarah lived in Accomack County, Virginia, nestled between the Chesapeake Bay and the Atlantic Ocean. Like most of the claimants featured in this chapter, Sarah represented a class of women, both black and white, newly widowed by the Civil War. However, Sarah's unmarried and childless status was not representative of most freedwomen's domestic experience. Whether they continued in marriages from slavery—many choosing to formalize them, others not—or whether they formed new or first-time relationships after emancipation, former slave women generally married and resided in two-parent or extended, male-headed households. Although some resisted and resented the government interference in their familial relationships that legalization represented, most freedmen and freedwomen embraced it and the protection it afforded their families.[17]

After generations of being denied the opportunity to do so,

freedwomen made family their primary concern. Many wanted to be at home for their families. When the limitations of men's employment made staying home impossible, freedwomen fought to control the amount of time they labored in the fields or for wages outside the home. Jacqueline Jones has said of the desire to put family first: "Blacks struggled to weld kin and work relations into a single unit of economic and social welfare so that women could be wives and mothers first and laundresses and cotton pickers second."[18] At home freedwomen cooked, cleaned, made clothing, and tended to gardens and livestock, as resources allowed; they cared for the old, the young, and those in need.[19]

Freedwomen married for love and in recognition of the importance of family, but practical reasons kept them in male-headed households. Economic reality dictated that families pool their resources in order to survive; though women's labor or wages often made a necessary contribution to the family economy, they hardly afforded women the opportunity to provide for themselves. As Laura Edwards has argued about freedwomen in North Carolina, "Economic insecurity ultimately propelled women into the orbit of male-headed households, if not as wives, then as daughters, aunts, sisters, and grandmothers."[20] Single women often moved in with other relatives or, less commonly, combined households with other single women to share resources. Though women could and did protect themselves, women in male-headed households were less vulnerable to the harassment and sexual exploitation of white employers or overseers.[21]

In spite of the difficulties they encountered, some freedwomen headed their own households, either by force of circumstance or by choice. Jones has pointed out that single women, particularly mothers with young children, left rural areas for towns and cities where they might find better opportunities to support their families. "As a result," Jones argued, "southern towns and cities were characterized by an imbalanced sex ratio in favor of women."[22] The fact that women alone contracted their own labor, took their grievances to courts and to Freedmen's Bureau agents, and took on government officials in their quests for pensions suggests that when it was necessary, freedwomen could operate effectively within what was considered the male realm.

Clearly a widow's pension promised Sarah some relief in the daily struggle to provide for herself. Initially her case seemed straightforward. Sarah could not provide material proof of her marriage to Riley Pitts. She claimed that she married him in Drummondtown, Virginia, on August 16, 1862; however, no public record of their union was ever made.[23] Like other widowed claimants, Sarah pointed out that she and Riley acted as husband and wife, "living and cohabiting" together, and were recognized as husband and wife by "friends and acquaintances."[24]

Sarah provided witnesses in lieu of documents to prove that she was indeed the widow of Riley Pitts. Among the several different men who claimed that they knew both Riley and Sarah quite well, two witnesses testified that "the said parties habitually recognized each other as man and wife and lived together as such for at least three (3) years before he enlisted and further that the said parties were recognized as man and wife by all their friends and acquaintances and that the said Sarah Pitts is now recognized as the widow of Riley Pitts by all her friends and acquaintances and also by the friends and acquaintances of the said Riley Pitts."[25] According to the requirements set down in the act of July 4, 1866, Sarah had supplied sufficient and proper proof of her marriage to Riley Pitts.

However, Sarah was not the woman who received the pension belonging to the widow of Riley Pitts. Sarah lost track of her claim after some years. She later explained that she had given her claim to "Mr. Samuel I. Walston of Accomack [County], Virginia to secure a pension and he let me have some goods from his store. He died about 1878, and I have had nothing since. I cannot say whether or not he secured a pension for me."[26] In the meantime, in October 1872 the Pension Office granted a pension on account of Riley Pitts's service to a woman named Sallie Cropper.[27] Was Sallie Cropper the real wife and Sarah Pitts an impostor, or vice versa? Was Riley married to both women at the same time, or to one after another? Why would two women claim to be the widow of the same man?

Sallie Cropper (also known as Sarah) had also applied for a widow's pension. Like the other Widow Pitts, Sallie had "no record evidence of her marriage," meaning, of course, that she could not furnish a marriage certificate. In her claim Sallie stated that she and Riley Pitts married "by mutual consent" and that she was "married by permission of Katy Cropper my mistress to Riley Pitts by permission of his master Edward Pitts."[28]

Though she possessed none of the necessary documents, Sallie legitimated her claim with white witnesses who appeared with her before the notary public in April 1872 to corroborate her claim. The witnesses stated that their "knowledge of these facts is obtained from being near neighbors to the owner and employer of Sarah Pitts she being owned by a member of their family seen her and Riley together often and know the relation between them."[29]

However, the testimony of Sallie and her two white witnesses proved inadequate. It happened that Riley's sister had successfully contested Sallie's earlier bid for Riley's bounty; now Sallie's claim was considered questionable. The Pension Office contacted the postmistress of the area in which Sallie lived and requested that she make the necessary inquiries as to whether Sallie and Riley were married. The postmistress responded that the witnesses to whom she spoke had indeed recognized Sallie and Riley as man and wife.[30]

Perhaps the most compelling evidence in Sallie's favor was the support of her mistress and Riley's master. Sallie's former mistress wrote a letter confirming that Sallie was Riley's wife for "seven years up to the time he entered the U.S. army, I considered her his wife at the time he left, they were both living in our family."[31] On the day Riley left for military camp, Sallie "packed the few things that he took with him and was very much distressed at his leaving." Riley's former master also offered to testify in Sallie's behalf.[32] The support of these two witnesses, coupled with the postmistress's findings, appears to have convinced the Pension Office of the legitimacy of Sallie's claim.

Who was the real Widow Pitts? Both stories appeared plausible. Neither woman could provide a marriage certificate, but both furnished witnesses who supported their claims. Sallie appeared to have what would be considered the more legitimate claim because she possessed the weighty evidence of her mistress's testimony. However, if Sallie was deemed the real widow, had Sarah filed a "fraudulent claim for the purpose of personating the legal widow of Riley Pitts," as one pension official would later contend?[33]

To ask who was the real Widow Pitts might be, in fact, misleading. It suggests that *real* and *legal* are synonymous, making the issue one of truth as opposed to one of legal definition. If a man, by law, can have only one wife at a time, then after he dies he should only have one legal widow. But if that man married, as Sarah put it, "not . . . in accordance with the laws and customs of the white people but in accordance with the customs of the colored people who were held as slaves," the question of a legal widow becomes much more complex.[34]

That two women claimed to have been married to the same man at the same time was not unusual for former slaves in the postemancipation South. In a letter home northern missionary Harriet Ware described a common scene: "A man who was sold six years ago to Georgia . . . [found] his wife here married again. He gave her leave to do so, however, when he was sold off, so had nothing to say."[35] Quite often couples were separated during slavery, either forcibly or voluntarily, and remarried, often without the other's knowledge. When slavery ended and couples found each other again, many a husband or wife found his or her spouse with someone else.[36] In many instances the sweeping marriage legislation passed in the South automatically married former slaves who were living together before they had the opportunity to sort out their various relationships.

Thus it happened, and quite frequently, that a former slave was married to someone he or she had never intended to marry, or even was married to more than one person. As Leon Litwack has pointed out, "The question facing numerous freedmen and freedwomen was not whether to formalize their slave marriage but which one should take precedence."[37]

The complicating factor in cases like that of the Widows Pitts was that there was no husband to determine which would be his only wife. Instead the task fell to pension officials prosecuting the claims to choose the legal widow according to their own conception of what constituted a legitimate marriage. Nothing in the pension legislation specifically addressed this problem. Although it was discussed in the congressional debate about the 1866 pension act, Congress left it up to the discretion of the commissioner of pensions to decide which woman would receive the pension.[38]

In the 1882 edition of *General Instructions to Special Examiners,* the Pension Office addressed the issue of contested widows' claims in general. A special examiner could determine which woman was the "lawful" widow by "ascertaining which one was first married to the soldier, and whether he was released from the first marriage by an absolute divorce, which permitted him to remarry."[39] Applying this formula to slave marriages was problematic at best.

In spite of the pension laws' ex post facto legitimization of slave marriage, slave and free marriage differed in ways for which such legislation could not account. The boundaries that marked the beginning and end of legal marriage were not the same for slave marriage. Marriages between whites were clearly bounded by civil law and ceremony; even common-law marriage was vested with legal status. To violate the marriage contract under the laws of freedom was to be held accountable by the state. The only way to end a marriage between free whites formally and legally was by divorce. Any other attempt to end a marriage left one open to the charges of abandonment, desertion, or even adultery.[40]

No such laws governed slave marriages, which varied according to the customs of a particular community and what particular masters would allow. Most slaves were married as Margaret and John Fields had been, by a black preacher "with the little ceremony observed by slaves, [where] there was no license and no record kept." Sometimes the master would perform a wedding ceremony, as pension claimant Rachel Walters recalled of her wedding. "We both belonged to old man Jim Allen," she said, and "he married us himself."[41] Mary Barbour, the daughter of slaves, described to interviewers her parents' more festive marriage celebration: "My mammy marry my pappy dar an' she sez dat de preacher from de Methodis' Church marry 'em, dat she w'ar Miss Mary's [her mistress] weddin' dress, all uv white lace, an' dat my pappy w'ar Mr. Charlie's [his master] weddin' suit wid a flower in de button hole. Dey gived a big dance after de supper dey had, an Marster Charlie dance de first set wid my mammy."[42]

Not all slaves married by ceremony, however. Harriet Berry explained, "The only ceremony we had consisted in procuring the consent of our owners, the slaves of each of our masters come together in the evening after the consent was granted and had a litter party and a supper." Freeman and Isabella Cherry married with their master's consent and "by their agreement to live and cohabit together as man and wife which was the usual form of marriage with slaves at that time." Some slaves, like Hagar and George Washington, had no event to mark the occasion but "just took up and lived together as man and wife."[43]

Divorce or other legal means of dissolving the marital union did not exist for slaves, nor did there exist a universal practice for ending a slave marriage. No matter how binding the marriage vow, it was not protected by the law and existed under the constant threat of the master's power to rupture or dissolve it. Some slave couples lived out their years together; others were forcibly separated by sale or by the death of their owner or, if they belonged to different owners, because one decided to move his plantation. Still others simply ended their marriages by choice, a practice slaves referred to as "quitting." Slaves faced no legal or social consequences for engaging in this form of "non-legal but community recognized divorce."[44]

During the 1890s, for reasons unknown, Sarah made another claim for a pension as the widow of Riley Pitts. In a special examination of the claim, questions arose about the veracity of her story. Witnesses argued that Sarah had been married to a man named Levi Bundick during the time she claimed to have been married to Riley. Underscoring the significance of naming, one witness testified that Sarah had only recently begun calling herself Sarah Pitts rather than Sarah Bundick, but another claimed that she had gone by both Bundick and Pitts since the war ended.[45] In her testimony under special investigation, Sarah attempted to clear up the matter of her marriages. Though she left some questions unanswered, casting suspicion on her claim, Sarah also presented a plausible story that accounted for the existence of Riley's other wife and Sarah's other husband. The crux of her case lay in the ambiguity of the boundaries in slave marriage and in her insistence upon distinguishing between, as she called it, "the laws and customs of white people" and "the customs of colored people."

Despite attempts of pension officials to treat slave marriage as a form of common-law marriage, Sarah did not acknowledge that any persons of color married during slavery, because, as she pointed out, "people did not marry in those days." Interestingly, both Sarah and Levi were free during the time of their alleged marriage, which meant that they could have been legally married if they so desired. Yet Sarah conflated her marital situation and that of slaves. Whether deliberately or not, Sarah's arguments played upon the complexity of differences between slave marriages and legal marriages that would enable a person to be married and not married at the same time. Of her marriage to Bundick, she argued: "I was not married to him. There was no marrying in those days." Indicative of the confusion borne of negotiating in and around the boundaries of nonlegal marriage, Sarah referred to Levi as her "husband"

in the very next breath and called herself his "wife."[46] Sarah
clarified the sequence of events, declaring that Levi had died
before she began her relationship with Riley. She tried to narrow in on Levi's date of death by pointing to significant markers of time during the war: "The white soldiers were down here
when he died. There had not been any battles fought that I
know of. There had not been any colored soldiers recruited at
that time."[47]

In this second claim Sarah acknowledged the existence of
Riley's other wife, but she still held fast to the assertion that
Riley had been her husband as well. Sarah insisted that she had
not married Riley in the sense that white people understood
marriage; she and Riley had not entered into any legal contract,
nor had they participated in any kind of ceremony. In this case,
the law did not allow marriages between slaves and free persons
of color. Emphasizing the distinction between slave and legal
marriage lent credibility to Sarah's story because by the varied standards of slave marriage, Sarah could very well have been
married to Riley. She offered compelling reasons, by the standards of slave culture, and told a persuasive story to argue that
she was Riley's wife. After her first husband died (sometime
around 1862), Riley began visiting Sarah. Although Riley officially lived at the Croppers' place, he and Sarah spent nights
together. Sarah claimed that this made them husband and wife,
even appealing to Victorian notions of propriety: "I must have
regarded myself as his wife," she argued, "or I would not have
lived with him."[48] Many slave (or slave and free) couples married "abroad," that is, they were married but lived on separate
plantations. In these cases the couples saw each other whenever
circumstances allowed. Spending the night together on occasion constituted living together.[49]

According to Sarah's testimony, she and Riley lived together
until he enlisted in the army. But even afterward the relationship continued, she argued, because Riley wrote her letters
from camp and sent her his photograph, suggesting his lasting commitment to her.[50] As further proof of their relationship

as husband and wife, Sarah turned to the pension system's standards, arguing that people within their community recognized them as such and that people knew her as Sarah Pitts. The two conditions of living and cohabiting together as man and wife and being recognized as such by others fulfilled the legal definition of a legitimate slave marriage.

The same line of argument served to suggest that Riley's marriage to Sallie might have ended by the time he and Sarah were together. Sarah admitted that Riley had lived with Sallie and that the two considered each other husband and wife. But, she argued, by the time Riley started visiting her, Sallie was no longer his wife. Sarah cited conditions that according to slave custom nullified the marriage: Sallie Pitts "took up with a white woman's husband. . . . She had a fuss with the man's wife Miss Ann Lilliston. . . . Ann had Mrs. Pitts thrown in jail. . . . After she got out of jail the white soldiers carried her to a fort down below. I did not see her anymore."[51] When asked, Sarah replied that she did not think Riley and Sallie ever divorced, but according to Sarah's way of thinking, if slaves did not marry as whites did, neither did they divorce in the same way. The fact that Riley and Sallie separated could have meant that they had quit the relationship, terminating it forever.

Sarah's testimony did not account for the fact that in her original application she claimed to have married Riley in 1859, three years before his enlistment, a discrepancy that called her story into question. Sarah's story also conflicted with that of Sallie's mistress, who stated that Sallie and Riley were together until he left for the army. Whether Sarah lied about being married to Riley is debatable; in retrospect it is impossible to tell. It is entirely possible that she merely lied in her original claim about the length of her marriage to Riley to make the marriage seem more substantial or that Sallie's mistress gave incomplete or untrue details of the last days of Sallie and Riley's marriage. Sarah's second claim, both the very fact that she reapplied for a pension and her argument within it, makes a strong case for the possibility that there were two Widows Pitts. The general upheaval in the South during the war years and the ease with which Riley might have dissolved or begun a marriage could have allowed Riley and Sarah to get together after Riley had ended his relationship with Sallie or could have enabled Riley to have two wives at the same time.[52] The truth of Sarah's identity as the widow of Riley Pitts was lost in the gap between the customs of slaves and the laws of freedom.

From the Pension Office's perspective, the aim in a case like that of the two Widows Pitts was not to determine why, by the standards of slave marriage, two women would claim to be the widow of the same man, because by legal definition a man could not have two widows. Instead agents had to determine which of the two marriages more closely approximated the criteria of legal marriage so they could choose the single legal widow. The problem with such cases lay in the paradoxical attempt of the Pension Office to discern a legal widow despite the fact that slaves did not legally marry one another.

In the end the special examiner responsible for Sarah's second claim concluded that she had filed her claim under false pretenses. Several witnesses testified that Riley's only wife had been Sallie Cropper, and thus the examiner argued, "It is a difficult question to see how we can apply any law or custom to make the claimant the legal wife of Riley Pitts: At the time Riley went into the army, he was living with his recognized wife Sallie."[53] Tellingly, Sarah's perception of the differences between slave and legal marriage could only be interpreted in terms of criminal activity. The Pension Office must have let the matter drop after this, though it could have prosecuted Sarah for filing what it deemed was a fraudulent claim.

In a similar case of two widows, the contesting claimant was not considered a fraud but an unfortunate victim of the capricious nature of slavery. The 1882 provision that determined which of two widows could be called the legal widow was based on the assumption that marriages ended by choice, not force. Accordingly, the most recent wife represented the husband's most recent choice. Rosetta Crandall had the misfortune of

being Ephraim Crandall's first wife; they were married sometime in 1844 in a ceremony presided over by a slave preacher.
Their master, David B. Perry, gave his consent and allowed the
couple to live together on his Rosedale, North Carolina, plantation where they lived as husband and wife for some ten years
and had four children. Though they might have suspected or
feared it, they were no doubt unprepared for what happened in
1855 when the joy of their fourth child's birth was met with the
bitterness of separation: Perry sold Ephraim to a slave trader.[54]

On his new master's plantation, Ephraim married Dolly, another slave. His reasons for marrying are unclear. Did his new
master force him to marry? Did he do so because he knew life
as Rosetta's husband was impossible? Was he lonely? Though
she admitted that Ephraim had a relationship with Dolly,
Rosetta claimed that he stayed in contact with her after he was
sold, that he continued in the capacity of her husband, even visiting her near the time of his enlistment. According to those
prosecuting the claim, Ehpraim's sale marked a clear break in
his relationship to Rosetta. His ensuing marriage to Dolly (corroborated by her former master and fellow former slaves), the
fact that he and Dolly stayed together until he enlisted nearly
ten years later, and that Dolly had three children by him appeared to supersede any previous attachment. Because Dolly
was Ephraim's wife at the time of his enlistment, she won the
title as his legal widow. Rosetta appealed this decision several
times. Although in each case her marriage to Ephraim was
affirmed, Dolly's claim to his pension prevailed.

Slave Relationships and the Issue of Morality

IN THE CASE of William and Alice Timmons, who applied for
a minors' pension, officials misapplied their own understanding
of proper marital relations and the related issue of morality.
Doubts about their mother's moral state ultimately nullified
William and Alice Timmons's claim to their paternity. When
they applied for their father's pension, William and Alice had

no idea that he had married another woman upon joining the
USCT or that his new wife had applied for his pension a few
years earlier.[55] William and Alice's mother, Jane, who never applied for a pension, died in 1872. Four years later William and
Alice, then sixteen and eighteen, respectively, applied for their
father's pension with the help of their guardian, Priscilla, a half
sister from their mother's previous marriage. Nothing came of
this first claim, and for reasons unknown William and Alice
waited until 1889 to follow up on it. Now, some forty years after
their parents' marriage, William and Alice would have to
demonstrate that they were the legitimate children of Abraham
Timmons by proving that their mother and father were married at the time of their births.[56]

Lack of sufficient documentation forced William and Alice,
like many other former slaves, to rely upon the recollections of
family and friends to account for their family history. Remark-
ably, they produced a number of witnesses who had known
their parents and could offer information about their relationship, among them their half sister, an old uncle, a cousin, a
woman who attended their mother at their births, and a white
woman who had known their mother's owner. From these witnesses William and Alice learned that Jane had lived in Florida
and belonged to a man named Higginbotham. Abraham's
owner brought him to Florida from North Carolina and sold
him to one of Higginbotham's neighbors. Abraham visited Jane
on Higginbotham's plantation once or twice a week over the
course of a few years before he left the area.[57]

William and Alice did not know for certain how their parents came together as husband and wife; they knew only that
their parents had been married "under slave customs." Lucinda
Williams, a woman who had lived on the same plantation as
Jane, recalled: "I was present at the ceremony of Jane Timmons
and Abram Timmons (the soldier) it was along in slavery time
when they married and they married according to the usealy
way they married people in them times . . . the Bosses of Colored people would give each one to whoever would want to

unite themselves as Holy Matrimony and they was a preacher called and would read the ceremony and then it was pronounced man and wife."[58] Because those present often recall events differently, some witnesses testified that Jane and Abraham married by ceremony, while others remembered no ceremony. They "simply lived together as man and wife by consent of their masters," William and Alice's half sister claimed. "Thats what they called marriage."[59] As the two versions of the marriage attest, slave customs varied from plantation to plantation, leaving William and Alice with no single founding event to designate as the origin of their parents' marriage and their own legitimacy.

In spite of the conflicting testimony, Walter Ayres, the pension official in charge of the case, acknowledged the existence of Jane and Abraham's marriage, but not without offering his reservations about it. He reported, "The examination thus far has tended to show a slave marriage . . . but said marriage has been stripped of the solemnity of ceremony." Reflecting the problematic nature of offering ex post facto validity to slave marriages, Ayres accepted the marriage as legitimate while simultaneously suggesting that it lacked the formality and seriousness of legal marriage. He further attributed the confusion over the Timmonses' marriage not to the vagaries of memory or the variance of slave customs, or even to the lack of laws codifying the guidelines of slave marriage, but instead to the "loose" marital relations between slaves, calling into question Jane's "character for chastity."[60]

The examination of the claim revealed that Jane had been with several men throughout her adult life. Before marrying Abraham, she was married to Milo Holland, with whom she had six children.[61] Sarah Williams, a woman who had known Jane during slavery, testified that after her marriage to Holland and before her marriage to Timmons, Jane had borne a child by another man. "Dan Woods was said to be the father of the child," Sarah claimed; "[Jane] was not married to Dan Woods."[62] Finally, a man named James Penny claimed to have had a relationship with Jane after Abraham's death. Although he professed to have lived with Jane and to have had a child with her, James stated that "I was not married to her. . . . She let me live with her after I had known her for about 6 months. . . . I did not promise to marry her, just took up with her."[63]

Within her own community, both during and after slavery, Jane's numerous relationships would not have raised questions about her chastity. As Deborah White has claimed, "Slaves rejected guilt laden white sexual attitudes"; sex was not considered sinful or impure, and premarital sex or sex outside of marriage was accepted within slave culture.[64] Such practices and attitudes, however, did not denigrate the marriage relation. Slaves, and later freed people, considered the marriage bond sacred—whether legalized or not—and held adultery as a heinous offense.[65]

Though Ayres concluded that Jane and Abraham had been married, William and Alice's claim was ultimately rejected. Upon reviewing an appeal of this rejection, Webster Davis, an assistant secretary of the Department of the Interior, argued that the evidence was insufficient to prove that Jane and Abraham had ever "habitually recognized each other as man and wife" or "were so recognized by their neighbors." William and Alice's inability to establish whether a ceremony occurred, which would have clearly marked the commencement of the marriage, proved detrimental to their case because of Jane's relationships with other men.[66]

Secretary Davis seized upon the question of morality, instead of the issue of legality, to explain the complications of slave marriage. Turning a blind eye toward slave customs or values and instead falling back on a common stereotype of black women, he pointed to Jane's relationships with the four men to argue that she had "no moral sense" because as far as he could see, there was no way to distinguish between her marriages and her more casual relationships: "It is said that she was not the wife of either Woods or Penny but was the wife of Holland and Timmons; the evidence, however, fails to show any basis for this distinction except that her relations with the two last named men were maintained for a longer time." Secretary Davis did not take into consideration that the evidence, provided by witnesses who knew Jane, demonstrated that slaves themselves made the distinction between getting married and cohabiting without "matrimonial intent," to use a term from domestic relations law, or that cohabiting in a nonmarital state was accepted within the slave community. For their part the witnesses were clear and consistent about which men Jane had married and which she had not.

In this case the grounds for determining pension eligibility rested upon the notion of morality inscribed within the legal definition of marriage. Davis argued that Jane's numerous relationships made it impossible to determine "moral matrimonial intent." He cited a precedent-setting case to point out that if slave marriage was to be treated as a valid institution, it had to be subject to the same standards as formal marriage. Therefore, it was not legal sanction but "the intent of the parties in such cases that is the governing factor, and if the moral matrimonial intent between the slaves was lacking, their outward matrimonial relation during slavery can no more be used as a foundation upon which to build subsequent legal marital status."[67] The contradiction in Davis's own thinking is clear: although slave marriages fell outside the bounds of the law, they could also, paradoxically, be considered illicit, or unlawful, relations. Pension officials judged the nature of slave relations according to Victorian notions of morality, a practice that precluded consideration of slaves' own standards of morality or their own sense of what constituted proper marital relations.

Finally, the assistant secretary argued that because Abraham had married another woman a year and a half after he left for the army, he obviously did not consider himself married to Jane or "bound to her by any permanent tie." Using this argument to prove Abraham's lack of moral matrimonial intent, Davis concluded that "a marriage between the mother of the appellants and the soldier Timmons is not proved."

Although there was no question that William and Alice were Jane's children, their relationship to their father depended upon their mother's relationship with him. Though the Timmons children could provide the requisite witnesses who testified that Jane and Abraham were married, the government's interpretation of their mother's relationships destroyed their chances not only for their father's pension but for his name as well. Because Jane and Abraham were not married, according to the government, William and Alice were deemed illegitimate; by law they had no father. In one of the many letters they wrote to the Pension Office as they chased their claim over the course of nine years, a testament to their persistence, William and Alice pleaded for their very identity: "We from our birth was called Wm and Alice Timmons and we know no other man to call our father save Abraham Timmons . . . please allow us a chance to Identify ourselves."[68]

Negotiating the Ambiguous Boundaries of Intimate Slave Relationships

IN THE Timmons case James Penny and others who described his relationship with Jane distinguished the relationship as nonmarital in intent by arguing that Penny "took up" with her. What slaves and former slaves called "taking up" covered a broad spectrum of relationships that occurred outside the boundaries of formal marriage. Slaves who claimed to have taken up with one another might have been referring to the nonlegal nature of slave marriage in general; in that sense, all slaves took up with one another.[69] Others used the term to mean beginning to live together as husband and wife without a ceremony, as the example of Hagar and George Washington demonstrates. Still others used "taking up" to describe involvement in an intimate relationship without "matrimonial intent," as Jane's case indicates.

After emancipation some former slave couples chose to take up and live together without formalizing their relationships.

Former slaves' reasons for making this choice included avoiding the cost of a marriage license, distrust of the government that had ignored their families for so long, and a sense of the redundancy of formalizing relationships that in their eyes were already legitimate. As Noralee Frankel has found, among freedmen and freedwomen what were called "took-ups" ranged from cases of long-term, committed cohabitation as husband and wife, to trial marriages between couples who intended to marry legally sometime in the future, and even to relationships between couples who preferred the ease of their old ways to the complications of marrying and divorcing in accordance with the laws of freedom.[70]

Interestingly, former slaves often used the term *took up* in their pension claims specifically to differentiate between marrying one another—entering into a relationship with the intent to stay together until death or separation—and engaging in a relationship with no clear "matrimonial intent." These distinctions mattered to pension applicants who might challenge a widow's claim or to widows whose intimate relationships threatened the acquisition or retention of their pensions. Whether relationships characterized as took-ups were actually lacking in marital intent or reinvented as such for the benefit of the claim, such characterization played off government officials' notions that no relationship that lacked legal sanction could be called a marriage. Tellingly, in his advice to freed people, Freedmen's Bureau assistant commissioner Fisk used the term *took up* in contradistinction to proper marriage, one vested with legal sanction and thus, as Secretary Davis put it, "moral matrimonial intent."

The case of Catherine Camphor, a ninety-year-old former slave living in Baltimore, Maryland, centered upon the ambiguity of the boundaries between marrying and taking up.[71] Catherine had been receiving a mother's pension for some eleven years when her son's posthumous contribution to her material support was suddenly interrupted by the appearance of a woman claiming to be his widow. According to her 1866 application for a pension, Catherine claimed that her son John left behind no widow, nor any children, which made her, as his mother, the next eligible relative to receive his pension.[72] By the testimony of several witnesses from her community in Baltimore, Catherine had been able to prove that she was indeed the mother of John Camphor and that she had been dependent upon him for material support before his enlistment, thus meeting the prerequisites for receiving a mother's pension.[73] By 1869 the Pension Office had approved Catherine's claim, and the case appeared to have been closed.

In 1880, however, Sarah Camphor made a widow's claim for a pension, explaining that she had not known until recently that she was eligible for her husband's pension. Testifying on Sarah's behalf, her former owner, Sarah Bounds, stated that Sarah and John Camphor were married in her dining room by a local preacher in 1849 and that they subsequently had five children, only one of whom was still alive in 1880. Sarah Bounds testified that Sarah and John lived and cohabited as husband and wife until the time of John's enlistment in the USCT.[74] In later testimony Sarah Bounds recalled that about a year before John had enlisted, she had had a falling out with him and forbade him to come to her home but that John and his wife still saw each other occasionally.[75]

Clarifying their living situation somewhat, Sarah Camphor recalled: "John lived and cohabited with [her] three nights a week until the war broke out. . . . Then Mrs. Bounds would not let [him] visit her regularly, but he would find occasion once or twice a week to come and remain overnight." After John left for the war, Sarah did not visit him at camp because, she claimed, she did not want to leave her mistress.[76]

With the additional evidence of several other witnesses who had attended Sarah and John's wedding and had known the couple to be married, Sarah's case was approved. Catherine Camphor was immediately dropped from the pension rolls, because the existence of the soldier's widow and child nullified a mother's claim to a pension.[77]

In cases of contested claims for a pension, there was always the possibility of perjury or that one of the claimants applied for a pension under false pretenses. In this particular case Catherine Camphor might have knowingly denied the existence of her son's widow because she had the advantage of making the first claim. But Sarah might also have made a false claim; she and her mistress could have concocted a story about a wedding in order to procure money falsely from the government.

As in the case of the Widows Pitts, however, in retrospect the question of whether one or the other was telling the truth cannot be resolved. What is more interesting, and more valuable in terms of understanding the transition to legal status, is the possibility that both stories were true. Again, like the case of the Widows Pitts, because there could only be one pensioner, the Pension Office had to determine which story to accept. It chose Sarah Camphor's story because her account was corroborated by her former mistress and supported by the law that favored the widow over any other family member.[78]

The differences between the customs of slaves and the laws of freedom played a crucial role in Catherine's claim. In this case, however, Catherine pointed to the varying bounds of slave marriage not to establish that a marriage existed where whites would not have considered it but instead to establish that a marriage did not exist where it appeared that one did.

When confronted with the information that Sarah had applied for a widow's pension, Catherine claimed that she knew John had a relationship with her, but she did not believe the two had been married. Catherine's argument rested upon the premise that no laws precluded slaves from living together without being married and that the practice of taking up was accepted within the slave community. She argued that she "never believed her son John was married to Sarah Jarrett, only supposed he 'took up' with her as he did with other women in the neighborhood. . . . [She] had heard that Sarah had children by John but never believed they were born to her in wedlock." By pointing out that John had taken up with other women in the neighborhood, Catherine called his matrimonial intent into question. She suggested that though John and Sarah may have lived together, it did not establish that they were married. Further, the fact that John may have had children with Sarah had little bearing on the case from Catherine's perspective; because within slave culture motherhood did not require marriage, having children together did not necessarily mark a couple as husband and wife. Many historians have pointed out that slaves viewed motherhood with deepest respect, regardless of whether or not the slave mother was married. This respect hearkened back, in part, to the traditional West African belief in the importance of motherhood, but in another regard it also derived from the experience of slavery. Because owners saw financial gain in the birth of new slaves, women who bore children were more likely not to be sold; reproduction could keep a family together. Bearing a child out of wedlock was not an immoral act, as Victorian notions of woman's purity would deem it, but one of "social and familial importance."[79] Finally, Catherine attested that Sarah had not acted in a wifely manner; Sarah had not visited John while he was in camp, as Catherine believed "any *wife* should have done."[80]

In the event that the Pension Office believed that Sarah and John had in fact been married, and in the absence of formal divorce for slaves, Catherine's testimony suggests that by the time John died, the marriage could have already ended. Sarah's former owner pointed out that she herself had thrown John off her place, forbidding him ever to come back, adding that Sarah and John only saw each other occasionally after that. If Sarah did not visit John in camp because she "did not want to leave her mistress," she may have displayed the same loyalty to her mistress in the year between John's exile from the Bounds place and his enlistment in the army. In other words, she might have refused to see him, effectively quitting their marriage.

Catherine offered explicit evidence that John himself had quit the marriage. She reported that she had visited John at camp. She noted that when she saw him, John had asked his captain to draw up a document leaving his belongings to her. When the captain asked John if he had any wife or child, Catherine testified that he had replied, "No! *none that he cared for*."[81] Catherine's story intended to show that by the time his mother had visited him at camp, John was no longer committed to the marriage. He needed no documents, no legal action to dissolve the relationship; by deciding that the marriage was over, he made it so. Although Catherine "verily believed herself entitled to the [pension] inasmuch as she as the mother of the deceased soldier had drawn his bounty and back pay, and that she had received his consent to such action," she eventually lost the pension to Sarah.[82]

Without Catherine's attempts to keep the pension, Sarah's widow's claim would have appeared deceptively simple. Sarah gained a pension on the strength of her mistress's testimony, which enabled her to prove that she and John married by ceremony and lived together as husband and wife. Catherine's efforts within the case illustrate that the apparently lenient requirements for a pension glossed over irreconcilable differences between slave and free marriage that were the result of the vastly varying contexts within which slave and free marriages occurred.

In another variation on the quandary of proving the nonexistence of a marriage, former slave Lucy Allen introduced the notion of marriages made by a master's orders rather than by a couple's mutual consent. In fact, Lucy deftly juggled two sets of competing relationships that threatened to undermine her case. Lucy applied for a pension from Lexington, Kentucky, in 1893. She had been taking care of herself for years since her husband had fallen ill and had gone to live in "the poorhouse," where he died in 1889. At the time she applied for her pension, Lucy was seventy years old, and though she described herself as a midwife and washerwoman, she clearly needed financial assistance. Lucy had married Charles Allen in 1868 under the laws of the state of Kentucky, and she had a marriage certificate to prove it. However, because both Lucy and Charles had been married to other people during slavery, pension officials wanted to be certain that the dates those relationships were terminated did not overlap with and thereby invalidate Lucy's marriage to Charles.[83]

Lucy explained that she had been married to Levi Parker during slavery but that the marriage ended long before the war began. She laid out the details of that marriage: "I was called Lucy Johnson until I was married to my first husband whose name was Levi Parker. . . . I do not know when I was married to [him] but it was long before the war, during slavery times and under the slave custom which in my case was the consent of my owner."[84] Her strategy seems to have been to undermine the marital nature of the relationship. She portrayed herself as unfamiliar with the most significant details of Levi's life: she did not know to whom he belonged under slavery, a fact she would have known if she had been married to him because both her owner and his would have had to consent to the marriage. She underplayed the closeness of their relationship. Lucy testified that she was married to Levi "only for about two years and during those two years I saw him about once in three months when he would come and stay with me over Sunday."[85] Where other former slaves might have pointed out that the circumstances that created separations in an abroad marriage did not nullify the existence of that marriage, Lucy seemed to be arguing that they did. In what might have been an appeal to the special examiner's own sense of proper marital conduct, Lucy confessed to conduct that would invalidate her union: "I had two children during the time I was cohabiting with Levi Parker and neither one was his child." In the course of her testimony, Lucy's language changed: she no longer referred to her marriage but to her cohabitation. Finally, Lucy claimed that the relationship with Levi Parker was "a matter in which I had no choice." Hers was a forced marriage, one in which she participated involuntarily.

But Lucy had a second problem to contend with: the Pension Office also required that she establish that Charles's marriage to Mary Redd had ended before theirs began. Testimony of several witnesses, including Mary's sister, revealed that although Mary and Charles had reunited after the war, Charles did break up with her before he married Lucy.[86] Lucy disputed the fact that the marriage had occurred at all, arguing that though Charles "had a woman named 'Mary' before the war and she had one child by him," Mary had not been his wife. In an effort to disqualify Mary, Lucy exploited society's own prejudices and played on the tenets of legal, and therefore moral, marriage by claiming that Mary was known as a "fast woman" and a woman of "lewd habits." Lucy was eventually successful in pursuing her case.

Remarriage and the Loss of Pension

MANY WIDOWS, both white and black, were vexed by the condition that made pension eligibility contingent upon remaining unmarried. Because widows' pensions were designed to replace the support of a husband who died as a result of his service to the nation, the pension system interpreted a woman's remarriage as a sign that government support was no longer necessary. According to the logic of the pension system, a new husband constituted a new source of support. Thus, by remarrying a widow forfeited her pension. Many widow pensioners tried to circumvent the system by taking up with a new partner rather than formally marrying him. In 1882, responding to allegations of such practices on the part of both white and black widows and swept along in the tide of increasing acceptance of state intervention in marriage, Congress enacted legislation that discontinued a widow's pension if she was found cohabiting with a man.[87] Other widow pensioners tried to hide their change of status, often by marrying under an assumed name, one that differed from the name on the pension rolls. A nosy neighbor or an inquisitive pension agent frequently foiled such attempts to outwit the government.

Certainly not every case of cohabitation represented a blatant effort to outsmart the pension system. As the phenomenon of taking up reveals, some former slaves simply continued the practice of marrying according to their own customs. Others took up together in relationships that they did not intend to be matrimonial, a practice which in their eyes would not constitute a new marriage. Complications in the pension system hinged on the issue of intent. What did a widow intend when she lived with another man or when she claimed to have remained a widow?

Mathilda Hubbard's case illustrates the frustration claimants and pension officials alike must have experienced as they navigated the murky waters of the question of a widow's intent. Mathilda applied for a pension in 1876 on account of her slave husband Richard Kearny, who had died in 1864. Included in Mathilda's case file is a copy of her certificate of marriage to Frank Hubbard, her present husband, dated 1873. Clearly making an effort to acquire only her just due, Mathilda requested a pension for the years 1864–73, the term of her widowhood. Mathilda's former master testified to the fact of Mathilda's marriage to Richard; he brought with him a meticulous family record which included the birth dates of Richard and Mathilda's children.

In the course of taking testimony, it came out that Mathilda had been intimately involved with a man named Richard Keyes in 1868, though the exact nature of that relationship was unclear. Mathilda maintained that she had not married Keyes, she had only taken up with him. Mathilda argued that though she had lived with Keyes and was known as Mathilda Keyes, "she was never married to said Keyes nor did they recognize each other as man and wife."[88] Not surprisingly, pension officials suspected that Mathilda lied about the nature of her relationship to Keyes in order to lengthen the term of her widowhood and thus receive more money from the government.

Had Mathilda lied? Had she attempted to manipulate the system by playing upon the differences between customs carried over from slavery and the norms and laws of free society? In her argument that she "took up" with Keyes, Mathilda characterized her relationship as nonmatrimonial, a perfectly acceptable form of intimacy within her own community. But the pension system could not accommodate this kind of taking up, in part because the practice of living together outside of formal matrimony was unacceptable according to the moral code implicit in pension requirements. Also, practical questions arose. How did one clearly distinguish between a marriage and taking up? Much like the concept of mutual and public recognition used to establish common-law or slave marriages, the best evidence one might offer of having taken up with a partner was one's own opinion about the relationship and the testimony of witnesses who could describe what others perceived the relationship to be.

In this case it appears that Mathilda's former owner held the most influence with pension officials. J. K. Kearny initially testified that Mathilda had not married Keyes, but his later testimony called this allegation into question: "She took up and lived with a man named Richard Keyes, with whom she lived as his wife until Christmas December 25 1869."[89] Though we cannot be certain that Kearny's testimony was the deciding factor, it is telling that Mathilda's term of widowhood was shortened to include only the years 1864–68. Ironically, though the practice of nonmarital cohabitation might have coincided with common stereotypes about African Americans' immorality, pension officials regarded Mathilda's claim that she had not married Keyes with the same suspicion with which they viewed any claim that a couple had been married.

Betsy Booker's case represents a more straightforward example of an attempt to evade the rules of the system in order to keep a pension. In 1874 pension officials learned not only that one of their pensioners was dead but also that she had been living under an assumed identity. In 1868 Betsy Booker, aged forty-two, won a pension on account of her slave husband Adam Booker, to whom she had been married for sixteen years. Adam died in Vicksburg, Mississippi, from typhoid malarial fever during the last days of the war. Betsy died in 1872, but the news did not reach the local pension agency for several months. A pension agent looking into Betsy's death learned from neighbors that she had been living with a man named David Grayer or Greer. She changed her name to Hattie Grayer or Greer and told people that she and David were married.[90]

According to pension law, had she been married to David, Betsy no longer would have been eligible for a pension because she no longer would have been widowed. Whether Betsy and David were actually married or whether Betsy took his name to create the illusion of marriage so they could live together without scandal is impossible to tell. Under either set of circumstances, however, if pension officials had learned of her relationship and especially of the fact that she claimed to be married, Betsy would have lost her pension. Betsy appears to have tried to hide the fact of her new relationship behind an assumed name; she continued to collect her pension under the name Betsy Booker, evading the government by keeping her new relationship a secret.

Amanda Van Buren's claim is suggestive not simply because she admitted to remaining unmarried to keep her pension but also because the special examiner in her case noted the prevalence of the practice. Amanda had received a pension in 1868 on account of her husband Martin Van Buren, whom she married during slavery in Louisiana. In her application Amanda stated that her master married the couple in 1860 and that Martin enlisted in 1863.

In 1879 John H. Benton, special examiner for New Orleans, discovered that Amanda had been living with a man for the past seven or eight years. Amanda had recently moved, and Benton was searching for her, though the records do not reveal if he was looking for her because she had moved or because he had learned of her relationship. When the two met up, Amanda admitted to Benton that she and James Johnson had been living together "as husband and wife, have owned each other as such among their neighbors and acquaintances, and have been supposed by them to be lawfully married . . . [and] that her intention . . . is . . . to live together as husband and wife till death shall separate them."[91] Amanda confessed to Benton that she had often considered surrendering her pension and marrying Johnson, and when her ploy was finally uncovered, she gave up her pension without regret. Benton recorded that "she now cheerfully surrenders her pension certificate."[92]

Interestingly, Amanda's description of her marriage to Martin changed significantly in the affidavit she gave to Benton. According to this 1879 affidavit, Amanda had not even known Martin during slavery. She claimed that "till freed by the war she was the slave of a Mr. Dougherty and worked on his plantation near Baton Rouge; and after the place was taken by the 'Yankees,' she came to New Orleans where she soon got acquainted with her husband."[93] In this telling of her story, Amanda married Martin at Camp Parrapet, where he was stationed, in a ceremony performed by a white preacher who belonged to the regiment. What accounts for the discrepancy between the two versions of her story? Either version would have qualified her for the pension in 1868, so the motivation to fabricate the details of her marriage is unclear. Benton seemed not to have noticed the discrepancy, perhaps because he did not have her original pension application on hand. In fact, Amanda's honesty impressed him to the extent that he described her as a "guileless creature" to his superiors at the Pension Office.

Amanda so convinced Benton of her remorse at having taken too long to give up her pension that he expressed his regret as well. Benton classed her in a separate category from other women who had done the same thing. Because Amanda had come to him "without the slightest hesitancy or reservation" once she heard he was looking for her, she was different from other women who "escape the just forfeiture of their pensions, under the false and persistent plea that their husbands, for such in fact they may be, are only boarders."[94] That all had the same goal of retaining their pensions seems to have escaped Benton's notice.

Amanda Van Buren's case seems a fitting place to end because it underscores how former slaves and pension officials exploited the range of the pension system, the simultaneous rigidity and malleability of its laws. For years Amanda stretched the bounds of the law; she successfully manipulated the terms of the pension system, replicating the experience of slavery by "marrying" Johnson outside of the realm of legal matrimony. Conversely, in spite of his wish to do otherwise, Benton was compelled to adhere to the law; he confiscated Amanda's pension certificate because the law could not distinguish between her good intentions and the intentions of those who cheated it without regret. In other instances it is not the evasion or the application of pension laws that demonstrates the amount of play within the system but the manner in which both pension officials and former slaves used the laws to interpret past and present relationships. Both groups took advantage of the ambiguities and loopholes in pension legislation, exploiting the gaps between the customs of slave marriages and the force of law either to support or to deny the pension claims under dispute.

FOUR

"The Order of Civilization"

Minors' Pensions, Legitimacy, and the Father-Centered Family

*B*ECAUSE A pension was a form of inheritance, the act of applying for a minor's pension forced many former slaves to grapple with their legitimacy, their legal identity as members of a particular family. In the case of William and Alice Timmons, the children were denied their father's pension because they could not prove that they were his legitimate children. Just as the law defined the legality of marriage, it determined the legitimacy of children, founding its construction on the marriage-centered, patriarchal family. A child was legitimate only if conceived or born within a lawful conjugal relation.[1] But if legitimacy appeared to derive equally from both parents and from their union, implicitly the hereditary relationship between father and child was primarily at stake. Legitimate status conferred upon the child the right to support by the father and the right to inherit his property, his family line, his name, and his status. As minors' pension claims generate issues of legitimacy and explore their implications, they also bring to the fore the shifting valuation of the parents' separate roles under the laws that governed families in free white society.

Familial Order and Disorder

IN HIS 1855 narrative *My Bondage and My Freedom*, Frederick Douglass argued that the slave family, unrecognized by the laws of southern states, fell into disorder:

> Slavery does away with fathers, as it does away with families
> . . . and its laws do not recognize their existence. . . . The
> order of civilization is reversed here. The name of the child is
> not expected to be that of its father, and his condition does
> not necessarily affect that of the child. He may be the slave of
> Mr. Tilgman; and his child, when born, may be the slave of
> Mr. Gross. He may be a *freeman;* and yet his child may be a
> *chattel.* He may be white, glorying in his Anglo-Saxon blood;
> and his child may be ranked with the blackest slaves. Indeed,
> he *may* be, and often *is,* master and father to the same child.[2]

Douglass lamented the loss of family ties produced by the laws
and circumstances of slavery that would separate a boy from his
mother, make him a stranger to his siblings, and keep his father
"shrouded in a mystery."[3] Yet the reversal Douglass referred to
was the subversion of the patrilineal, patronymic family, the
family in which the father was featured prominently. The institution of slavery had no place for the legal paterfamilias, the
source of family lineage and the bearer of the inheritable: property, status, and the family name.

Douglass declared that slavery "does away with fathers."
Read literally, Douglass's statement might mean that male
slaves did not father children because slave owners forcibly im-
pregnated their female slaves, as appears to have been the circumstance of Douglass's own birth. But slaves did father children. Fathers figure prominently in Douglass's statement; it
is not their absence that is evident but their disordered relationship to their offspring. The institution of slavery had not
done away with the figure of the father; rather it was the loss of
the legal hereditary relationship between fathers and their children that Douglass decried. He stated that "the name of the
child is not expected to be that of its father, and his condition
does not necessarily affect that of the child." Douglass seems
to have been less concerned with the handing down of property
or wealth—which slaves generally did not formally possess—
than with the systematic transmission of identity from gener-

ation to generation.[4] The laws that did not recognize slaves'
families also did not recognize the father's prerogative to pass
on his family line to his children, leading Douglass to conclude
that "genealogical trees do not flourish among slaves."[5]

In Douglass's own case this disordered relationship res-
onates with particular force and emphasizes that it was not necessarily slave fathers who disappeared but any man who fa-
thered a slave. Douglass's master, at the highest rung of
southern society, may also have been his father, but the master-
slave relationship took precedence over that of father-son. No
acknowledged legal or social connection existed between them.
Reversing the order of paternal succession, the law deemed
Douglass neither white nor free, and if he was by blood a member of his master-father's family, by law he was not. The non-
bequeathing father (master) could thus sell his children without censure or remorse.

Douglass's claim that slavery reversed the order of civilization can refer not only to the elimination of the bequeathing father but also to the creation of the visible, bequeathing mother.
Unspoken in the cry "He may be a *freeman;* yet his child may
be a *chattel*" was the operation of the law of the South that de-
creed that the child inherited the condition of bondage from
the mother. Unspoken in the lament "He may be the slave of
Mr. Tilgman; and his child . . . the slave of Mr. Gross" was the
effect of the law that made the child the property of the
mother's owner.

Yet to call the situation of the slave mother a reversal of the
free family suggests that slave and free families were polar op-
posites and thus that slave mothers could be equated with free
fathers as the head of the household. But neither slave mothers
nor slave fathers possessed the legal or material means by which
one could assert control over the other.[6] Unlike free white fathers, for example, neither slave parent controlled the child's
person or earnings.[7] And though they attempted to protect, so-
cialize, and care for their children as best they could, neither
slave parent possessed any legal authority over their children.

Such authority belonged exclusively to the master and to those to whom he delegated it.[8]

Perhaps Douglass was referring to the idea that the nature of the institution of slavery and slaves' own cultural heritage gave mothers a central role in slave families. However dubious the recognition—because it was related to economics rather than concern for slave families—the mother-child bond was consistently acknowledged by the law and by slave owners. Masters valued female slaves for their reproductive function: the more children a slave woman produced, the larger the master's labor force became. Sexual reproduction and economic production were inextricably linked. Motherhood thus affected a female slave's life and determined her worth and her place in a way that fatherhood did not for the male slave.[9] And though slave mothers had to manage feeding and caring for infants in addition to their usual work schedule, their reproductive and child care activities created a connection between mother and child that masters were least likely to sever by sale or some other kind of separation. The owner's recognition of the mother-child bond also meant that if slave parents married "abroad" or lived apart on the plantation, the children lived with their mother.[10] Deborah White has argued convincingly that "relationships between mother and child [in slavery] still superseded those between husband and wife. Slaveholder practices encouraged the primacy of the mother-child relationship, and in the mores of the slave community motherhood ranked above marriage. In fact, women in their role as mothers were the central figures in the nuclear slave family."[11]

The mother-child bond not only was a central function of slavery as an institution but was rooted in slaves' own culture, dating back to African family structure. The origin of slaves' families lay in a complex of varying African cultures whose systems of descent were both matrilineal and patrilineal and had at their core the extended kinship group rather than the two-parent family. Generally, the conjugal unit was not centered but functioned as an element of a larger family that spread across multiple generations. A married couple's primary responsibility was to reproduce; parenting and socialization were the responsibility of the larger family group. White pointed out that in West Africa mothers raised children in separate living areas, either alone or with the help of other women. The mother-child tie was thus strengthened beyond those of father-child and husband-wife.[12]

Certainly in free families mothers were responsible for caring for and nurturing their children, both because such duties were viewed as a natural outgrowth of a woman's "femaleness," her biological capacity to reproduce, and because they were considered a wife's reciprocal responsibility to the husband who provided for her, a matter of keeping up her end of the marriage contract.[13] Rather than doing away with or eliding the father's role, the free mother's responsibilities toward her family complemented those of the paterfamilias. On the other hand, the centering of both the mother and the mother-child bond in slavery might have been interpreted as a departure from the civilized or the proper family because it occurred simultaneously with the denial of the father's privileged place in the family.

Douglass's white abolitionist contemporaries argued with certainty that "slavery destroyed traditional family structure and corrupted morals."[14] Douglass's agreement is evident as he bemoaned the elimination of the father and the "disorder" that it produced. Yet Douglass knew from his own situation that slaves often experienced a family life in which kin provided emotional support and nurturance. His attitude toward his grandmother shows his respect and regard for the mother, offering the clear sense of the order she restored to the situation of the slave family. Although he was separated from his own mother, Douglass's description of his childhood in his grandparents' home suggests the strong influence of female kin in his life. Throughout numerous pages of discussion, Douglass mentioned his grandfather only in passing, devoting the majority of attention to his grandmother, who was held in high esteem within the community, was an excellent gardener and fisherwoman, and took great care in raising her grandchildren.[15] Although Douglass was not raised in a two-parent household, one that was "traditional" in the way that he or white abolitionists understood the term, in his early childhood he experienced an ordered family existence.

According to the principle that slavery reversed the order of civilization, once the oppressive yoke of slavery was lifted, former slave families would be free to develop according to the proper order of things. Fathers would again be fathers: whole again, restored to their position as head of the family, they would bequeath their name and their condition to their children. And mothers would assume a role befitting a helpmeet. Yet the acquisition of regulation and protection under domestic relations laws would not reverse the roles of mother and father. Rather, it would endow the male with new legal and social power over his wife and children, a power that had not existed for any family member under slavery.

Legitimacy in Historical Perspective

SINCE THE first colonists set foot in the "new world," the issue of legitimacy has concerned American judges and lawmakers. Bastardy laws appeared in the earliest colonial legislation, meting out punishment for sex outside of marriage and the subsequent birth of illegitimate issue. Many historians agree that initially the concern over illegitimacy stemmed from the fears of colonial officials who believed immorality threatened the stability of their communities. The laws regarding illegitimacy, like those regarding fornication, adultery, drunkenness, and blasphemy, served, in theory, to preserve the moral and social order.[16]

More tangible issues of economics also affected colonial bastardy legislation and decisions. In a society which held the male legally responsible for providing material support for his family, the birth of an illegitimate child immediately raised questions about support. During the late eighteenth and the nineteenth centuries, the courts and lawmakers concerned themselves less with using bastardy legislation to control morality and paid increasing attention to the financial burden that illegitimate children posed for society. In the courtroom fathers remained the focus of bastardy cases as judges attempted to compel them to support their children.[17]

Beyond the issues of morality and economics, however, lay that of the preservation of a society ordered by lawful marriage and the patriarchal family. Punishing the parents of an illegitimate child reinforced this norm. Stripping the bastard child of his or her lineage and inheritance rights was meant to protect the sanctity of the individual family by keeping the unlawful element out after the fact. Doing so obviously punished the victim as well.[18]

Compelled by the growing conviction that illegitimate children should not be held accountable for their parents' sins, jurists and legislators in the late eighteenth and the nineteenth centuries enacted significant reform in bastardy legislation. However, this reform did not alter the privilege given to the patriarchal family in the legal construction of legitimacy. Grossberg has argued that in part this reform consisted of less stringent conditions for lawful marriage, as well as the passage of legislation that made it easier to legitimate children. The law also came to recognize common-law marriage, to assume that all children born in wedlock were legitimate, and to grant legitimacy to children of annulled marriages or children whose parents married after their birth.[19] As a manifestation of one such reform, Grossberg pointed to the liberal use of legislation in the South to enable the legitimization of the children born during slavery whose parents married after emancipation or whose parent or parents may have died during slavery.[20]

Grossberg argued as well that lawmakers and judges created a legal relationship between mothers and their illegitimate children by allowing mothers custody and conferring upon these children the right to inherit from their mother's line, though such provisions varied widely from state to state. Colonial law had automatically granted fathers custody of legitimate children; prior to such reform illegitimate children had been considered "outside of the legitimate patriarchal household, and thus of custody law." Such children were, as Grossberg pointed out, "*filius nullius*, the child and heir of no one."[21] The reforms granting mothers custody of their illegitimate children thus enabled these children to enter into a lawful familial unit, complete with lineage and inheritance rights. None of this, however, made the illegitimate child a member of the paternal family, nor did it make the female-headed family an acceptable alternative to the established norm.

This climate of reform that pervaded the nineteenth century no doubt influenced the passage of pension legislation that automatically legitimated the children born in what were now to be considered legitimate marriages between slaves or between slaves and free persons of color who lived in slave states. The pension act of June 6, 1866, and its subsequent amended version set down the conditions for what the government would accept as legitimate slave marriages. This included marriage by some sort of ceremony and/or mutual and public recognition that a couple considered themselves to be husband and wife. This act further provided that the offspring of any such marriage would be recognized as the soldier's lawful children, giving legal status to the children while simultaneously reinforcing the paternal origin of legitimacy.[22] Lawmakers might also have legislated automatic legitimacy for ex-slave children to allay their concern—stemming from the belief that former slaves had no regard for the marriage bond—that illegitimacy among former slaves would place a moral and economic burden upon free white communities.

Although the legal institution of their masters branded all children born of slaves as illegitimate, most former slaves might have found alien the concepts of legitimacy and illegitimacy, as well as the moral and economic questions they raised. Although slaves did bear children out of wedlock, the legal issues and implications associated with illegitimacy in white society had no

significance within the slave community. What meaning would
a legal concept like legitimacy have to those whom the laws ignored? And free society gave no weight to illegitimacy within
slave families. Regardless of the laws, no slave was ever prosecuted for bastardy, because, as Robert V. Wells has pointed out,
"no white ever seems to have worried about whether or not
black children were bastards . . . the only social condition that
mattered was that the children of slaves were also slaves."
Margaret Burnham has argued that the courts were "unclear
as to the exact legal status of the child. Illegitimacy implied
wrongdoing, and the concept did not fit the slave family which
was denied the opportunity to be 'legitimate.'" Martha Hodes
has suggested that the issue of bastardy mattered to whites
when it involved free white women and enslaved black men because the existence of a "free child of partial African ancestry"
threatened definitions of blackness and whiteness and upset the
connection between racial identity and status.[23] The bearing of
children out of wedlock did not offend the moral sensibilities
of slaves; they valued motherhood regardless of a woman's marital status. Furthermore, that masters provided material support for their slaves rendered moot the question of who would
provide for the "fatherless" child.

    The marriage–centered notion of family that tied a child's
identity exclusively to the conjugal relation of his or her parents thus had little relevance to slave culture. The legal relationship created between father and legitimate child was also
alien to it. Precisely as Douglass argued, the laws of free society
did not recognize a relationship of legal heredity between a
slave father and his offspring. The provisions for inheriting a
minor's pension rested implicitly upon this concept of the bequeathing father. As former slaves grappled with the parameters of lawful marital and parental relationships, minors' claims
for a pension illustrate how unfamiliar were these male–centered legal concepts of legitimacy and inheritance, and in spite
of that unfamiliarity, how former slaves laid claim to the prerogatives of legitimate, inheriting children.

The Children of Slaves and the Quest for Legitimacy and Identity

ACCORDING TO the act of July 14, 1862, if a soldier's widow either had remarried or had died, the soldier's legitimate child or children under the age of sixteen were entitled to receive his pension. Minors' claims for a pension were often complicated by the need for the child to prove the legitimacy of his or her parents' marriage. Sorting out the former slaves' marriages was a complex process of finding the right kind of evidence and believable witnesses. The process was further complicated by the ambiguous parameters of the relationships, which had to be defined as marital both under slavery and under the pension system. But precisely because of the difficulty and frequent confusion, the tangled issues and the equally tangled responses, minors' claims provide invaluable insight into the transformation of slave families in freedom.

The first case unfolds like the fascinating tale of the sixteenth-century Frenchman Arnaud Du Tilh, a clever impostor who came to the village of Artigat and claimed the identity of Martin Guerre, a troubled young man from a prominent family who had been absent from the village some eight years. Bearing a likeness to the man and armed with enough pertinent information about him, the impostor became "Martin Guerre" and reaped the benefits of the man's life: he lived in intimacy with Guerre's wife, acquired Guerre's business and social status, and inherited his wealth. Though his ruse eventually was discovered, Du Tilh's successful stint as Martin Guerre speaks to the relative ease with which one could assume a new persona in a world where identity could never be authenticated with any degree of certainty. That a stranger could take up someone else's life demonstrates that personal identity was not rooted very deeply in any kind of essential permanence but rested primarily upon the credibility of a person's storytelling and the acceptance of others that he was who he claimed to be.[24]

The tall, slender young man who claimed to be John Robin-

son does not appear to have possessed quite the same compelling motivation as Arnaud Du Tilh, yet the conditions for
a former slave to establish his or her identity in the postbellum
South were not unlike those of sixteenth-century Artigat. If he
was the son of former slaves Adaline and Elias Robinson, if he
was the only surviving child of Private Elias Robinson of Co. F,
13th USCT, he stood to receive just over $1,000 from the gov-
ernment, a considerable sum at the time, especially for an
African-American man who worked as a daily farm laborer.[25]
Yet more was at stake if the stranger who called himself John
Robinson could prove that he was who he claimed to be. He
could inherit a valid identity in free society: an identity as the
child of a lawful union, a proper family name, and a family line
to pass on to future generations.

The young man who claimed to be John Robinson had
grown up as an orphan during the late 1860s and the 1870s in
the Nashville, Tennessee, home of a man named Mills, who was
the chief of police. He had come to live in the Mills home
around the age of five with his mother, Adaline, who worked
there as a servant during the war. Mrs. Mills testified that Adaline took John to visit his father several times at his camp in
Gallatin and that a man wearing a Federal uniform and claiming Adaline as his wife came to visit at the Mills home.[26] John's
father died of smallpox in 1865, and his mother died of consumption three years later. Throughout his childhood John
stayed on with the Mills family, apparently in the capacity of a
servant. He frequently ran away and worked stints as a cabin
boy on the Cumberland River. John ran away for the last time
around 1879, a year before he initiated his pension claim. In
an 1884 letter to the commissioner of pensions, he expressed
regret for having run away and also offered an underlying sense
of the tumultuous emotional state of a young black man growing up alone in a white home. "I love Mrs. Mills as a mother,"
John wrote. "I did not appreciate her kindness till grown."[27]

Initially the young man could not offer pension officials

much information about his early past. In 1883 he told an
agent, "I can at this time throw no light upon where I was from,
where I was born, if a slave who owned me, if my owners are
living or dead."[28] He offered a date of birth, Elias and Adaline
Robinson as his parents' names, that his father had served and
died in the USCT, and that his mother died shortly after. He
knew that Elias had served as a cook for his regiment, which
was stationed at Gallatin.

Over the course of several years, pension officials pieced together the scattered remnants of John's past out of information
culled from interviews in Nashville with Elias's comrades, Adaline's friends, and Elias and Adaline's relatives and former owners in DeKalb County where they had been enslaved. They
learned that Elias and Adaline had been slaves owned by a
family named Robinson. The couple left DeKalb County during the war and traveled some fifty miles west to Nashville,
where Elias enlisted in the army. Some of the witnesses recalled
that Adaline frequently brought John, who was remembered as
"a spoiled brat," to visit his father at the military camp.[29]

The principal questions in the case centered on John Robinson's legitimacy. Was the marriage between Elias and Adaline
legitimate? Did they have a son named John, born during that
marriage? These questions were answered in DeKalb County
where pension officials found Elias and Adaline's former owners (or their family members), Elias's brother, and Adaline's sister and mother. They learned that Adaline and Elias came to
live on neighboring plantations when Wingate T. Robinson acquired Elias as part of his new bride's dowry. Adaline belonged
to a relative of Wingate named John Robinson, and she married Elias in 1857 or 1858. The validity of the marriage was confirmed by both owners and by Elias and Adaline's relatives. All
remembered that a slave preacher had performed a ceremony
and that the couple had lived together as man and wife until
they left the county during the war. The witnesses further reported that after they married Elias and Adaline had a son

whom they named John. If the man claiming to be John Robinson could prove that he was the John Robinson in question, the crucial issue of his legitimacy would be established.

A ready-made past had been waiting in DeKalb County for someone to claim it. Was the young man the same boy of four or five who left with Adaline and Elias? The young man's "return" to DeKalb County reads like the return of "Martin Guerre." A stranger made his way into the community claiming to be someone who had been absent for years. He could not offer proof of his identity—he might have claimed that he was not given a birth or baptismal certificate—nor did he possess some precious memento that belonged to one of his parents— his mother's locket, perhaps, or the buttons from his father's uniform—personal items that might have connected him to them. The stranger shared memories of living with his mother and visiting his father at the army camp. He remembered a sister but could not recall whether she was older or younger than he; he recalled only that she died when he was young. He bore some vague resemblance to his parents, gone from that community for two decades. Those who remembered the Robinsons did not have pictures of them that might have refreshed their memories, but they did see Elias in John's strong facial features and Adaline in his tall, graceful stature.

The dark mark on the front of the young man's neck captured the attention of several witnesses. Some, like the son of his mother's master, a doctor who claimed to have been present at John Robinson's birth, remembered a birthmark. "I recognize upon the front of this man's neck one of the little freaks of nature that said John was borne with . . . a little rough thickening of the skin resembling a rasberry or mulberry which the aforesaid John borne of Adaline and Elias had at birth."[30] The presence of such a mark upon the stranger's neck convinced the doctor that he was indeed John Robinson. Yet others remembered a scar from a burn received as a child and believed the mark upon the stranger's neck to be one and the same.[31] Was this mark a birthmark or a scar? How far might a person go to create an identity? As far as burning his flesh to replicate a mark that no one had seen for twenty years? What might such a mark look like after all that time had passed?

The stories of Arnaud Du Tilh and the man claiming to be John Robinson bear comparison because of the strikingly similar manner in which the sometimes vague, sometimes vivid memories of others provided the foundation for each man's identity. Unlike Arnaud Du Tilh, however, the man claiming to be John Robinson could offer up witnesses to account for most of the missing years between the young family's departure from DeKalb County and his lone return. The Pension Office concluded that the man in question was indeed John Robinson. Yet the possibility of fraud was rife in his case, predicated as it was upon the memories of others. I raise the specter of dissimulation here not to cast aspersion on the man deemed John Robinson but to demonstrate what was at stake in the case. To rename oneself or to create a new past was hardly difficult, but here was an identity already forged, valid not simply because such a person once existed but because he had been born into the right circumstances according to free society, as the product of a legitimate union. At their center minors' claims for pensions were about money, about recovering the loss of the material support that a father provided for his children. Yet enmeshed in the economics of such claims was a quest for identity and legitimacy in a society that centered the father in a family consecrated by marriage.

The second case provides a telling example of this quest for identity and legitimacy as a young man attempted to situate himself along his paternal line. James Frazier's parents had been married for little more than a year when James's father died. Neither the brevity of the union nor the fact that James had no recollection of his father would have undermined his chances for a pension as long as James could prove that the marriage did exist and that he was his father's son. Although these standard provisions proved beneficial to James, they reveal something arbitrary about the concept of legitimacy, in this case a relationship based in law and not in personal relationships. James never knew the father to whom his legitimacy was tied, and he knew little about him. "I don't know where father was born nor where he came from, and I can't describe him," James told a pension official. What he did know about his father came from his mother: "All I know is that he died in Little Rock in the time of the cholera and ma said so."[32] Yet James would strive to establish a connection between them to prove his case.

James, a farm laborer living in Pulaski County, Arkansas, was already twenty-eight years old when he first applied for a pension in 1895. James's file offers no clue as to why he initiated his claim so late; he had been eligible for a pension for quite some time because his mother, Eliza, had been dead for many years and had never drawn a pension. James's father, Simon Frazier, had belonged to a family named Frazier during slavery in Bradley County, Arkansas, not far from the Louisiana border. He and several other men—two of whom were Frazier slaves and also called themselves Frazier, another from a nearby farm owned by a relative of the Fraziers—fled thirty-six miles north to Pine Bluff and enlisted together. Fortunately for James, these men, as well as some of their comrades, all settled in the same area in Arkansas and remembered clearly the fact of his parents' marriage and his birth.

James's parents met in a contraband camp during the war: Simon was a soldier, and Eliza Mitchell was a refugee from slavery. Within fifteen months of their meeting, Simon and Eliza were married by an army chaplain in a legal ceremony and had a son. A few weeks after James's birth, Simon fell ill and died. Throughout his childhood James lived with his mother and her second husband, Henry Blackman, who had served with Simon during the war. Though Eliza died when James was fourteen years old, he continued to live with his stepfather until he reached adulthood.

The collection of testimony in James's claim dealt primarily with establishing his legitimacy. Although a number of witnesses could testify that a marriage had occurred, only one witness was actually at the wedding, and that man could not remember any of the details some thirty years later. Several witnesses claimed that an army chaplain presided over Simon and Eliza's wedding, but no record of the marriage existed, and the chaplain had since died. Because none of the other witnesses had attended the ceremony, there were discrepancies in the testimony as to when, where, and by whom Simon and Eliza had been married.[33]

Initially the Pension Office rejected James's claim, stating that the evidence of his parents' relationship was not sufficient to classify it as matrimonial. However, James was able to appeal this decision successfully on the grounds that many of the witnesses recognized his parents as husband and wife. According to section 4705 of the *Revised Statutes,* the government would accept this recognition as proof of a legitimate marriage. This section specified that if a "colored" soldier's widow could prove that the couple was married by some ceremony they deemed obligatory or if they habitually recognized each other as husband and wife and were so recognized within the community, then the government would recognize theirs as a legitimate marriage and would consider their children the soldier's lawful children.[34]

Although much of James's own testimony was devoted to proving his parents' marriage and his own status as their legal offspring, he also attempted to establish his identity as his father's son. Implicitly at least, he seemed to understand that what was in question was not simply that he was the product of a legitimate union. One witness remembered that on his deathbed Simon claimed James as his son. "He spoke his last words to me when he died," Brum Harrison testified. "He told me to tell Eliza to take care of his boy."[35] James argued that this testimony established his legitimacy because the *Revised Statutes* deemed a child legitimate if his or her father acknowledged the child as his own. Unfortunately, the legislation he referred to applied to children born before their parents' marriage and was not pertinent to his case.[36]

James also sought to establish a connection with his father by taking his surname, an echo of the actions of former slaves some thirty years earlier. He gave the pension official the history of his surname, acknowledging that before he initiated his pension claim, he had used his stepfather's name: "Mother's next husband [after Simon] was Henry Blackman, whom she married when I was quite young. . . . I go by the name James Blackman mostly. That is the name I farm under, but since commencing my pension [claim] I have taken the name James Frazier. After I got old enough to know my correct name, I have gone by the name Frazier."[37]

That he farmed under the name Blackman and thus entered into contracts under that name implies that Blackman was James's legal name. It also suggests that Henry Blackman had become a father to James, who had come to live with Henry when he was "a small boy in his mother's arm" and stayed until he was twenty-one.[38] Already a man at the time of emancipation, Henry would have developed his understanding of family relationships and responsibilities during slavery. Influenced by West African traditions of extended kinship and shaped by the conditions of slavery that regularly ignored family ties, slaves developed a dynamic concept of kinship that transcended spatial and consanguineous boundaries. According to Ira Berlin, Steven Miller, and Leslie Rowland, "Early on, American slaves extended the bonds of kinship beyond the boundaries of individual farms and plantations, uniting family members who were forced to live apart by the circumstances of their enslavement. The language of kinship expressed a broad range of mutual obligation. Slaves . . . confer[red] the status of kin upon fellow slaves who were unrelated by blood. By the nineteenth century, kinship ideology and practices had extended to the larger Afro-American community."[39] Undoubtedly Henry's affection for the boy, coupled with this understanding of kinship responsibilities that extended beyond one's immediate blood relatives, compelled him to care for James in the years after his wife's death.

It is unclear whether James began calling himself Frazier to support his claim or whether he had come to understand that his biological father's name was his correct name in free society. Whatever his reasons, by taking the name Frazier, James reversed the order and the significance of the naming process. James took his father's name not because he was legally entitled to the paternal name that had preceded him but because he meant to link himself to his father, after the fact, and offer the name as proof that he was his father's legitimate son.

In the end James won his pension on appeal and became a legitimate inheriting son. He acquired both the monetary reward of a pension and, symbolized by his surname, formal recognition of his right to his paternal line. Because the government regarded Simon and Eliza Frazier's marriage as valid, Simon Frazier was posthumously restored to his proper position as a bequeathing father, just as Douglass might have imagined.

The fact that the owner rather than the father was the legal guardian of slave children gives further emphasis to the sometimes arbitrary nature of legitimacy. Richard Martin's children knew their father only slightly, in part because he died when they were all under the age of ten but also because of the circumstances of slavery that gave their owner the power to determine their living situation. When they initiated their claim in 1882, David, Bluford, and Lida's legitimacy was not at issue because Thomas Harris, their mother's former owner, testified that Richard and Jane Martin were married in his home in Calloway County, Missouri, by a minister of the gospel sometime in early 1855. Nor was there a question about the legitimacy of their half sister Elizabeth, also a claimant in the case, for her mother's former young master deposed that Richard Martin had married Hannah Lawrence, a slave on another plantation, sometime following Jane's death.[40]

Though Richard Martin's oldest son, David, was certainly old enough to have remembered his father, their contact had been limited because Jane and Richard belonged to different owners. By law their children belonged to the mother's master, and so David, Bluford, and Lida resided with Jane on Harris's plantation. It was not until sometime around 1860 (when David was five years old) that Jane's owner hired Richard from his owner "in order that he might be with his family."[41] It is not clear how often Richard had been able to see his family before that time, but typically in abroad marriages fathers in close proximity visited their families once or twice a week.

The war tore the family apart. Jane died in 1862 when, according to Harris, "some troops came to my place, and wanted the cabin that Jane was in. They took her out of her own cabin, that was warm and comfortable and put her into another one where there was little or no fire, and she took cold, and lingered along, and finally died."[42] Not long after Jane's death, Richard married Hannah Lawrence, a slave belonging to one of Harris's neighbors. The claim does not reveal whether Harris returned Richard to his owner or whether Richard lived with his new wife after they were married. His children belonged to their mother's owner and had to stay on his place; even if Richard stayed there too, visiting Hannah would have lessened the time he had for contact with his children. The laws of slavery still applied in Missouri, even in the midst of war, because Missouri was a border state. Desperate to preserve Missouri's loyalty to the Union, President Lincoln guaranteed the protection of the institution to the state's powerful slaveholders who upheld this loyalty. Although conflicts between proslavery and antislavery forces, the actions of fugitive slaves, and the recruitment of black men into the service weakened the institution, slavery did not officially end in Missouri until January 1865.[43] Within a year after his marriage to Hannah, Richard joined the tide of fugitive slaves that swept across Missouri and into the ranks of the Union army.

Harris appears to have been a constant adult presence in the lives of David, Bluford, and Lida. Five years David's junior, Lida was only two years old when her mother died. She testified: "I was a very small child when [her father] enlisted. And I have no recollection of what my father's general physical ap-

pearance was."[44] Richard's death in the army left David, Bluford, and Lida orphaned. None of the children lived with their
stepmother until 1886, when she took in Bluford, just before he
was declared insane and was taken to the Missouri State Insane
Asylum where he subsequently died.[45] Lida lived on Harris's
place until 1876, when she was sixteen. She moved to neighboring Mexico, Missouri, and married Turner Jamison, with
whom she was "keeping house" when she was interviewed for
her claim. David too lived with Harris for several years after his
father's death; one acquaintance claimed that when he met
David, who was a boy at the time, David was "employed at Mr.
Thomas Harris, his old master."[46] As an adult, David married
and worked as a cook at the same insane asylum where Bluford
would live out his last days. David died in 1884 after suffering
from consumption.

After emancipation, the children might have been appren-
ticed to Harris, though the record is silent on that score. In the
years immediately following the war, the Black Codes allowed
African-American children who were orphans or whose parents were deemed incapable of taking care of them to be ap-
prenticed to white employers. Ultimately, as Eric Foner put it,
the apprenticeship system "seized upon the consequences of
slavery—the separation of families and the freedmen's
poverty—as an excuse for providing planters with the unpaid
labor of black minors."[47] Southern judges often gave former
owners the first opportunity to "hire" their former slaves,
which might have been the situation for David, Bluford, and
Lida. Peter Bardaglio has described the mixed motives of
planters who found themselves with orphaned former slaves
under their care. Apprenticeship enabled planters to exploit
and control the labor of their former slaves while making simultaneous claims to paternal concern for them.[48] After vehe-
ment protest from African-American parents and other family
members called the system into question, Reconstruction gov-
ernments in southern states and federal legislation later nullified the apprenticeship system.

It is difficult to imagine with any certainty how David, Bluford, and Lida felt about their former owner. Former slaves often reflected back upon their owners as Georgia resident Celestia Avery did in the 1930s. "Mr. Heard was a very mean master," her interviewer reported, "and was not liked by any one of his slaves. Secretly each one hated him. He whipped unmercifully and in most cases unnecessarily."[49] Many freed people took whatever steps were necessary to keep their former owners out of their lives, to cut off any association with them. One ex-slave recalled: "De slaves was freed when I was 'bout ten years old. Many of de slaves, i'cludin' my folks, lef' deir masters de very day we got our freedom."[50] Mississippi ex-slave Frank Williams told interviewers that when his father tried to leave his old master, Tom Williams, in the spring after emancipation, the man tied his hands to a tree, whipped him until he bled, and kept him chained up for a week. So great was Frank's father's desire to leave that he stood his ground and finally convinced his former owner to let him go.[51]

Yet some former slaves maintained ties to their old masters, perhaps out of genuine affection but particularly out of familiarity and practicality. Hannah Austin's parents stayed on with their former owner "even after freedom and until their deaths."[52] Hannah emphasized her former owner's kindness and his considerate treatment of her family, suggesting that her parents had formed an attachment to him that they would not break after emancipation. Ezra Adams from South Carolina gave more ambiguous testimony, offering the sense that material security played a significant role in his continuing relationship with his former owner:

> You ain't gwine to believe dat de slaves on our plantation
> didn't stop workin' for old marster, even when they was told
> dat they was free. Us didn't want no more freedom than us
> was gittin' on our plantation already. Us knowed too well dat
> us was well took care of, wid a plenty of vittles to eat and
> tight log and board houses to live in. De slaves, where I lived,

knowed after de war dat they had an abundance of dat somethin' called freedom, what they could not eat, wear, and sleep
in. Yes sir, they soon found out dat freedom ain't nothin',
'less you got somethin' to live on and a place to call home.[53]

Necessity also cemented ties between former slaves and their
owners. Many former slaves needed their former owners' testimony to provide evidence in their pension claims. A former
owner might also have been the most convenient source of employment or housing after the war.

The gamut of feelings between former slaves and former
owners mirrors the complexity of human relationships. How
the figure of the master must have confused slave children! The
master wielded full power over his slaves, and his authority superseded that of parents or other adult kin over their children.
Slave parents tried to raise their children as best they could, socializing them in the norms of slave life and offering them
strategies for survival. As the case of Harriet Jacobs's brother,
William, illustrates, slave children frequently got caught in the
tug of war between the competing demands of owners and parents. Jacobs described: "One day, when his father and his mistress both happened to call him at the same time, he hesitated
between the two; being perplexed to know which had the
strongest claim upon his obedience." William responded to his
mistress and earned his father's reproach.[54] Predicated on the
belief that "slaves raised properly on the home place from infancy proved more loyal and obedient than slaves purchased on
the auction block," owners often curried favor with small children in an attempt to win their affection, proffering small gifts
or granting them special favors.[55] How might David, Bluford,
and Lida have responded to the imposing figure of the master
who treated them with both authority and affection and who
offered a measure of stability in their parents' absence?

Evidence in the claim suggests that the Martin children developed a strong familiarity, perhaps even a closeness, with their
former owner over the years. Lida testified that her former

master and mistress were the best source of information about her parents: they "will know more about the history of my father and mother and their family than any other persons that I can refer to."[56] Although Lida may have been referring to the written records of their slaves that masters usually kept, the fact that she stayed on the Harris place ten years after emancipation (well beyond the existence of the apprenticeship system), coupled with the Harrises' own continued efforts to help her with her claim, suggests that they knew about Lida's family because they had close ties with them. Even the pension official noted that Thomas Harris was "apparently a friend to his colored people."[57]

While making his claim for pension, David Martin used his father's surname. Yet the prosecution of his claim revealed that throughout his life, up until his death at the age of twenty-nine, David Martin was also known as Atch Harris. When David married, he gave his legal name as David A. Harris. After David died, his widow explained that he "always went by the name of Harris because he was raised and belonged while a slave to Mr. Thomas Harris."[58] She might have been referring to the practice of calling slave children after the name of their mother's owner. She might also have meant that David deliberately kept the name Harris because he felt entitled to it or because it belonged to his master, who had been a constant figure in his young life. Either of the latter seems likely because in freedom David could have chosen any name he wanted.

That David deliberately retained his master's name is underscored by the fact that he continued to use the name Harris even when calling himself Martin for his pension claim. Did this mean that David felt closer to his master than to his father, choosing his master's name over his father's when most others were doing just the opposite? Or did it mean that David was making a connection to his mother? Perhaps not all former slaves felt compelled to reassess their familial identity as the pension regulations forced them to do. David's retention of his master's name may suggest less about his relationship with his father than it does about the effect living in the custody of his master had upon his sense of personal and familial identity. But David apparently knew that according to the ordering of descent in free society, he was more likely to be recognized as Richard Martin's son if he possessed his father's surname. Although David's legitimacy was not in question, calling himself David Martin according to the proper order of paternal succession could only strengthen his case.

The Mother's Place in the Concept of Legitimacy

WE MIGHT ASK how the reordering of the father's position affected the mother's family position. Minors' claims for pensions highlight the mother's absence in the legal and social concept of legitimacy and in the configuration of genealogical lines in free society. Although the slave mother did not possess formal or legal authority over the members of her family, slaveholding society accorded her a notable relationship to her children. She took care of the children, she passed her status on to them; her master became her children's master regardless of who owned their father. The emphasis on the father-child relationship in minors' pension claims demonstrates a shift of the mother's visible public position to one that was obscured by the centrality and authority of the father's new status as paterfamilias.

This change, of course, meant the loss of the mother's terrible responsibility of bequeathing the status of slavery to her children, something no mother relished. And it does not obscure the significant roles that freedwomen played in their families and communities. The value of freedwomen's labor in their own homes and in waged work outside the home, their preservation of the ethos of mutuality developed in slavery, and their frequent challenges to the imposition of absolute male authority all clearly demonstrate African–American women's crucial presence in the daily survival of their families and communities and the continuing importance of the mother's place in the family. Nevertheless, the mother's shifting position illustrates that male dominion over the rest of the family was the rule of law in American society at the time and shaped the way former slaves and pension agents addressed the issues of legitimacy and lines of descent.

In 1880, at the age of seventeen, Toney Sharp initiated a pension claim from his home in Hertford County in northeastern North Carolina. Toney was only an infant when slavery ended and when his father died in the service of the USCT. He was eligible to apply for a pension because he was a minor at the time of his father's death and because his mother had remarried before he reached the age of sixteen. Toney's parents, Violet and Benjamin Sharp, had belonged to Jacob and Starkey Sharp, brothers who had owned neighboring farms in North Carolina before the war. The brothers had given their consent for Violet and Benjamin to live together as man and wife on Jacob's farm; though they had no ceremony, their masters' consent and the act of living together bonded Violet and Benjamin as marriage partners.[59]

The main objective in Toney's case was to prove the existence of his parents' marriage, a relationship that Toney could not recollect but of which he had learned from his mother and others who had known his parents. "At the time they became by custom man and wife," Toney explained of his parents' marriage, "there was no such law as colored people having to obtain license before they could be man and wife."[60] Several witnesses, including Violet herself, helped to establish the fact that the couple had lived together as husband and wife and were so recognized by their masters as well as by other slaves.[61]

According to the conditions set down by the Pension Office, Toney also had to establish that he was his father's only surviving child and prove his date of birth.[62] If there were other minor children, the pension money would be divided among them; as the only surviving son, Toney was entitled to the full amount of the pension himself. Presumably, Toney had to verify his date of birth to confirm that he had been a minor at the time of his father's death. Perhaps he also had to prove that he had been conceived or born during the time of his parents' marriage. Unlike many former slaves, Toney knew his date of birth. When asked if she had recorded it in a Bible, Violet testified, "I keep no record, I don't know that I can tell you why I remember [Toney's birth date], but as he grew up, I used to tell it to him often."[63]

The only material evidence of his date of birth that Toney could produce was a slip of paper given to him by his mother upon which the date was written. He had no birth certificate or baptismal record, nor had his parents any family record. Toney had no material proof that he was his father's only son, but he declared that his mother often told him that he was the only child born during his parents' marriage. What information his former owner may have recorded disappeared with him when he died.[64]

The gaps in Toney's evidence and knowledge were filled in by former slaves who appear to have known him well and may have been considered part of his extended family. Harriet Sharp, another of the Sharps' former slaves, remembered the approximate date of Toney's birth because she had a daughter near his age, and she also testified to his being Benjamin Sharp's only child. When the examiner asked how she could be positive of the fact, Harriet noted the intimacy of slaves who had lived on the same plantation: "Because we were all living together at the time of Ben's enlistment and death, [I] have known them all since I was twelve years old, and had there been any other children, I certainly would have known it."[65] Benjamin Pruden, who had lived on Dorsey Pruden's place only a quarter of a mile from Jacob Sharp's farm, pointed to the same sense of family and familiarity to explain how he knew Toney to be Benjamin Sharp's only son. "I was an older man than Ben," he told the examiner, "but we formed a liking for each other which made us very intimate and I knew all about him."[66]

In white culture genealogy was determined exclusively by fathers and sons, ensuring through the male line the continuation and preservation not simply of individual families but of history itself. Beyond the matter of invisible bloodlines attaching one generation of males to the next, beyond the intangibility of patrimony, lies the act of recounting family history, a literal (oral) act of passing on or passing down. What part of his familial identity did Toney actually inherit from the father he did not know? Toney's mother supplied the critical information, repeated his birth date to him over and over again, and finally had it written down for him so that even when she was gone, he would not forget. As White has argued, "When fathers were separated from their offspring, mothers were the crucial kinship link between the child and his or her unknown father. *She* supplied the information that made the father live in the child's mind."[67] Other former slaves knew his parents intimately, described his father to him, and told him of his parents' marriage. Toney's genealogy was not simply a straight line progressing from father to son but a network of strands, the product of active, living history passed down and carried on through a multiplicity of voices.[68]

Though Violet was an important genealogical link, providing Toney with crucial knowledge of his family and himself, within free society's system of domestic relations, Violet's role as mother was important only as a means to establish that Toney was his father's legitimate son. The only white witness in Toney's case had no pertinent information to offer. Henry Clay Sharp, the son of Violet's former owner, recalled that his father had owned Violet and stated that he knew Toney and "have always known him as the son of Violet."[69] But Toney's maternity was not in question, and because Henry Sharp did not remember Benjamin Sharp, he could not establish that Benjamin had been Toney's father or that Toney had been Benjamin's only son. That Henry Clay Sharp's testimony was irrelevant helps make it clear that the mother's public role had become obscured in the transition from slavery to freedom.

If naming practices make it possible to see former slaves forging ties to their fathers, they also reveal the shifting position of the bequeathing mother. In the 1880s the three surviving children of Laney Jane and Jack Joiner, all in their late twenties and early thirties, applied for a pension. Because their mother had remarried in 1876 and had never received a pension, Jack, George, and Arena believed that they were eligible for a minor's pension. At the time all three lived near their mother in Nash County, North Carolina, the same place where they had lived as slaves. The Joiner children had little trouble finding witnesses for their claim because they lived among many of the same people they and their parents had known in slavery. Their neighbors included Mary Batchellor, their mother's former mistress; several of her daughters; Lewis Joiner, the son of their father's former master; and several former slaves from both the Batchellor and the Joiner plantations, including an uncle and an aunt.

There seemed to be little question that Jack, George, and Arena were the children of Laney Jane and Jack Joiner. Though Laney Jane and Jack were not married by ceremony, they had been husband and wife by their respective owners' consent for fourteen years before Jack ran away to join the USCT. During that period Jack made the mile journey from his master's place to Laney Jane's two or three times a week. In addition to Laney Jane's own testimony, the fact of their marriage was supported by the testimony of Laney Jane's former mistress and her daughters and that of Laney Jane's kin.[70]

Long before lawmakers granted mothers custody of their illegitimate children, the abroad marriage in slavery represented one of the rare instances where white society considered genealogies to be matrilineal. Because ownership was passed through the mother, only the mother's master recognized and recorded the births of children born within abroad marriages. In fact, as Brenda Stevenson has argued, slave owners "routinely identified the child's parentage solely with the mother, often denying any acknowledgement of the father's role—biological, emotional, social, or material."[71]

Mary Batchellor offered her own family record as evidence

in the case because it contained the dates of birth of Laney Jane's children. It was not unusual to find information about slaves in the family records of owners because owners often considered their slaves to be an extension of the family. Neither Mary Batchellor nor her husband could read or write; the schoolteacher "or others who happened along and were able to write" had written the "age paper" she presented to the special examiner.[72] In the record three of the five children were noted as Jack Joiner's children, suggesting that their paternity, or Jack Joiner's place in their lives, was not inconsequential.[73] But they acquired their place in the Batchellor family record though their connection to Laney Jane.

Witnesses pointed to the use of the surname Joiner as a means of establishing the familial connection between Jack Joiner and the claimants. When Lewis Joiner, the son of Jack Joiner's former master, cast doubt on George's paternity, those in support of the children responded as if the paternity of all had been jeopardized. Lewis Joiner alleged that Jack "parted from [Laney Jane] for a while—after she had the yellow one, George, [h]e was not Jack's child. Anyone could tell from looking at him, that he was not Jack's child. And Jack did not go back to see her again for nearly twelve months."[74] In response to the issue of Jack, George, and Arena's paternity, their uncle, John Joiner, pointed to the surnames by which people recognized them. He recalled, "These children have been known by the name Joiner, ever since the surrender, Before that they were called Bachelor, after their owner."[75] When they belonged to Batchellor during slavery, they carried his name. However, like many of their contemporaries, after emancipation Jack, George, and Arena had taken their father's surname.

Mary Batchellor's daughter Ann Eliza argued: "They were all recognized as Jack Joiner's children, and . . . [they] are still called Joiner, although none of them were ever owned by any Joiner, as owner, or master."[76] Ann Eliza made a point of distinguishing between paternity and ownership in her use of the surname Joiner. By calling the children after their father, according to the law of her own culture, Ann Eliza established their familial connection and, as the law dictated, accorded Jack the position at the head of the family.

The unintended consequence of the emphasis on the use of the father's name was to obscure the mother's place in the family's genealogy. Clearly what was notable about the change from Batchellor to Joiner was its indication of their shift from the status of property to the status of free people. However, if the name Batchellor signified ownership and, in the case of abroad marriages, the separation of children from their fathers, it nonetheless represented the tie between Laney Jane and her children. The name Batchellor represented slave owners' practice of configuring slaves' genealogies along the mother's line, assigning the children of an abroad marriage to the mother's master. Although the use of the name Joiner was meant to illustrate the association of the father and his children that slavery had ignored, it also served as reminder that in free society family lines were patrilineal.

In spite of what others called them and their uncle's and their mother's claims that they were called Batchellor in slavery, Jack, George, and Arena insisted that they had always been called Joiner. Speaking on behalf of his siblings, Jack testified: "I remember my father Jack Joiner, before he went away to enlist. As long as I can recollect I have always been known by the name of Jack Joiner and never by any other name. My brothers and sisters have also always been called by the name of Joiner, and not by any other name."[77] This insistence on having always been called Joiner in a sense represented yet another reversal of naming practices. "The name of the child is not expected to be that of the father," Douglass had said of slavery, but these children of slavery took their father's name in spite of that expectation and in the process reinvented themselves as their father's children in accordance with the rules of free society. As in other cases, it is not certain why Jack, George, and Arena took their father's name, to claim him as their rightful father or for the benefit of their pension claim. Whatever the reason, in a society that equated lineage with the surname, this action, as well as their denial of having ever been called Batchellor, underscored the process that reordered descent along the male line.

The Joiner children had worried unnecessarily about the blemish on their family record: the special examiner had no doubt that they were all Jack Joiner's legitimate children. In response to the issue of George's alleged illegitimacy, the examiner referred to the law that presumed the legitimacy of children born in wedlock. But there was an ironic twist to the story's end. Jack, George, and Arena failed to acquire their pensions. Their eligibility for a minor's pension was contingent upon their having been under the age of sixteen when their mother remarried. Because Laney Jane had remarried after all her children had reached adulthood, neither Jack, George, nor Arena could reap the rewards of their father's service to the Union.[78]

Legitimacy in Parents' Pension Claims

PARENTS' PENSION claims reversed the order of inheritance so that the child bequeathed to the father or the mother. Ned Barnard's case demonstrates that the same issue of legitimacy applied to fathers' claims as it did to minors' claims and that even a father's acknowledgment of his child might not have sufficiently assured the legal relationship between them. Ned lost his second bid for a father's pension because the Pension Office determined that his son was illegitimate.

The reviewer in Ned's case concluded:

> This claimant presents a nice question not to my knowledge decided authentatively before. . . . [Ned] was a slave; the soldier . . . is said to have been his son by marriage with Peggy Gregory, a free woman. This marriage, so called, according to [Ned] was a relationship by "consent" of Peggy Gregory and being adverse to the wishes of

[Ned's] owner was abandoned and a marriage more agreeable to the owner was consummated with another woman
by whom [Ned] had a family. I do not see that we can hold
that soldier was the legitimate son of [Ned]. Under the
circumstances it is very uncertain that he was in any sense
[Ned's] son.[79]

Ned claimed to have been married to Peggy by her consent,
thus meeting one of the standards for a legitimate slave marriage. Yet, true to the practices of the pension system, the case
reviewer appears to have put more weight upon the fact that
Ned's owner was against the marriage. In seeming accordance
with the tenets of slavery that held that slaves could not marry
if the master did not give them his consent, the owner's disap-
proval was translated to mean that the marriage was not valid.
The reviewer's emphasis upon Ned's "more agreeable" second
marriage supports this conclusion, especially because the reviewer appears to have accepted its validity without question.

The outcome of Ned's claim implies that though the concept of illegitimacy protected the sanctity of the paternal family
in theory, it also worked against fathers as it did their children.
In spite of the fact that Ned claimed his son as his own, the government's failure to recognize his marriage to Peggy severed
any legal tie between father and son.

Reminiscent of slavery's attention to the mother-child bond
and in accordance with the construction of a legal relationship
between mother and illegitimate child under the reform in bastardy laws, the son's ability to bequeath to the mother does not
appear to have been dependent on the status of her marriage.
Just as an illegitimate child might inherit property and his or
her familial identity from the mother, so too could a mother inherit a pension from an illegitimate child. After Rachel Holden
had escaped slavery with her five children, she moved to Kansas
and kept house for her son Peter, who "farm[ed] upon rented
land" to support her for some six months before he enlisted in
the army. In her claim Rachel reported that she had never mar-

ried and that "the children that were born were illegitimate children."[80] In spite of her declaration, Rachel received a pension; clearly she was not penalized for her son's illegitimacy.

In her claim for a mother's pension, Priscilla Hagan testified that "at the time of my son Oliver's birth, I was a slave[;] I was never married. My son Oliver Hagan the soldier was an illegitimate child but he was known and recognized . . . as my child."[81] Priscilla further cemented her son's illegitimacy by pointing out that Oliver's father "never recognized the Boy as being his child."[82] Yet, like Rachel, Priscilla too received a pension.

Legitimacy and Identity in the Twentieth Century

BECAUSE relatively few former slaves applied for minors' pensions, the question arises about the representative value of their stories. Were they typical of the stories of former slaves, if it can be said that any former slaves were typical? They were the last generation of slaves and had not lived in slavery long before emancipation, the same generation that would be interviewed in the 1930s by workers in the Federal Writers' Project. Though the WPA interviews do not appear to make explicit reference to the issue of legitimacy, it is present nonetheless.

The circumstances of slave marriage figured prominently in the collective memory of slavery. J. W. Whitfield of Little Rock, Arkansas, reported to WPA interviewers: "My father told me how they married in slavery times. They didn't count marriage like they do now." South Carolina former slave John Collins responded to questions about his background: "My daddy was name Steve Chandler. My mammy was called Nancy. I don't know whether they was married or not." Whether the interviewer or Collins raised the question of his parents' marriage is impossible to tell. Demonstrating how automatic had become the association of legality and morality with marriage, Julia White remembered that her parents legitimated their relationship after emancipation. "My father and mother had the kind of wedding they had for slaves. . . . After peace a minister came and married my father and mother according to the law of the church and of the land."[83]

Remnants of the question of legitimacy also lay in the practice of taking the father's surname after emancipation, which interviewees claimed to have done with relative frequency. Like Whitfield or Collins, most former slaves seemed undaunted by the issue of legitimacy in their responses to questions about the identity of their parents. John C. Brown explained in his interview: "After freedom [Shelton Brown] tell me he was my real pappy. Him took de name of Brown and dat's what I go by." In this case the father's word alone was sufficient proof for the son.[84]

That many of the former slaves applying for a minor's pension had not known their fathers well or at all was typical of their generation, though certainly it did not characterize the experience of all slaves. In spite of Douglass's claim that slavery did away with fathers, slave fathers did function as fathers and were considered as such by their wives, their children, and other slaves. Still, many fathers and children lived apart either because of abroad marriages or because of separations created by the economic needs or personal circumstances of slave owners. The absence of fathers in the lives of those applying for minors' pensions gives emphasis to the centrality of the slave mother's position, a position buttressed by the laws of slavery, the predilection of masters toward matrifocality, and the practices of slave culture.

FIVE

"My Master . . . Supported Me"

Parents' Claims and the Role
of the Provider

*T*HUS FAR it has been clear that slave familial relationships did not fall neatly into pension law categories. Free society's ideal family, regulated by the law and Western cultural tradition, differed significantly from the lived experience of slave families, regulated by the master, the circumstances of slavery, and slaves' own cultural tradition. To compare the two is to compare apples and oranges. The pension claims of mothers and fathers who lost a son (or sons) to the war not only underscore the problem of this incongruous comparison but also suggest its continuation in freedom. The disparity between former slaves' families and free society's ideal remained in part because former slaves' historical and cultural background did not change dramatically with emancipation and partly because everyday survival in the postwar South dictated a very different kind of family organization. The experiences of these former slave parents make it clear that in spite of what the law or social convention prescribed, family structure and organization in general varied considerably in lived experience according to one's access to vital resources such as education, employment opportunity, and social and political privileges.

To argue that the model of family inscribed in pension legislation had little in common with slave or ex-slave families is not to say that those differences could not be bridged or that the pension system could not bend to accommodate circumstances that varied from what it construed as the norm. Although pension officials were careful to test the soundness of a claimant's eligibility and to root out fraud whenever they could, it is fair to say that the Pension Office was not in the business of denying pensions. Strict application of the requirements for pension might have protected the system from undeserving claimants or saved the government money by paying out for fewer pensions, but ultimately such stringent treatment of pension claims might have undermined the pension system's very purpose of compensating soldiers and their families. Not every American family actually lived according to the model inscribed in pension legislation. To adhere strictly to the provisions of those laws would have denied countless deserving claimants the benefits of a pension. Examining dependent parents' claims further develops the distinct model of family structure and organization inherent in pension legislation and reveals, just as widows' claims did, how claimants and pension officials alike attempted to interpret and apply the laws, and in some cases even change the laws, to suit the experiences that varied from this ideal model.

A Hierarchy of Family Relationships

THE PROSECUTION of parents' claims for pensions exposes a hierarchy of familial relationships within pension legislation. Although Catherine Camphor, the mother who lost her pension to her son's widow, did not convince pension officials that her son John had not been married to Sarah Jarrett, her argument raised an important question about whether the husband–wife relation should have been given priority over the mother–son relation. Catherine's testimony implied that she had been closer to her son than his wife had been, especially after John had enlisted in the USCT. Sarah never visited John after he enlisted because she did not want to leave her mistress, but Catherine had visited him. According to Catherine, at the time of her visit, John expressed the desire that his mother should have all his possessions in the event of his death and had his captain draw up a document to that effect. In the pension process Catherine's version of the truth and the fact that John and

Sarah had been married lay at the heart of one of the crucial differences between slave and free familial relations: how and why certain relations were considered more important than others.

If the government believed that Sarah was John's widow, there was no question of choosing the more legitimate relative, as was done in the cases where two or more people claimed to be the same relative. The pension laws already determined that a widow received a pension before any other relative. Although the act of July 14, 1862, provided that the mother could receive a pension only if the soldier left no widow or minor children, the act of July 27, 1868, established an order of succession for relatives eligible for pension: widow, child, mother, father, and orphan brothers and sisters under sixteen years of age.[1] Just as the pension laws reflected the norm of the two-parent, male-headed household, they also established a rigid hierarchy of familial relations. By giving priority to the soldier's wife and then to his minor children, the laws held the conjugal relation as central and the children of that relation as next in importance. Any relationships that fell outside of the two-parent household also fell below it in terms of importance, regardless of the dynamics of an individual family. Even if John had been closer to his mother than to his wife, had left his belongings to his mother, and had decided that his marriage was over, the law held that his widow was to receive a pension first and foremost. Although the law did not deny that Catherine was John's mother, as it might deny that a couple had been married or that a child was legitimate, it recast their relationship by subordinating the mother-son relation to that of husband-wife.

The relegation of older parents to secondary status in the immediate family was derived in part from the Anglo-American conception of the adult husband as a provider. The pension laws assumed that the relations between family members operated upon the principle of reciprocity, just as they assumed in the relation between father and child. The relations between the husband-father and his wife and children were not equal because the husband-father was vested with authority over his family by the de jure and de facto forces that deemed him head of the household. But these familial relations were characterized by a degree of give and take, an exchange of duty and obligation.

The reciprocal relations between husband and wife were clear under the law, especially because spouses were punished for failure to fulfill their obligation to one another. The husband, the paterfamilias, was obliged to support the wife, who in return cared for the children and the household and gave her obedience and earnings to her husband.[2] Relations between the father and children were less clear under the law but came to take on the same characteristics of support and dependence in practice as the husband-wife relation. The traditional Western conception of reciprocal relations between parent and child was based upon the notion that the parent owed the child protection and maintenance for bringing the child into the world and the child owed the parent obedience and honor for his or her very existence. At common law a father had full control over the child's earnings. Although common law did not compel the father to support his children, poor-law statutes in England and the colonies made such provisions.[3]

In the unquestioned assumption that the husband-father would support his wife and children, pension laws situated the wife and children at the top of the hierarchy of familial relations. Relations between adult children and their parents were also cast in terms of dependence and support under the pension laws. In order to receive a pension, relatives other than the soldier's widow or orphans had to prove that they had been dependent upon the soldier for material support. In a congressional debate over the establishment of widows' and orphans' pensions in 1818, advocates argued that the widow "lost her husband who supported her" and the orphan lost the "parent, on whose exertions alone it depended for maintenance and education." Representative William Henry Harrison from Ohio argued further, "You cannot, indeed, restore the husband to the widow, the parent to the child,—but you can supply their places to a considerable degree, and I think it is your duty to do it."[4] Because the soldier's service to the government deprived the wife and/or child of their provider, the government became a surrogate provider for as long as such a role was necessary. Once a widow remarried and had someone else to support her, once a child reached the age of sixteen and could support him or herself, they were no longer eligible for a pension. Parents' subordinate status under pension law was related to the fact that they were not the primary recipients of the adult male child's support.

In free society an adult child assumed the role of provider for his or her parents when the parents became old and infirm and unable to provide for themselves. The assumption that adult children would provide for their parents was also rooted in reciprocity. According to traditional Western thinking, a child's very existence became a debt owed his or her parents, lasting as long as the parents lived. Under this principle, if parents were in need, it was the adult child's responsibility to care for them. Though not established in common law, in America this sense of obligation would become law by statute in many states in the twentieth century.[5]

The conception of the family inscribed in pension laws projected a particular moment in the life cycle of a specific form of family organization, creating a picture of family arranged in descending order of importance from the male head of household: wife, children, mother, father, and siblings. Initially this fixity could not acknowledge that the boundaries of family fluctuated, embracing different members as social, emotional, physical, and economic needs dictated, that roles and relations shifted according to these same needs, or that the marriage relation may not have been considered the essence of family organization.[6] This conception of family could not incorporate the dynamic, resilient nature of slave and ex-slave families as they adjusted to the harshness and uncertainty of both slavery and freedom. Exclusion from laws that governed and protected free families, the tradition of the extended family in African culture,

the centrality of the mother-child bond in this tradition, the
forced separation of slave family members, "abroad" marriages,
strong extended family ties, including ties to nonblood or "fictive" kin, difficult economic times in freedom, all these factors
played a part in shaping former slave families that did not operate according to the rules and principles of familial relationships in the dominant white culture.[7]

Multiple Providers: Subsistence in Slavery and Freedom

FOR SLAVES, basic subsistence depended upon a varied complex of social and economic relationships. Theoretically it was
the master's responsibility to provide for the material well-
being of slaves, a return upon the labor he coerced from them.
But in addition to, often in lieu of, the master's provisions,
slaves contributed to their own material survival through a
number of activities, which included tending gardens and provision grounds, raising livestock, hunting, fishing, and gathering indigenous plants. Within their own internal or informal
economies, slaves bartered or sold their surplus crops and livestock and other items they themselves produced such as furni-
ture, baskets, and horse collars.[8]

The function of a primary male provider, as the crafters of
pension legislation understood it, was simply inconsistent with
lived experience under slavery. As Ira Berlin and Philip Morgan have stated, "Slaves worked in a variety of ways, but almost
always the slaves' economy was a family economy."[9] As much
as the husband-father, the wife-mother and other relatives provided for their families whatever they managed to obtain. One
example Deborah White used to illustrate this argument is that
of Frederick Douglass's grandmother. White also pointed out
that men and women alike shared the responsibility of sup-
plementing the material goods provided by the master.[10] No
prescribed role governed which parent or even which family
member assumed this responsibility. Opportunity, physical

proximity to family members, particular skills, and access to off time, land, and materials determined who would contribute to the family economy.

In her narrative Harriet Jacobs described how her grand-mother convinced the mistress to let her bake crackers at night to sell in their neighborhood. The mistress's response illus-trates how slave owners benefited from allowing slaves to work for themselves: Grandmother "obtained leave to do it, provided she would clothe herself and her children from the profits."[11] After Harriet's parents died her grandmother supplied her with food and clothing, because her master gave little thought to them: "I gave myself no trouble on that score, for on my vari-ous errands I passed my grandmother's house, where there was always something to spare for me. . . . I was indebted to *her* for all my comforts, spiritual or temporal. It was *her* labor that sup-plied my scanty wardrobe."[12] Even children contributed to the family economy. In her pension claim Nancy Woods explained that her son worked a plot of land the master gave her and "he used to raise vegetables and corn for her, and his earnings for her support."[13]

The ideal of the father-provider clashed with the everyday experience in the postwar rural South, as it had with the slave experience. The circumstances of freedom lent themselves to the continuation of multiple providers within former slaves' families. The nature of rural life in general, the debilitated southern economy and agriculture, the extreme poverty of the recently emancipated, and the inability of families to survive on the meager wages paid to black men meant that every mem-ber of the family had to work to contribute to the family econ-omy whether by laboring in the fields, "hiring out" for wages, or "foraging" for small animals, fish, and fruits and vegetables.[14]

This collective approach to survival overlapped with the "ethos of mutuality" developed in slavery, which continued to characterize freed people's family and community relations. In her discussion of how freedwomen ordered their familial re-sponsibilities in the face of the Freedmen's Bureau's "narrow model of family and married life," Leslie Schwalm pointed to the same conception of helping those in need: "Marriage was not the only, or even most important, familial relationship; many freedwomen spent the years immediately following the war caring not only for their children, but also their grand-children, nieces and nephews, cousins, sisters, parents, aunts, and grandparents. Still others adapted their intimate relationships to the range of responsibilities and duties that lowcountry African Americans recognized not only as legitimate but also obligatory in their tightly woven families and communities." In striking contrast to the notion of the nuclear family as a separate and independent economic unit, among former slaves a person in need could turn to a variety of kin and community networks for assistance.[15] Although the law and white culture may have asserted the male as head of the household and labeled him the primary provider, in freedom as in slavery providers varied according to availability of resources, economic opportunity, and family structure.

The concept of the male provider played a significant role in efforts to facilitate the transition from slavery to freedom. Northern officials encouraged former slave men in their roles as heads of household precisely so that they would assume the role of the provider. As Schwalm has argued, northern officials believed that making freedmen responsible for their families' economic support would promote the success of a free labor system and would prevent former slaves from becoming dependent upon the state or upon charity from the Freedmen's Bureau for day-to-day survival. Schwalm was careful to note that giving black men power over their families did not constitute giving them the same power and status in society that white male heads of household enjoyed:

> Yet, curiously enough, the effort by Northern agents of Reconstruction to bring freedwomen and children into legally sanctioned families as dependents of black men offered only illusory promises of increasing freedmen's range of power or

authority. The prerogatives of black masculinity envisioned by white bureau officials were apparently constrained to freedmen's domination over their wives and children. Reconstruction-era family policy attempted to transfer women and children from either autonomy or dependence on the state into legal and economic dependence on and subordination to men who were significantly disempowered themselves.[16]

If laws regarding parents' pensions reinforced the significance of the male provider, the cases examined in this chapter reveal the near impossibility of imposing the role of provider on the freedman in his newly appointed capacity as head of household.

Even former slaves' advocates, those who exhorted them to be just like free whites, understood that the family roles they prescribed did not coincide with the reality of ex-slaves' situation in freedom. The words of the Reverend Isaac Brinckerhoff suggest as much. In a section titled "Provide for Your Family," he wrote: "All the members of your family have heretofore been accustomed to work in the field, or at some other labor. The father, mother, and children together have toiled the livelong day. At present this cannot perhaps be changed. It is to be hoped, however, that the time will come when the wife and mother will be able to devote her whole time and attention to family and household duties. . . . In this case the support of the family will rest on the husband and father. He will be obliged to earn enough for all, and thus supply all their wants."[17] The conditional nature of his advice is readily apparent. Though he could only offer the hope that "the time will come" when former slaves could take up white familial roles—indicating his understanding that families functioned differently according to varying circumstances—Brinckerhoff continued to hold up a single ideal model of family organization, with the father as the sole support of his family.[18] The double standard apparent in Brinckerhoff's advice is indicative of the impossible bind such expectations placed upon former slaves. Their present condition was unacceptable from the perspective of free society, but the acceptable condition was impossible to attain in the immediate future.

Former slaves themselves recognized the impossible bind of living up to these ideal notions of male and female roles. Yet, as Laura Edwards has observed, rather than seeing themselves as inadequate, former slave men and women forged their own definitions of manhood and womanhood that took into account the realities of their lives. Particularly significant in terms of shaping these definitions was the reality of economic insecurity, which meant that men could not be sole providers and women could not stay at home. In their own definitions many former slaves affirmed manhood and womanhood in the very ways that elite whites would have seen it denied. Manhood might be measured by the effort to make a living wage rather than the achievement of it, womanhood by contributions to the family's well-being in both the fields and public spaces.[19]

Defining Dependence and Support under the Pension System

BECAUSE OF the requirement that parents prove their dependence upon their children, parents' claims for pensions demonstrate precisely how slave and ex-slave familial relations did not immediately fit into reciprocal relations of dependence and support inherent in the pension laws' conception of family. Claims of mothers and fathers show how the role of the master shaped and affected slaves' notions of the provider and how slave and ex-slave support systems developed and functioned according to their own needs and resources instead of what free society had prescribed.

Despite the obvious absence of a central provider within the slave family, pension officials based decisions about parents' and siblings' claims on a relationship of dependence upon the soldier until the new law in 1890 dropped the requirement for all parents' claims. Martha Taylor's case exemplifies the basic stumbling block encountered by former slaves who filed a claim based upon prior dependence. In the midst of the war, Martha ran away from Northumberland County, Virginia, to Baltimore, Maryland, with "seven head of children." Her husband, who had been sickly for many years, died in 1866, the same year that Martha applied for a pension on behalf of her son Walter's service. Typically slow-moving, the Pension Office sent Martha a letter in 1871 requesting the date that she "ceased to live with or rely upon her master for support," implying that before her emancipation she could not have been dependent upon her son for material support. Blind to the instances where an internal slave economy flourished, the pension system seems to have operated upon the general principle that as property themselves, slaves could not possess, let alone distribute among their family members, the fruits of their own labor.[20]

Martha attempted to demonstrate that her son Walter had supported her for a time after she had run away from her master and before he enlisted in the army. She claimed to have run away in 1862 and argued that before Walter enlisted, he had worked on a farm to make money for her rent, food, and fuel.[21] She also offered evidence that her son desired to send her money from his army pay but thought better of it because he "feared it would not reach her, owing to the insecurity of the mails—and also because he feared she had moved away from their previous home and he was not certain as to her address and her whereabouts."[22] Martha's former master claimed that the Emancipation Proclamation of January 1, 1863, freed her, inadvertently narrowing the gap between the time Martha was a slave and the date Walter enlisted in the army. In the end the Pension Office rejected Martha's claim on the grounds that she had been a slave up until her son's enlistment in the army and, because he had not sent her any of his pay thereafter, she could not have been dependent upon him for her daily survival.[23]

Apparently Martha shared her predicament with countless other former slaves. In his annual report to Congress, W. W. Dudley, commissioner of pensions from 1881 to 1884, made a plea for slave mothers because they could not meet the requirement of dependence: "The exact terms in which this section controls the character of evidence required practically excludes from its benefits slave mothers. I therefore recommend that it be amended so as to provide that when the soldier died while the mother was yet in a condition of slavery, she shall not be denied a pension because of her inability to show that her said son contributed to her support, or that he recognized his obligations to do so."[24] Dudley recognized the contradiction of demanding that enslaved parents have been dependent upon their offspring. Although Dudley's recommendation and similar suggestions on the part of individual pension officials did not result in legislation that specifically addressed former slave parents' claims, they can be seen as part of the larger effort in the latter half of the 1880s to eliminate the requirement of prior dependence in order to allow all parents easier access to pensions. As Megan McClintock illustrated in her work on Civil War pensions, white parents often experienced difficulty meeting the narrowly defined terms for parents' pensions. Many could not supply the requisite evidentiary material to prove prior dependence upon the soldier, particularly as the gap increased between the date of the soldier's death and the date of filing a claim.[25] The resulting law of 1890 clearly demonstrates that just as claimants conformed to the dictates of the law, so too could the law conform to citizens' needs when necessary. Whether such accommodations broadened the definition of family upon which pension laws were modeled to include slave families is hard to say. In light of the perseverance of the ideal of the single male provider and the reciprocal relations of dependence and support, it seems most likely that the situation of the slave family was considered to be the exception to the rule rather than an alternative family model.

Rooted in the principle of a parent's dependence upon an adult child was the contingency that a parent must be incapable of fully supporting himself or herself. A pension was designed as a surrogate for a provider lost to the war. Consequently, just like the widow who remarried and had someone new to provide for her or the child who had reached the age of sixteen and could take care of himself or herself, parents who could feasibly support themselves were considered to be their own providers and therefore were not in need of a pension. As McClintock has noted regarding parents' claims in general, the state of dependence differed for mothers and fathers.[26] A mother had to demonstrate the absence or incapacity of a husband or other sons who could provide for her. For example, in addition to proving that her son sent her money, clothing, and coffee during the war, Tennessee pension claimant Patsey Sneed successfully demonstrated her condition of dependence in 1867 by pointing to the fact that in the last years of his life, her husband was incapable of supporting her. Witnesses testified that after emancipation Patsey's husband Washington (also called Quash) "in consequence of old age and infirmities . . . was unable to procure a living by manual labor but was an encumbrance and a tax on his . . . wife Patsey up to the day of his death."[27] Presumably if Quash had been able to make a living in those couple of years after emancipation, Patsey could not have claimed to be in a state of dependence upon her son, because her husband would have been her primary provider.

A father's claim of dependence usually was accompanied by proof of some physical infirmity that prevented his assumption of the position of provider.[28] Interestingly, pension officials appeared reluctant to label any fathers, whether black or white, slave or free, as dependent, perhaps because dependence was considered a female trait. As Commissioner James Tanner noted in 1889, "If the father of the soldier was living [at the date of soldier's death], proof of the condition of dependence would be likely to show the father's inability to provide a sufficient support for his family."[29] With dependence came the stigma of a father's failure to live up to his responsibility as head of household.

Proving a state of dependence was not entirely impossible for former slaves. In 1865 former Missouri slave Nancy Woods took in washing and hired herself out as a servant in order to support her five children, ranging from age nine to sixteen. Regardless of her need at the time, Nancy was compelled to prove a state of dependence upon her two oldest sons, Price and Henry, who had served in the USCT and died three months apart. Fortunately Price and Henry had not enlisted in the USCT until four months after their emancipation. In the interim they both worked on farms and supplied their mother with food and money for rent from their earnings. Nancy could prove this fact with testimony from both her former young master and the man for whom Price had worked. Nancy's former master added a measure of certainty to the success of her claim when he reported that he had seen Price give his mother money and heard him tell her to use it to pay the rent.[30]

Eliza Williams's son, Theodore, worked as a farmhand during 1862 and 1863. His wages went directly to Eliza, who used the money to pay her rent and to buy her groceries. At the center of Eliza's case lay the testimony of Hugh Hambleton, who stated that he had hired Theodore for two years and had paid Eliza for his services. Other witnesses claimed that Eliza's son sent her money while he was away in the army. Coupled with the fact that Eliza's husband was a heavy drinker up until his death in 1865 and therefore was not a sufficient provider, the evidence of her son's support gained Eliza a pension.[31]

Juda Gray's case illustrates the problematic nature of defining dependence and need in the context of slavery. When she filed a mother's claim in 1880, Juda had already experienced a lifetime's worth of loss. Residing in Scott County, Virginia, Juda had spent most of her seventy years in bondage. During the war Juda lost all but four of her twelve children; as she explained, "I haven't seen any of the other children since the war and I don't know whether they are dead or alive."[32] Juda's present state of need was readily apparent to all who knew her. Witnesses assessed the value of Juda's property, a cow and "a poor bed and bedclothing," at a total of $16. Juda worked as much as her age and her feeble condition allowed and survived upon what her remaining children and her neighbors could afford to give her.[33]

Juda claimed a pension on behalf of her son Alfred, her fourth oldest child, who was a slave until he ran away to enlist in the army. Because Alfred remained behind enemy lines until he died and Juda had no contact with him, she could not claim that Alfred had supported her after emancipation, as a claimant such as Nancy Woods might. Furthermore, Juda herself noted that Alfred could not have fully supported her during slavery in the manner that the pension system expected. As she put it, "The soldier Alfred Gray worked for his owner[;] he got no wages from him for his work, he was hired to other persons to work sometimes by his owner but his owner always got the pay."[34] Yet Juda claimed a condition of dependence upon her son and insisted that he did indeed support her while they were enslaved. Although he performed most of his labor for his master without pay, during off time—on Sundays, "wet days," and in the evenings on "long winter nights"—Alfred made baskets, horse collars, and brooms, which his master allowed him to sell for his own profit. Alfred used part of the money he earned to provide his mother with the food and supplies she needed in addition to what her master gave her. Rather than rejecting Juda's claim outright, pension officials were compelled to assess the extent to which Alfred had supported his mother and to which Juda was in need of that support.[35]

The ensuing evaluation of Juda's claim proved complicated, particularly because pension laws did not address the issue of dependence in the context of slavery. Most likely, those who crafted pension legislation assumed that a male slave's condition prevented him from providing anything for anyone. The original Civil War pension law stated simply that a mother could receive a pension if she was dependent upon her son "in whole or in part." The revised act of March 3, 1873, defined "when [a] mother [was] assumed to be dependent upon her son," but clearly it was not referring to slaves: "a mother shall

be assumed to have been dependent upon her son, within the
meaning of this act, if, at the date of his death, she had no other
adequate means of support than the ordinary proceeds of her
own manual labor and the contributions of said son or of any
other persons not legally bound to aid in her support; and if .
. . the son had recognized his obligations to aid in support of
said mother, or was by law bound to such support."[36]

Applying this definition to slavery raised more questions
than it answered. What constituted adequate support? Because
slaves did not work for pay, could the master's provisions be
considered the "proceeds of [their] own manual labor"? Because the master was not legally bound to provide for his slaves,
did his contribution count? Individual pension officials grappled with such questions in prosecuting the claims of dependent relatives and often answered them according to their own
sense of dependence and need. As one official's lament suggests, there were no easy solutions: "The question of dependence on the part of a Mother who was a slave up to within a very
time of her son's enlistment is one difficult to settle unless some
fixed principle is laid down."[37]

Juda's owners' sense of the degree to which she depended
upon her son underscores the difficulty of defining a slave's dependence, especially from vastly varying perspectives. In early
affidavits several members of their master's family testified that
Alfred had contributed to his mother's support by supplying
her with extra food and clothing. In later testimony the master's family members changed their story. Their new insistence
that Alfred could not have supported his mother because the
master did so more than adequately suggested a realization that
to say otherwise might make them appear remiss in providing
for their slaves. Juda's young master, Harvey Gray, recalled that
Juda had been well cared for: "My father, who owned Juda, always provided well for her the same as he did for other slaves.
. . . I cannot say that Juda Gray was in any way dependent upon
the son Alfred for support because she was well cared for until
she was made free."[38] Harriet Gray, Juda's former mistress,

added, "While these people remained with us, they wanted for nothing, and [Juda] always had enough to eat, drink, and wear."[39] Members of the master's family were all quite clear that although Alfred might have given his mother some things, she had not been in need of them.

A master's sense of his slaves' basic needs and the slaves' sense of those needs did not necessarily coincide, however, which raises further questions about the importance of intermittent and supplemental contributions to the master's provisions. Sometimes what was added appears to have been variety. Alfred supplemented Juda's staple diet of cornbread and meat with other kinds of food, and he bought her an extra pair of shoes because the master provided only one pair a year. Juda elaborated: "Alfred helped me a good deal before he left [for the army]. He used to help me along. He gave me clothing and things to use. He used to give me handkerchiefs occasionally. He gave me two dresses during the war. He brought coffee and one thing and another . . . this was during the war and while he was in bondage. I was a slave also at the time and my master provided me with clothing and supported me every bit as he did other slaves."[40] But sometimes what was added appears to have supplemented a fundamental insufficiency. Another of the Grays' former slaves reported that Alfred brought his mother food to soothe her weak stomach, implying that the food supplied on the plantation was not always nourishing or adequate. "The owner did not at all times furnish his slaves with enough to eat and wear," he recalled. "I have wanted myself for clothing at times, while a slave, and sometimes my stomach would be weak . . . but usually our master provided his slaves with the comforts of life."[41] Did support have to be constantly life-sustaining? Did Alfred's contributions that kept Juda nourished and comfortable constitute support? In what sense and to what degree did Juda need the extra clothing, shoes, or food that her son supplied? Though the terms *support, dependence,* and *need* may have defined free familial relations, they lack any precision when applied to slave families. In other words, what was understood as their meaning in terms of free families could not be transferred to slave families.

While wading through Juda's case, pension officials addressed some of these issues, but the case as a whole offered no resolution to the problematic status of a slave's dependence. Because Juda had been free for approximately two years before Alfred died and he had not supported her during that time, the Pension Office rejected her claim. The case reviewer found that Juda was "not dependent upon [her son] in any measure for support." Juda managed to survive without Alfred's assistance and therefore was not in need of it. Furthermore, the reviewer pointed out, Alfred did not meet the reciprocal requirements of a legal provider: "Alfred . . . then about 30 years old was under no legal obligation to aid in her support." Had Alfred been a minor, his mother might have been entitled to his pension as she would have been to his wages; had Alfred sent Juda any money or material goods, he would have been acknowledging that she needed his support. Despite the fact that Alfred had voluntarily helped his mother throughout his young adulthood in slavery and was unable to contact her during the war and thus could not help her then, Juda failed to gain a pension.[42]

That very same ambiguity in the concept of dependence, the lack of precise definition, could also work in a claimant's favor. Edward Jackson applied for a pension in 1882 after a decade of hard luck. Advancing in age, growing increasingly ill, barely making a living in a depressed agricultural economy, Edward encountered his final misfortune when a mule and two milk cows drowned as the Mississippi River flooded his neighborhood in East Carroll Parish, Louisiana.[43] Edward could only offer minimal evidence of support by his son Jefferson in his pension claim. Two witnesses reported that Jefferson "lived in the same house with [his father] before he enlisted and would cut wood and help his father . . . up until he left for the army."[44] By Edward's own admission he was a slave when his son enlisted, so this help must have been administered during his enslavement. Edward also stated that Jefferson did not send him any money while he was in the service. And yet in 1887 the Pension Office approved Edward's claim.

Why did Edward get a pension? His seems to be an example of how pension officials might apply the law liberally to satisfy their own personal concerns about a particular case. Edward's infirmity and inability to support himself appear to have made his claim successful. Friends, former employers, and the doctor who had taken care of him when he first fell ill in 1863 all attested to Edward's weak physical condition and his clearly dependent state. Perhaps his misfortune moved a particularly sympathetic pension official, one who also might have been impressed by the affirmation that Edward "has always shown a willing disposition to labour when able," as his doctor testified.[45] Perhaps the men who adjudicated his case were among the many who pushed to redefine the requirement of dependence; Edward's case anticipated by a few years the new law that made a claimant's present condition of dependence the deciding factor in awarding parents' pensions.

Although it was fraudulent, Lydia Gregory's claim for a pension on account of her nephew's service in the USCT was one of those by applicants who fell outside the list of eligible relatives and consequently were denied any consideration as dependent family members.[46] Sometime shortly after the war, a former slave named Hannah Gregory received the bounty and back pay of Thomas Gregory, a young man she claimed was her son. In reality Hannah's daughter, Matilda, was the soldier's mother, but Matilda had been sold off during slavery and never heard from again. Had Hannah purposely attempted to defraud the government by pretending to be her own daughter? Or had she applied for the bounty and back pay thinking it was her right to do so because it was she who raised Thomas and acted as his mother after Matilda was sold away? Her motivation is unclear.

In 1884 Hannah's other daughter, Lydia, applied for a mother's pension under the name Hannah Gregory. Perhaps it was Hannah's earlier success that made Lydia believe she could simply assume Hannah's character and claim to be Thomas's mother. When Special Examiner H. P. Maxwell looked into the case, he soon learned that Hannah Gregory had died in 1882, and he subsequently managed to uncover Lydia's scam. Unlike her mother's case, which might have been justified, Lydia's was a blatant effort to outwit the government.

Yet Lydia's case presents a plausible scenario and thus raises an interesting point about who should have been eligible for a pension. Lydia asserted that her sister's absence and the death of both Thomas's grandmother and his father made her his rightful heir, but the principles of inheritance and the laws of the pension system denied Lydia this status. However, had Thomas lived, without any parents or grandparents, might his aunt have been his only family? Might he have lived with Lydia while he got on his feet after the war? Might he have worked alongside of her in the fields, contributing to their household's share of the crop? Certainly the Civil War pension system could not have accommodated every possible type of family relationship for fear of bankruptcy or excessive fraud by claimants who invented all kinds of relationships. Lydia's case does not suggest that it should have but rather demonstrates just how far lived experience could vary from the ideal family type inscribed in the pension laws.

Dependence and Support beyond Slavery

ALTHOUGH THE government denied Ned Barnard's second claim as a parent because it decided that his marriage had not been valid, the facts of the case, even if unique, illustrate the inability of the provisions for parents' pensions, rooted as they were in the notion of single male provider, to capture effectively the economic reality of former slaves. Approximately twenty years before the war, Ned, then a slave, had married a free woman named Peggy Gregory and had a son with her. Though he would later testify that his master was "bitterly opposed to a slave marrying a free woman," in his first claim Ned explained that he and Peggy married with his master's permission and Peggy's consent ("she being free born" needed no other permission).[47] Their son Zachariah was born in 1841, and because his mother was free, he was free, too. Zachariah lived with his mother near the Barnard farm and called himself Zachariah Gregory after her. Because Ned's owner was "dissatisfied" with their marriage, Ned and Peggy separated, and later Peggy moved from North Carolina to Virginia with Zachariah. Sometime later Ned married a woman "more agreeable to the owner" and began a new family.

Although Ned was a slave, he appears to have exercised the same right as a free father and laid claim to the fruits of his son's productive labor, hiring out Zachariah and using his son's wages to provide goods for his slave family. Zachariah's assistance allowed Ned to position himself in the role of provider. "At the time he was working for me while in the service I was burdened with a large family of small children," Ned explained, "and his labor helped me considerably in my family's maintenance."[48] Thomas Barnard, a former slave who appeared to have been freed before the war, reported that he had hired Zachariah from his father. "Zach was some twelve or fifteen years old when I had him," Thomas recalled. "I think I hired him two or three years [but] do not recollect what I paid his father for him, it was small wages though—as he was a small gruffy boy."[49]

It is doubtful that Ned had any legal right to his son's wages, but he might have expected his son to assist him in his survival, as regularly happened among slaves. It might have been customary among free women of color who married slaves to hire out their children (who inherited their mothers' free status) in order to improve their slave husbands' material conditions. In this case, even though Peggy and Ned were no longer married, either Peggy or Zachariah might have generously offered to support Ned. It is also unclear why Peggy did not take Zachariah's wages during this time, especially because she was free and Zachariah was living with her. After Peggy moved to

Virginia, Zachariah helped to support her. Ned testified that this change was his doing: "I did not take any of my sons wages while they live in Portsmouth, Va. but let it go to the support of his mother. . . . At the time of my son's death I was living with my owner Grandy Barnard and was supported by him."[50]

That Ned did not take his son's money but "let it go" to Peggy implies that he wielded unusual de facto authority for a slave. Whether this is suggestive of the power some male slaves held within their families or is an early example of a slave man seizing a power exercised by males in free white society is impossible to tell. In her discussion of the free women of color living in Petersburg, Virginia, Suzanne Lebsock argued that "when a free woman cohabited with a slave, here were the materials for a complete sex-role reversal, for the woman assumed all legal rights and responsibilities for the pair." If this legal role reversal was the same for slave men and free women who "married" in other states—and the fact that slaves lacked any legal rights as such suggests that possibility—Ned's case becomes that much more unusual.[51] Perhaps Ned was expressing his sense of self, reconstructing his slave self as a forceful and decisive individual who acted as a free man might have. But Ned was hardly in a position to assume the role of provider. Taking the wages of one's child in free white society was a practice based on a relationship of reciprocity that Ned as a slave was unable to fulfill. Rather, Zachariah played both roles; he was simultaneously supplemental provider and son, handing over his wages to his father.

Throughout his testimony Ned insisted that Zachariah "would have been a great help to me in my old age had it not been for the war." Ned pointed to the future, to when he might be struggling and in need of his son's support, both because of the difficult economic times after slavery and because Ned would be getting older and less capable of supporting himself and his family. In an 1892 affidavit Ned described how Zachariah could have helped him after slavery. (Note that Ned's testimony conflates Zachariah's help before his enlistment dur-

ing 1863 with Ned's need for such help later on.) "At the time
of enlistment, or thereafter, I could have got more than $5 per
month had he stayed with me . . . and if [Zachariah] had not
enlisted it would have helped me more as he was becoming
more able bodied, demanding higher wages. I was poor and was
a tenant on other's lands, thus he was great service to me in helping to support my family. During the soldier's time in the war I
could have gotten from [$8 to $9] per month for his labor."[52]

Ned's argument is worthy of attention because it illustrates
an important point that in a sense rendered moot the question
of dependence upon the soldier during slavery. Before 1890,
when the law regarding dependence changed, the pension
process looked only to the past to determine if the claimant's
relationship with the soldier warranted future support. It did
not look at what the soldier's role would have been in the
claimant's present situation in freedom. Regardless of who had
supported the claimant during slavery, a new set of needs arose
as the master-slave relationship was eradicated and the family
took over the full responsibility of providing for its members.

How valid was Ned's assumption that Zachariah would have
helped him in freedom? Quite possibly Ned assumed that as he
had determined the allocation of his son's wages in slavery, so
would he in freedom. But Zachariah would have been an adult
by the end of the war and would have had more say about his
own earnings. Ned might have believed that his son would care
for him out of a sense of reciprocal duty, despite the fact that
during slavery he had been unable as the father to fulfill his side
of the mutual obligation, that is, to support or protect his son.
Perhaps Ned simply looked around him and imagined that he
would be taken care of in the same manner as other needy former slaves. Like Ned, many parents had become "old and infirm, and unable to support [themselves] and family comfortable" after years of harsh labor.[53] As they had done in slavery
when the master turned them out, these parents relied upon
their children, their kin, and their community for help.[54]

The pension records support the notion of the continuation

of care for the elderly as well as the notion that many diverse, fluctuating households were created after slavery so that families could survive. Some parents, like Margaret Fields, lived full time with their married children. Margaret lived with her daughter from the end of the war until the end of her life. In the years after the war, Margaret contributed to the family economy by working in the fields. As she grew older and unable to perform such strenuous labor, she began to keep house for the family.[55] Miles Cartwright, a younger man, had been badly injured while performing heavy labor for his regiment in the USCT. Afterwards, he was often incapable of laboring at more than one-third his earlier capacity. A friend asserted: "He was in a hard place till his son got big enough to help him. He was not able to keep his family up. His son is about 20 or 21 now."[56] Other parents lived with their children temporarily as needed. Eliza Tyler resided in her daughter's home on and off for ten years before her death. Benjamin B. Manson's son moved in with him and "took care of [Benjamin] in [his] old age." Finally, Huldah Gordon's son sent her money whenever he could spare it.[57]

Support networks not only included older children helping their elderly parents, however. William and Alice Timmons lived with their half sister after their mother died. Typical of the many former slaves in the rural South, Rena Eason lived and worked with her children on a piece of land. Yet, unlike most, Rena owned the land, having purchased it with her bounty money. After escaping slavery in Missouri, Rachel Holden moved to Kansas and built a home for herself and her youngest daughter. The local postmistress noted that "the other children have found a home with her when they chose to stay." Lucy Nichols described how her stepuncle came to live with her, her sisters, and her mother during the war: "My step-father's brother . . . stayed at our house [and] waited on and cared for and protected us, and helped to support us, as he was unable to [become] a soldier." During this time Lucy's sisters also "hired out to make the support."[58]

In addition to the strong extended kin ties or the ethos of mutuality that might have created such a diversity of households, sheer economic necessity made the role of provider impossible for a single person to fill. Ned described himself as a "poor . . . tenant on other's lands," which meant he was a tenant farmer or renter; he did not own the land upon which he farmed but most likely labored upon a designated piece of land for a portion of the profit from the crop he harvested. Most rural freedmen worked as sharecroppers, as hired laborers who received a portion of the crop or profit as compensation, or as waged laborers who worked for cash. Ned may have worked in any or all of these capacities.

Traditionally renting has been viewed as a step up from sharecropping or working for wages because it afforded the laborer a measure of independence, protection from the planter's prying eyes and the potential, limited though it may have been, to get ahead economically. Laura Edwards's discussion about labor in the tobacco region of Granville County, North Carolina, about 125 miles west of Ned's home, demonstrates the error of assuming that Ned was better off than others and thus that he might not have needed his son's help. Edwards pointed out that renting did not always afford economic or social independence, especially for African Americans, who often were given the worst land to farm and who had to struggle with white landowners' conception of them as a permanently dependent group. Ned's description of himself as poor suggests that renting had not necessarily garnered him economic independence. Edwards argued further that poor families frequently combined renting with other kinds of labor in order to survive. With this in mind, Ned's insistence that Zachariah's waged labor would have been helpful seems quite plausible.[59]

In pointing to what his son would have done for him, Ned identified yet another juncture at which the concept of the single provider could not embrace the slave family and other families that did not function according to this ideal. In freedom it was quite likely that the family as a whole would have

depended upon the former soldier's wages or labor—his contribution to the family economy—as part of a larger system of
support. Just as the war deprived the wife of the "husband who
supported her" and deprived the child of the "parent on whose
exertions alone it depended," it deprived whole families of a
crucial link in their support systems. However, they would receive no recompense after the war. The pension law's conception of the husband-father as sole provider could not embrace
the preponderance of ex-slave and other families who were
obliged to organize their family economy differently.

Ned lost his first bid for pension because he could not prove
his dependence upon Zachariah. He reapplied (under the new
law of 1890) and failed again when the Pension Office declared
Ned's marriage invalid and his son therefore illegitimate. Because Ned had no legal connection to his son, he had no
grounds upon which to claim a pension.

The 1890 Law: Redefining Dependence and Support

IN 1890 Congress loosened the requirements for Civil War pensions. The act of June 27, 1890, the Dependent Pension Act, allowed a pension to any veteran who had served in the Union
army for ninety days, had been honorably discharged, and had
some disability that prevented him from making a living. Unlike the previous legislation, under this act a soldier did not
have to prove that his disability was service-related; the emphasis of the new law was on the soldier's service in the military, not the nature of his disability. This law was the first in a
series that granted pensions based on service, "each more liberal than its predecessor."[60]

Among its provisions the 1890 act addressed the question of
"would have," enabling parents to claim pensions on the principle that they would have been dependent upon the soldier if
he had survived. Evans Haynes's case demonstrates how parents benefited from this new law. His 1879 claim had been rejected because he could not prove that he had been dependent

upon his son Anthony before the latter's enlistment in the USCT. In 1845 Evans, who had belonged to Thomas Haynes of Wilkinson County, Mississippi, had married Mandy Land, a slave belonging to Nathan Land, and they had several children together. As the law dictated, their son Anthony and their other children also belonged to Nathan Land and lived on his farm with their mother. Although his marriage to Mandy had been deemed "legal and valid," Evans could not claim that he was dependent upon his son during slavery because, as his former owner pointed out, Anthony "as a slave could not aid [his father] in his support as the profits of his labor belonged to the master."[61] This generalization is not entirely true, as other cases have shown, but apparently Anthony did not help his father. Perhaps he was too young, or perhaps his father did not need any help, or, yet again, the fact that Anthony lived on another plantation might have precluded any desire to assist his father. Nor could Evans claim that Anthony had supported him after his emancipation. Anthony was a slave up to the time of his enlistment, and he died after a month in the service.

Evans's general state of dependence may also have been called into question in the examination of this first claim. During the years 1879–82 he was assessed for taxes with 72¾ acres of land valued at $144.[62] Witnesses quickly pointed to the poor condition of the land, which was "so broken that it is useless for cultivation." Suggesting that the tax assessor had overvalued the land, these witnesses argued, "There is a large quantity of the same quality of land belonging to the state in this county that no one will buy at [$1.25] an acre."[63] Nonetheless, Evans's claim was rejected in 1883.

After gathering more testimony, Evans filed another claim in 1890 under section 1 of the new act, which required only examination of the relative's present state to determine dependence. The relative no longer had to have been supported by the soldier in some way before his enlistment or during his military service. Henceforth it was necessary "only to show . . . that such parent or parents are without other present means of support than their own manual labor or the contributions of others not legally bound for their support."[64] The difference in terms of pension payment was that the pensioner received money from the date of filing the claim, rather than the date of the soldier's death as the earlier laws had provided.

Clearly this provision was not made exclusively for ex-slave parents because white parents were also having trouble meeting the rigid terms of dependence in the pension laws. Over the course of the decade before the act was passed, some commissioners of pensions, among them W. W. Dudley, pointed to the "injustice" done to all parents by the "narrow construction" of the terms of dependence. Dudley used an example to illustrate the nature of this injustice: "The son is killed in battle; he does not in fact contribute to the support of his mother at the date of his death, but in reality has been supported by her up to the time of his enlistment. Increasing years and adversity overtake the mother, and she becomes dependent upon the charity of friends. Had the son lived, this would not have been the case, and yet we are obliged to deny her a pension because, at the date of the soldier's death, it cannot be shown that she was dependent upon him for support, in whole or in part."[65] According to Dudley the problem with the earlier definition of dependence was precisely that it did not consider what the son's role would have been in his parents' life as they grew older and became incapable of caring for themselves.

The assumption that the son would have supported his parents in their old age rested upon the principle of reciprocity. Arguing before the House for the need to enact new legislation regarding parents' claims, Representative Edmund N. Morrill of Kansas noted, "The bill is based upon the assumption that the father or mother who gave their son to their country is entitled to the grateful consideration of the Government in their old age and poverty, and that it is reasonable and just to assume that the gallant boy who bravely and loyally gave his life to his country would, if that life had been spared to him, have tenderly cared for the mother who bore him and carefully watched

over him in his years of helplessness."[66] Morrill suggested that
the young man who felt a sense of duty and loyalty toward his
country would have felt the same toward the parents who raised
him. Yet it is not simply loyalty or gallantry that would move
a young man to help his parents. Morrill's explanation called
upon the original relationship of reciprocity. The son would
care for his mother (and/or father) in her "old age and poverty"
just as she cared for him when he was young and helpless. It
was this same sense of reciprocity, "grateful consideration" for
having given up their son, that would compel the government
to grant the parents a pension.

Under the new law Evans was able to prove his present dependent state with prior testimony from his former master, his
doctor, and his neighbors. Evans's doctor, T. F. Haynes,
summed up Evans's condition in 1883:

> Evans Haynes . . . has been more or less disabled by chronic
> Ghonorrhoeal Rheumatism, since [1865] and now that his
> children have all left him does not make a support, nor has
> he paid a dollar on his medical account for years—His wife
> [deceased] has a few acres of worthless Pine Hill Land, and
> [Evans has] one idiot son to support. . . . I know that even
> with the aid of his children the land of his wife was so poor
> that it never paid for the cultivation, and consequently that
> Evans has not paid the merchants who trusted him and now
> cannot get advances from any of them, as they see no chance
> of getting their pay.[67]

Caught in a vicious cycle of poverty so familiar to ex-slaves in
the South, failing in health, responsible for a son with special
needs, Evans was desperate for financial assistance, most likely
beyond what his family and friends could spare. Whereas similar conditions had not been sufficient to earn him a pension
in 1883, the new law changed his luck.

The new law also helped Joe Payne, an ex-slave living in
Missouri who had been separated from his family during slav-

ery and therefore would have been unable to prove a relationship of dependence upon a son he rarely saw. As a young man Joe was one of a few slaves who belonged to Gilliard Roop of Lafayette County, Missouri. Sometime in the early 1840s Roop consented for Joe to marry Agnes, a slave belonging to the Tarlton family who lived approximately two miles from Roop's property. Joe explained the logistics of his abroad marriage: "I visited Agnes every Wednesday night and Saturday night and stayed with her until the next morning."[68] During the course of their marriage, Agnes and Joe had two sons named Samuel and Joseph.

About four years after the marriage, Gilliard Roop died, and Joe was sold off as part of his estate. Joe's new master, a "hemp raiser," took him to a plantation thirty miles away from his family. Joe recounted that his new master "was a hard master and worked me hard." Two years passed before Joe was able to visit his wife and children. He did not describe how he got there, whether he made the thirty-mile journey on foot or was able to catch a ride at least part of the way. When Joe returned to the plantation after his visit, his master told him that the trip took too long and that Joe could no longer see his family. Approximately ten years later, just before the war broke out and no doubt due to the unsettled nature of the time that might have softened a slave owner's resolve, Joe's master allowed him to visit his family again. "[I] went to Lexington to see my boys and I took along a big book for them to read and they could read and write," Joe recalled with pride. He claimed that at this time Agnes was still his wife. Although he could not see them during the war, he kept track of his family and learned that Sam had entered the military and that Agnes had married a man named Nathan Evarts or Nathan Stone.[69]

Joe applied for a pension under the new law in 1892 according to his own understanding of the relationship of reciprocity between the government and its citizens. In a letter addressed to the commissioner of pensions, Joe described his desperate situation. "I need help badly. I am old and poor," he wrote. "I wish you could realize an old man's condition. Possum is mighty spa[r]se in these woods and hard to get. Corn bread, cracklins and coon grease are getting to be strangers on the old man's table. The white man keeps his chicken house locked and wild turkeys are done gone forever."[70] Rather than making the case that his son would have helped him in his time of need, Joe demanded his rights, pointing to the government's responsibility to him as the father of a soldier. "My son died for his country and now the country should help me." After proving that Sam was his son by the testimony of members of the Tarlton family, Joe received his pension. Had he applied under the old law, Joe would not have been able to prove that his son helped him to survive because he saw his son only twice in twelve years.

When Joe applied for his pension, he did not know that Nathan and Agnes, in the capacity of Sam's parents, had received Sam's bounty and arrears of pay in 1867. Joe was unaware that Nathan had claimed to be Sam's father. After his investigation of the case, Special Examiner Victor L. Dodge determined that Nathan had committed perjury back in 1867 because Nathan himself testified in 1892 that Joe was Sam's father.[71] In his own defense, though, Nathan claimed that he believed a father and a stepfather were one and the same under the law. Evidence in the case suggests that Nathan certainly could have been a father figure to Sam. Although Joe recalled that Agnes did not marry Nathan until during the war, Nathan asserted that he married Agnes not long after Joe was taken from his family. Perhaps the marriage had been hidden from Joe; it is possible that when Joe came to visit after a ten-year absence, Agnes did not want to tell him that she had taken a new husband. Nathan and Sam had enlisted together and served in the same company and regiment. A former comrade testified that though he did not remember whether Nathan was called Sam's father, "the two always bunked together and Nathan took care of the soldier in many ways as a father might do for a son."[72] The special examiner was convinced that Nathan was a liar, but perhaps this newly freed man did not fully understand the legal difference between a biological father and a stepfather.

If much of this study has emphasized the problematic elements of acquiring legal family status, Joe's case underscores how extremely beneficial such status could be. Here was a man who was denied the opportunity to have any kind of relationship with his son, dependent or otherwise. Yet the government awarded him a pension by virtue of the fact that he was the child's biological and legitimate father.

The New Law and Old Complications

ALTHOUGH THE 1890 act removed the tangled issue of prior dependence in slavery, the notion of dependence between parents and children remained problematic because questions of familial relations did not translate simply from slavery to freedom. In 1882 Arkansas resident Harriet Gray filed a mother's claim for a pension. Although her first claim had not yet been adjudicated, in 1890 she filed another claim under the new act. The Pension Office treated Harriet's two claims separately, rather than consolidating them, perhaps under the same rule that allowed a soldier to file claims under different laws as long as the payment of the claims did not overlap. On October 3, 1899, the Pension Office rejected both claims, stating that it was not certain that Harriet's son, Harvey Gray, had ever been a soldier.[73]

Several factors led to the rejection, all of which could be attributed to the lack of communication and information that characterized the end of slavery and the early years of emancipation. Because Harriet did not know which company her son had joined, pension officials searched the rolls of the 88th Regiment of the USCT and found that no one had enlisted under the name Harvey Gray. There had been a soldier named Abner Gray, however. These results suggested that Harvey Gray might have enlisted under another name, that his name had been recorded incorrectly, or that he had never enlisted at all.

In addition, the Pension Office found discrepancies between the dates of Abner Gray's enlistment and Harvey's alleged enlistment. Whereas Harvey was believed to have enrolled in 1863, Abner Gray did not enroll until late 1864. Furthermore, while Abner Gray's height had been recorded as five feet three inches, Harvey's master remembered his former slave as being some five or six inches taller.[74]

Approximately a year later Harriet appealed the rejection, offering testimony that proved her son had been a soldier and explained why he might have enlisted as Abner Gray. Harriet Shannon was a former slave who had lived on the same plantation as Harriet and Harvey Gray and had known Harvey since his childhood. She testified that she knew Harvey had been a soldier because he had come to visit her wearing "blue clothes" and that she had cared for him when he had taken ill during his military service. George Johnson, who had "lived on Stephen Johnson's place adjoining Gray's," reported: "I knew [Harvey] when he was only 7 or 8 years old and I know that he was the claimant's son. I knew him afterward as a soldier in Memphis, Tenn. He belonged to the 88th colored regiment. . . . I helped to bury him. . . . I was practicing the drummers of the 88th; and at his funeral marched out to the graveyard with part of my drum corps and part of his. He was a drummer in his regiment. I reckon he was not more than 17 when he died."[75] Among others, Harriet Gray's former young master, Harvey Gray, explained that her son had a nickname. "Harvey was also called Hab. My name is Harvey and he was named for me. I am frequently called Hab."[76] The Pension Office accepted the notion that Harvey may have called himself "Hab" or even "Ab" when he enlisted and that his full name had thus been recorded as Abner. This evidence convinced the authorities that Harvey and Abner Gray were the same person and that Harriet's case deserved to be adjudicated.

Continuing to treat Harriet's claims separately, the Pension Office accepted her claim under the 1890 act but rejected the earlier claim on the grounds that she had not been dependent upon her son because he had been away from home without contact for two years before his death. Harriet's lawyer promptly appealed the latter decision, pointing to Harriet's newly acquired rights as a parent: "The soldier being a minor up to the date of enlistment and to the date of his death, the parent would be entitled to his services if he were living, and therefore, to a pension if he were dead."[77] Accordingly, under the principle of reciprocal relations between parent and child, because Harvey was a minor when he died, Harriet was entitled to his pension. Perhaps as Ned Barnard had, Harriet assumed she could take up the rights of a parent as they were offered to her in freedom.

Yet, like Ned, Harriet had not fulfilled her role as a parent during slavery in the manner that reciprocity demanded, as her final rejection would state. The Pension Office upheld its rejection on the grounds that having lived two years on his own before his death, Harvey had been "emancipated," not from his master but from his mother. F. L. Campbell, assistant secretary of the Department of the Interior, explained that if a parent's right to his or her child's earnings was based on providing for the child's maintenance, then the parent's failure to provide for the child negated that right. (The parent was assumed to be the father, just as the child was assumed to be the son.) Campbell stated, "When, however, the parent does not maintain the child but on the contrary, permits him to use his time as his own, taking no interest in his welfare, providing no home for him, and allowing him to go his own way unmolested and uncared for by such parent, such a procedure, amounts, in law, to an emancipation of the child."[78] According to the principle of emancipation, the fact that his mother did not support him freed Harvey from the obligation to turn his wages over to her. Because the reciprocal tie between them had been severed, Harriet had no grounds to claim that her son would have supported her later in life. It is the irony of the story that even if Harvey had remained with his mother during those two years, Harriet could not have maintained him or provided a home for him as the pension system defined such conditions. Nor could she have allowed him to go his own way because she had been a slave and had no formal authority to allow him to do anything.

Harriet Gray's case serves as a striking example of the extent to which the operation of the pension system was fraught with tension. The issues raised in parents' claims about the hierarchy of family members and the reciprocal relations of dependence and support underscore the extent to which the model of the male-headed, two-parent family shaped the pension system. But if the temptation is to focus on the narrowness of the laws or the extent to which citizens might have had to conform to the model in order to receive the benefits of the pension system, parents' claims make it clear that there was also a considerable amount of play within the pension system, just as the widows' pensions demonstrated.

Harriet Gray must be seen in relation to claimants like Ned Barnard, who insisted that the "would have" mattered; or Joe Payne, who demanded that the government live up to its responsibility to him; or even Juda Gray, who did not receive a pension but whose case, representative of the myriad cases that called the notion of dependence into question, led pension officials and lawmakers to reconsider the requirements for pensions. Undoubtedly the constant, persuasive demands of former slaves played a role in the enactment of the 1890 law. Although free parents encountered similar problems of proving prior dependence, it is easy to imagine that the questions raised about the condition of dependence in former slaves' cases led to a reassessment of the concept in general. Rather than maintaining a rigid position, the system was continually modified by those who were seeking what they considered to be rightly theirs.

Epilogue
The Storytellers

L OUISA CALDWELL'S case appears at the outset of this book. Her pension file is rather unremarkable in general, a slim affair containing only a few yellowed and tattered documents. She left no popular legacy to speak of, no great speeches, no essays or books; she was and is virtually unknown. Because it recorded the fact of her existence, Louisa's pension claim reveals her as an actor in the extraordinary drama that was the era of emancipation. The scantiness of Louisa's pension file makes it necessary to surmise or to imagine most of the details of her life, but the few documents reveal that she was a wife and then a widow, a mother of six, a member of a community in Lexington, Kentucky. She possessed the tenacity necessary to pursue a pension claim, and the success of that claim no doubt gave her some measure of satisfaction, in terms of material reward and perhaps in knowing that she had demanded and received recognition from a government that was now hers. Louisa's story may have been brief, but it survives because she filed a pension claim.

I have sought to raise here specific questions about what it meant to have legal or legitimate family relationships in nineteenth-century America. I have endeavored to illustrate how issues of family relationships and citizenship coincided in the pension process, how efforts to acquire a pension thus reflected the challenges former slaves faced in claiming the status of citizen. At the heart of these cases are particular individuals and the stories they told, situated as they were at the threshold of entry into American society and culture. America was not necessarily unwelcoming, as the acceptance of former slaves' pension claims suggests. Here at least was an agency of the federal government trying to uphold the goals of citizenship and the rights thereof granted in the Fourteenth and Fifteenth Amendments. This was not the Freedmen's Bureau, a temporary agency created specifically to aid former slaves, but the Pension Office, a permanent institution that processed the claims of any citizen who applied. Yet clearly the Pension Office was not standing with arms outstretched, waiting to embrace its formerly enslaved brethren. Undaunted by their lukewarm reception, pursuing goals that ranged from the practical—getting money—to the lofty—getting one's just reward for services rendered to one's country—former slaves told their stories to pension agents. Theirs were stories of finding or making a place in a society that simultaneously expected conformity and rejected the notion that blacks could ever live up to its standards. Their stories reflected the promises of Reconstruction—promises of freedom, civil and political rights, land, opportunity—both fulfilled and unfulfilled.

Former slaves' pension records demonstrate how individual stories shed light on collective experience. The broader themes of these stories announce what were to emerge as the significant themes of African-American history and literature in the United States in the later nineteenth and the twentieth centuries, themes of identity, displacement, assimilation, resistance. The sentiments expressed in these narratives filed away in the pension records would resonate in the writings of those who became the voices of their own and future generations. In some we find the conviction of Ida B. Wells Barnett as she decried the injustice and inhumanity of a government that would not protect its citizens against lynching. Others echo with the ambiguity that W. E. B. DuBois described, the impossibility of living with a "double-consciousness . . . an American, a Negro; two souls, two thoughts, two unreconciled strivings; two warring ideals in one dark body, whose dogged strength alone keeps it from being torn asunder."[1] All reflect that sense of entitlement expressed by Martin Luther King Jr., who told members of the bus boycott in Montgomery, Alabama, "We are here in a general sense because first and foremost we are American citizens, and we are determined to apply our citizenship to the fullness of its means."[2] It was a simple thing that King was asking—the right to get on the bus in the front, to sit in any seat, to be treated with dignity—but in its simplicity it represented the fullest claim to the rights of citizenship. When former slaves applied for pensions, their demand too was simple, but it represented an essential right of American citizens, the right to compensation for services rendered their country.

Notes

All pension records cited are found in Records of the Veterans' Administration, Record Group 15, National Archives, Washington, D.C.

INTRODUCTION

1. Cited in Wood, *Creation of the American Republic,* 124.

2. On the moral foundations of American conceptions of virtue, see ibid., 91–124.

3. Kerber, *Women of the Republic,* 199–200. Kerber's concept of "Republican Motherhood" rests upon the assumption that the family is the source of a virtuous citizenry. See also Bloch, "The Gendered Meanings of Virtue," 56–57; Blankenhorn and Glendon, *Seedbeds of Virtue,* 2, 55–56.

4. Burnham, "An Impossible Marriage," 211; Tushnet, *American Law of Slavery.*

5. Morgan, *American Slavery, American Freedom,* 376.

6. Shklar, *American Citizenship.*

7. Amy Dru Stanley argues that the "rights of family" were fore-

most among those rights considered to define the difference between slavery and freedom ("Conjugal Bonds and Wage Labor," 471).

8. Pension claim of Louisa Caldwell, widow of George Caldwell, Co. G, 116th USCVI.

9. Berlin, Reidy, and Rowland, *Black Military Experience;* Litwack, *Been in the Storm,* esp. chap. 2. Estimates of the number of black soldiers who died in the army vary; see Foner, *Reconstruction,* 125; Berlin et al., *Free at Last,* 477.

10. On the battle over state or federal control of citizenship rights in the creation of the Thirteenth and Fourteenth Amendments and the Civil Rights Act of 1866, see Kaczorowski, "To Begin the Nation Anew," 45–68.

11. Foner, *Reconstruction,* 68–70.

12. On the Black Codes, see Nieman, *To Set the Law in Motion,* 72–102; Foner, *Reconstruction,* 199–201; Litwack, *Been in the Storm,* 366.

13. Nieman, *To Set the Law in Motion,* 109; Lively, *Constitution and Race ,* 45–48; Foner, *Reconstruction,* 244.

14. Kaczorowski, "To Begin the Nation Anew," 48.

15. James, *Framing of the Fourteenth Amendment,* 21–23; Foner, *Reconstruction,* 252.

16. James, *Framing of the Fourteenth Amendment,* 78.

17. Gettys, *Law of Citizenship,* 3–4. Repudiation of *Scott v. Sanford* had begun during the war with such actions as a statement by Attorney General Edward Bates in 1862 proclaiming the citizenship of free blacks born in the United States, the 1862 repeal of the Fugitive Slave act, and the issue of the Emancipation Proclamation (Litwack, *North of Slavery,* 63; Lively, *Constitution and Race,* 39–40).

18. Lively, *Constitution and Race,* 49–52.

19. Berlin et al., *Black Military Experience,* 5–6; Litwack, *Been in the Storm,* 64–103, 502–56; Foner, *Reconstruction,* 110–18.

20. Gutman, *Black Family in Slavery and Freedom;* Litwack, *Been in the Storm,* 240–44; Bardaglio, *Reconstructing the Household,* 132–33.

21. Bardaglio, *Reconstructing the Household,* 132.

22. *Preliminary and Final Reports of the Freedmen's Inquiry Commission,* 38th Cong., 1st sess., 1864, S. Exdoc. 53, 5; Litwack, *Been in the Storm,* 230.

23. Grossberg, *Governing the Hearth,* 130.

24. McFeely, *Yankee Stepfather,* 131.

25. Leslie Schwalm describes the way in which northern middle-

class notions of gender roles and relations shaped Reconstruction policy and affected the ways in which Freedmen's Bureau agents dealt with freed people's families (*A Hard Fight for We*, 234–68).

26. Special Order No. 15, issued March 28, 1864, stated: "Any ordained minister of the Gospel, accredited by the General Superintendent of Freedmen, is hereby authorized to solemnize the rites of marriage among the Freedmen" (cited in Berlin et al., *Black Military Experience*, 712 n. 1). On northern missionaries and Freedmen's Bureau agents taking up the practice of encouraging former slaves to marry, see Litwack, *Been in the Storm*, 240–42.

27. The law in North Carolina stated "that if any such persons shall fail to go before the clerk of the county court . . . and have their marriage recorded before the first of September, one thousand eight hundred and sixty-six, they shall be deemed guilty of a misdemeanor, and punished at the discretion of the court, and their failure for each month thereafter shall constitute a distinct and separate offense." For a complete list of marriage laws passed in southern states immediately after the Civil War, see *Freedmen's Affairs: Laws Relating to Freedmen*, 39th Cong., 2d sess., 1866–67, S. Exdoc. 6. Herbert Gutman discusses some of these laws in *The Black Family in Slavery and Freedom*, 418–25; see also Clinton, "Reconstructing Freedwomen," 307. On the construction of the North Carolina law, see Edwards, *Gendered Strife and Confusion*, 32.

28. "Freedmen's Bureau: General Orders No. 8," *Report of Commissioners of Freedmen's Bureau*, 39th Cong., 1st sess., 1865–66, House Exdoc. 70, 108–11. For the Freedmen's Bureau's treatment of slave marriages in South Carolina, see Schwalm, *A Hard Fight for We*, 239–48.

29. Though Peter Bardaglio makes the important claim for a distinctive domestic relations law in the South, shaped by the South's transformation from a slave to a free society, both Michael Grossberg and Bardaglio point to increasing state intrusion in family life throughout the nineteenth century (Bardaglio, *Reconstructing the Household*, xi–xviii; Grossberg, *Governing the Hearth*, 3–30; see also Bardaglio and Boris, "The Transformation of Patriarchy," 70–93).

30. Bardaglio, *Reconstructing the Household*, 176–89. Michael Grossberg describes the practice of apprenticing poor children in the nineteenth century in *Governing the Hearth*, 263–68.

31. Berlin, Miller, and Rowland, "Afro-American Families in the Transition from Slavery to Freedom," 89–91.

32. For examples of the kinds of cases that came to the fore in this era, see Grossberg, *Governing the Hearth,* 134–36; Bardaglio, *Reconstructing the Household,* 133–34; Edwards, *Gendered Strife and Confusion,* 57–58.

33. Both Margaret Burnham and Peter Bardaglio point to Winthrop Jordan to this effect. Jordan states that "while statutes usually speak falsely as to actual behavior, they afford probably the best single means of ascertaining what a society thinks behavior ought to be; they sweep up the felt necessities of the day and indirectly expound the social norms of the legislators" (Jordan, *White over Black,* 588; Burnham, "An Impossible Marriage," 206; Bardaglio, *Reconstructing the Household,* xvii).

34. See esp. Gutman, *Black Family in Slavery and Freedom;* Blassingame, *Slave Community;* Stevenson, *Life in Black and White;* Malone, *Sweet Chariot.*

35. The WPA interviews with former slaves have been reprinted in many publications, including Rawick, *American Slave.*

36. Schwalm, *A Hard Fight for We,* 149–54.

37. Berlin et al., *Black Military Experience,* 14. The estimate of 10 percent represents African Americans in both the Union army and navy combined.

38. In this sample 22 of 35 pension claims filed on behalf of an African-American soldier, or approximately 65 percent, were filed after 1890. Of 507 claims on behalf of white soldiers, 290, or approximately 57 percent, were filed after 1890. Theda Skocpol finds that the "take-up" rate for all veterans jumped from 16.85 percent in 1885 to 39.34 percent in 1891 and 62.85 percent in 1895 and continued to rise in the first decades of the twentieth century (*Protecting Soldiers and Mothers,* 109, 138).

39. I measured success rate by counting any approved claim on behalf of a soldier's service. Out of a total of 507 claims on behalf of white soldiers' service, 444 were successful. Out of a total of 35 claims on behalf of black soldiers' service, 23 were successful. For the figures to speak more broadly to the pension files as a whole, a larger sample is needed. Donald Shaffer compared the success rate of 545 white and 545 black Civil War pension applicants and found that "white applicants had a significantly higher success rate in their pension applications than African Americans" ("I Do Not Suppose," 133–34).

40. On general problems faced by former slave applicants, see Skocpol, *Protecting Mothers and Soldiers,* 138; Shaffer, "I Do Not Suppose," 132–47.

41. Several of the case files contained more than one applicant for the soldier's pension. For example, several files contained the applications of two women claiming to be the widow of the same soldier. Other files contained the applications of both the widow and the children, who might have applied if the widow died or if she had remarried. The number of applicants in each minor's claim ranged from one to five, depending upon the number of children a soldier had and whether they were minors at the time of the soldier's death. Regardless of the number of children within it, each minor's claim was counted as a single case.

42. Since I first began this project, several studies have come out that concentrate on the question of freed people's attitudes toward legalized marriage. I address these studies more extensively in chap. 4.

43. BRFAL, "Letters Received," 1866–67.

ONE The Pension Process: A View from Both Sides

1. Pension claim of Harriet Berry, widow of Joseph Berry, Co. A, 37th USCT, Harriet Berry affidavit, Feb. 20, April 2, 1884, Feb. 1, 1868.

2. Leon Litwack describes many such journeys (*Been in the Storm,* 52–59).

3. On May 9, 1863, Captain Charles B. Wilder, superintendent of contrabands at Fort Monroe, estimated that some 10,000 refugee slaves had come under his control (Berlin et al., *Destruction of Slavery,* 88–90).

4. Ibid., 90. Initially uncertain of the status of runaway slaves, Union officials referred to them as "contrabands," signifying that they would be protected like other property seized by the enemy. Although the Second Confiscation Act of July 1862 freed such runaways, the name stuck.

5. On Union army recruiters, see Berlin et al., *Black Military Experience,* 114–15. On the wartime experiences of slaves from this region, see Berlin et al., *Destruction of Slavery,* 59–70.

6. Berlin, *Slaves without Masters,* 136. Berlin cites Virginia's free black population at 58,046 in 1860.

7. Harriet Berry pension claim, Polly Wilson affidavit, April 2, 1884.

8. Berlin et al., *Destruction of Slavery,* 68–69.

9. Ibid., 61.

10. Berlin et al., *Black Military Experience,* 659. Robert F. Engs argues similarly that in Hampton, Virginia, where Fort Monroe was located, the Union army offered assistance to former slaves "grudgingly and ineffectually" (*Freedom's First Generation,* 26).

11. Jones, *Labor of Love, Labor of Sorrow,* 60–65.

12. Harriet Berry pension claim; Constantine Nitzsche, near Raleigh, N.C., to Harriet Berry, Norfolk, Va., April 18, 1865, copy in Harriet Berry affidavit, Portsmouth, Va., Feb. 1, 1868. Another example of such a letter is William H. Cheney, Donaldsville, La., to Priscilla Atwood, Aug. 29, 1865, in pension claim of Priscilla Jane Atwood, widow of Alexander Atwood, Co. E, 11th USCA.

13. For a discussion of this and other acts relating to black soldiers' bounties, see Berlin et al., *Black Military Experience,* 766 n. 3.

14. Harriet Berry pension claim, Harriet Berry affidavit, Feb. 20, 1884. Within Harriet's pension file is an affidavit taken in 1868, suggesting that Harriet had tried to apply for a pension earlier, but the application process does not appear to have been completed at that time.

15. Jacqueline Jones argues that "the categories of cook, servant, and laundress were fairly flexible" (*Labor of Love, Labor of Sorrow,* 74). On black women's labor as servants, cooks, and laundresses, see Hunter, *To 'Joy My Freedom,* 50–65.

16. The monthly sum of $8 for a widow was specified in the act of July 27, 1868, and was to be provided until her remarriage or death. Additionally, widows received an extra $2 per minor child belonging to the soldier. On March 19, 1886, the amount of a widow's pension was increased to $12 a month. The increase applied to all existing widow pensioners and to new claimants who were married before March 19, 1886. Additional increases to widows' pensions occurred well into the twentieth century. According to the original act of 1862, if a soldier did not file for a pension within a year from the date of his discharge, his pension would be granted from the date when the last piece of evidence was filed. Originally, no such time limitations applied to widows and other dependents. The acts of July 27, 1868, and March 3, 1873, allowed a soldier five years after his discharge to file a claim for benefits from his date of discharge; any claims filed after that period would pay benefits from the date the last piece of evidence was filed. Under these acts widows and other dependents (with some exceptions for minors) were also subject to the five-year time limit. The Arrears Act, signed into law January 25, 1879, provided that all pensions, both those already approved and those approved in the future, would start from the date of the soldier's death or discharge, with no limitations on the date of filing the claim. Under this act pensioners could reopen their cases and receive arrears in one lump sum (on the acts of July 27, 1868, and March 19, 1886, see Glasson, *Federal Military Pensions,* 139–41; on the

Arrears Act, see ibid., 151–53, 164; Skocpol, *Protecting Mothers and Soldiers*, 115–18. The Arrears Act can be found in *U.S. Statutes at Large* 20 [1879]: 265).

17. Harriet Berry pension claim, Harriet Berry affidavit, Feb. 20, 1884.

18. Before 1881 Harriet's claim would have been sent to the Widow Division, which reviewed the claims of widows, children, and other dependent relatives. In 1881 the Pension Office was divided according to region; the restructuring included the creation of a review board, which examined all cases before the Pension Office rendered a final decision (*RCP,* 47th Cong., 1st sess., 1881, H. Exdoc. 1, 731–32).

19. The activities of pension agencies in the South were suspended when the war began, and pensions to disloyal persons were prohibited. At the war's end, and as the need arose, these southern pension agencies were reopened (*RCP,* 39th Cong., 1st sess., 1865, H. Exdoc. 1, 775–76).

20. Pension claim of Hagar Washington, widow of George Washington, Co. E, 58th USCT, Hagar Washington affidavit, Dec. 29, 1894.

21. The 1862 act can be found in *Statutes at Large of USA* 12 (1859–63): 566–69. On the creation of the pension system, see Glasson, *Federal Military Pensions;* Weber, *Bureau of Pensions,* 15–19; Skocpol, *Protecting Soldiers and Mothers,* 102–51; Vinovskis, "Have Social Historians Lost the Civil War?" On the benefits of Civil War pensions for widows, see Holmes, "Such Is the Price We Pay," 171–95. Whether Holmes's study includes black widows is difficult to tell; she refers once to "white widows" and to "widows" in general, without reference to race.

22. Harriet Berry pension claim, Harriet Berry affidavit, April 2, 1884.

23. Ibid., Feb. 1, 1868.

24. Cited in Lyons, *Exemplum,* 83.

25. We do know that Harriet was still working on the claim from her end. In 1883 she filed another affidavit taken from witnesses who had known Harriet during slavery (affidavit of Jane Arnold and Harriet Fruby, Feb. 16, 1883).

26. *RCP,* 45th Cong., 3d sess., 1878, H. Exdoc. 1, 827.

27. Harriet Berry pension claim, J. W. Bostick, special examiner, Washington, D.C., Feb. 21, 1884.

28. Ibid., John G. Greenwalt, special examiner, Norfolk, Va., to commissioner of pensions, Washington, D.C., April 7, 1884.

29. *Statutes at Large of USA* 17 (1871–73): 571. See Glasson, *Federal Military Pensions,* 142, for a discussion of pertinent legislation.

30. Harriet Berry pension claim, Polly Wilson affidavit, April 2, 1884, Willis Sandler affidavit, April 2, 1884, Henrietta Wilson affidavit, April 2, 1884, Elijah Copeland affidavit, April 5, 1884, Lewis Jackson affidavit, April 5, 1884.

31. Ibid., Martha Burgess affidavit, April 3, 1884.

32. Ibid., Mary Burgess affidavit, April 3, 1884, Robert H. Berry affidavit, April 3, 1884.

33. Pension claim of Tanya Butler, mother of William Butler, Co. C, 12th USCT, M. M. Cloon, claim agent, Pulaski, Tenn., to [illegible], chief clerk Pension Office, Washington, D.C., March 21, 1870.

34. *RCP,* 48th Cong., 1st sess., 1883, H. Exdoc. 1, 352–54.

35. Before 1881 the authority to conduct special examinations had been granted by the act of July 4, 1864, which authorized the commissioner of pensions to send clerks from his office to investigate claims that he suspected to be fraudulent. This act was later consolidated in section 4744 of the *Revised Statutes of the United States* (1873–74).

36. Concern over fraudulent cases had been expressed in many annual reports of the commissioner of pensions. See, for example, *RCP,* 40th Cong., 2d sess., 1868, H. Exdoc. 1, 448–51; ibid., 44th Cong., 1st sess., 1875, H. Exdoc. 1, 442–44.

37. Ibid., 40th Cong., 3d sess., 1868, H. Exdoc. 1, 448.

38. Ibid., 41st Cong., 3d sess., 1870, H. Exdoc. 1, 434.

39. Ibid., 44th Cong., 1st sess., 1875, H. Exdoc. 1, 443. On claim agents and fraudulent claims by black applicants, see Shaffer, "I Do Not Suppose," 139–40.

40. Ibid., 45th Cong., 3d sess., 1878, H. Exdoc. 1, 815. Interestingly, the Arrears Act of 1879 repealed earlier legislation limiting the use of parole evidence (Glasson, *Federal Military Pensions,* 165).

41. Skocpol, *Protecting Soldiers and Mothers,* 119.

42. *RCP,* 42d Cong., 3d sess., 1872, H. Exdoc. 1, 13. Baker continued to complain about this problem in his report of 1873 and in a letter to the House of Representatives in 1874 (*Letter from Commissioner of Pensions,* 43d Cong., 1st sess., 1873, H. Misdoc. 221, 2).

43. *General Instructions to Special Examiners* (1882). See section on "Colored Claimants," 23–25. This booklet was first printed in 1881. It was revised in 1882, 1886, and 1897. I was only able to locate the 1882 and 1897 versions in the National Archives and the United States Bureau of Veterans' Affairs in Washington, D.C.

44. Skocpol, *Protecting Mothers and Soldiers,* 138.

45. See pension claim of Nancy Alexander, widow of Westley

Alexander, Co. E, 110th USCT, J. A. Bentley, commissioner of pensions, Washington, D.C., to Nancy Leatherman [Alexander], c/o P. Harris, Pulaski, Tenn., Oct. 8, 1874; pension claim of Martha Taylor, mother of Walter Taylor, Co. C, 1st USCT, notice from Pension Office, Nov. 12, 1875.

46. *General Instructions to Special Examiners* (1882), 23.

47. Mechal Sobel offers a compelling comparison of black and white conceptions of time in *The World They Made Together*. See especially pp. 30–43 for slaves' conception.

48. Botume, *First Days amongst the Contrabands*, 49; Towne, *Letters and Diary of Laura M. Towne*, 27.

49. Pension claim of Nancy White, widow of John White, Co. I, 6th USCT, Nancy White affidavit, Oct. 26, 1885.

50. *General Instructions to Special Examiners* (1882), 24–25.

51. Pension claim of Isabella Cherry, widow of Freeman Cherry, Co. B, 37th USCT, Starkey White affidavit, Sept. 29, 1879, citation from a completed claim application; see also pension claim of Betsy Proctor, widow of James Proctor, Co. I, 118th USCT, Mary E. Proctor affidavit, April 17, 1868, and 1873 completed claim application.

52. Pension claim of Tennessee Lissia, widow of Henry Lissia, Co. G, 12th USCT (includes claim of William Lissia, brother), O. Miller, special agent, Nashville, Tenn., to J. A. Bentley, commissioner of pensions, Feb. 1, 1877; pension claim of David Martin et al., minor children of Richard Martin, Co. E, 68th USCT, B. P. McDaniel, special examiner, Bowling Green, Mo., to John C. Black, commissioner of pensions, May 23, 1888.

53. For example, in the pension claim of Hannah Gregory, mother of Thomas Gregory, Co. E, 35th USCT, the former owner's testimony helps to expose a fraudulent claim. The case is examined more fully in chap. 5.

54. Pension claim of Rena Eason, widow of Miles Eason, Co. A, 37th USCT, Grafton Tyler Jr., special examiner, Gatesville, N.C., to Green B. Raum, commissioner of pensions, Aug. 6, 1890.

55. Pension claim of Laney Jane Joiner, widow of Jack Joiner, Co. I, 37th USCT, Mary Batchellor affidavit, May 9, 1884. Interestingly, the agent in this case argued, "I do not think the promise of pay had any influence to bias her testimony or make her state other than the truth." Witnesses did not often admit to accepting money for testimony because such an admission generally nullified their disinterested status.

56. David Martin et al. pension claim, B. P. McDaniel, special ex-

aminer, Bowling Green, Mo., to John C. Black, commissioner of pensions, Washington, D.C., May 23, 1888.

57. *General Instructions to Special Examiners* (1882), 24. Theda Skocpol argues that though some suspicions of black claimants are noted in the 1882 version of the booklet, "similar suspicions are expressed elsewhere in the pamphlet, especially about widow applicants." However, because the process of special examination was designed to uncover fraudulent claims, examiners were instructed to determine whether particular relationships were legitimate, or that a widow had not remarried, or that relatives met the general requirements for pension. Only black claimants were overtly singled out as the possible perpetrators of fraudulent claims (*Protecting Mothers and Soldiers*, 596 n. 131). By 1897 the section entitled "Colored Claimants" had been removed from the booklet.

58. Douglass, *My Bondage and My Freedom*, 116–17.

59. *Preliminary and Final Report of the American Freedmen's Inquiry Commission*, 38th Cong., 1st sess., 1864, S. Exdoc. 53, 4.

60. Fisk, *Plain Counsels for Freedmen*, 51–54.

61. Nancy White pension claim, E. M. Clarke, special examiner, Natchez, Miss., to John C. Black, commissioner of pensions, Washington, D.C., Nov. 4, 1885.

62. Pension claim of William and Alice Timmons, minor children of Abraham Timmons, Co. G, 33d USCT, Priscilla Gary affidavit, May 1896; the actual "age book" can be found within William and Alice's file in the National Archives.

63. Ibid., Walter S. Ayres, special examiner, Buffalo, N.Y., to D. J. Murphy, commissioner of pensions, Washington, D.C., July 15, 1896.

64. Jones, *Soldiers of Light and Love*, 141.

65. Rose, *Rehearsal for Reconstruction*, 100–101.

66. Pension claim of Toney Sharp, minor child of Benjamin Sharp, Co. B, 37th USCT, L. Turner, special examiner, Norfolk, Va., to Hon. Hiram Smith, acting commissioner of pensions, Washington, D.C., Sept. 30, 1889.

67. *RCP*, 50th Cong., 1st sess., 1887, H. Exdoc. 1, 1123.

68. Pension claim of Charles Anderson, Co. K, 17th USCI; Rena Eason pension claim; pension claim of Rachel Walters, widow of Henry Walters, Co. C, 66th USCT; pension claim of Catherine Camphor, mother of John Camphor, Co. G, 30th USCT.

69. Tanya Butler pension claim, M. M. Cloon, pension agent, Pu-

laski, Tenn., to chief clerk Pension Office, Washington, D.C., March 21, 1870.

70. Pension claim of Spriggs Barney, father of Thomas H. Barney, Co. C, 23d USCT, A. Sterling Jr., U.S. attorney for Maryland, Baltimore, to E. B. French, Esq., Dec. 29, 1870.

71. Pension claim of Milly Martin, widow of Richard Martin, Co. I, 35th USCT, 1868 Application for Widow's Pension, G. N. Ragsdale, special agent, to J. M. Baker, commissioner of pensions, Washington, D.C., July 29, 1873. As of 1897 Milly still had not heard about the outcome of her second claim.

TWO "We All Have Two Names": Surnames and Familial Identity

1. "General Orders No. 8, Marriage Rules," *Report of Commissioners of Freedmen's Bureau*, 39th Cong., 1st sess., 1865–66, H. Exdoc. 70, 109.

2. Brown, *John Freeman and His Family*, 20–21.

3. Ibid., 22.

4. Botume, *First Days amongst the Contrabands*, 45–49, 60. Botume was a missionary in the South Carolina Sea Islands during and after the war.

5. Ibid., 49.

6. Despite the owner's power to do so, most slaves gave their children their first names (Gutman, *Black Family in Slavery and Freedom;* Cody, "There Was No 'Absalom' on the Ball Plantations," 563–96). In his work on Carolina slave-naming practices, John Inscoe calls into question Gutman's assertion of the prevalence of naming for fathers, suggesting not only that slaves named their children for mothers also, but that their naming practices varied widely ("Generation and Gender as Reflected in Carolina Slave Naming Practices," 252–63). On the relationship between slave names and African naming patterns, see Wood, *Black Majority*, 181–86; Thornton, "Central African Names and African-American Naming Patterns," 727–42.

7. Cited in Rawick, *American Slave*, vol. 14, *North Carolina Narratives*, pt. 1, p. 296.

8. Leon Litwack discusses the names former slaves took and the reasons they took them in *Been in the Storm*, 247–51.

9. Cited in Rawick, *American Slave*, vol. 16, *Kansas Narratives*, 11.

10. Cited in ibid., vol. 4, *Texas Narratives*, pt. 1, p. 54.

11. Cited in ibid., Supplement, ser. 1, vol. 6, *Mississippi Narratives,* pt. 1, p. 20.

12. Charles Anderson pension claim.

13. Cited in Rawick, *American Slave,* vol. 4, *Texas Narratives,* pt. 1, 225.

14. Gutman, *Black Family in Slavery and Freedom,* 232, 248; Genovese, *Roll, Jordan, Roll,* 446. Eric Foner discusses the symbolic nature of the names some former slaves chose in freedom in *Reconstruction,* 79; see also Williamson, *After Slavery,* 310.

15. Cited in Baker and Baker, *WPA Oklahoma Slave Narratives,* 21.

16. Cited in Rawick, *American Slave,* vol. 14, *North Carolina Narratives,* pt. 1, p. 139.

17. Pension claim of Lucinda Twine, mother of Anderson Twine alias Toyan, Co. D, 1st USCC, Mills Jordan affidavit, 1896.

18. Ibid., Benjamin Hendle affidavit, April 22, 1896.

19. Ibid., Lucinda Twine affidavit, 1896.

20. See Wright, *Black Boy,* 153–54. For an interpretation of this incident and a discussion of naming in African-American literature, see Benston, "I Yam What I Am," 3–11.

21. Before the war the education of slaves had been outlawed in every southern state except Tennessee. In 1860, 90 percent of the adult African-American population in the South was illiterate (Foner, *Reconstruction,* 96).

22. Herbert Gutman used John C. Cahoon's plantation records in *The Black Family in Slavery and Freedom,* 123–43. Huldah and Robert appear in these records as "Huldah Jr." and "Little Bob." Suggestive of the value of the pension records, although the plantation records enabled Gutman to provide extensive information on slaves' first names, little if any information about surnames appears to exist. Interestingly, as the claim itself indicates, even whites were not immune to having their names misspelled or misunderstood. "Cahoon" was apparently "Cohoon," as Gutman's records suggested. I use "Cahoon" because it is the spelling used in Huldah's pension file.

23. Ibid., 129.

24. Ibid., 124, 131–33.

25. Ibid., 196–97.

26. Pension claim of Huldah Gordon, mother of Miles Gordon, Co. H, 1st USCC, Huldah Gordon affidavit, March 29, 1883.

27. For background on the Freedmen's Bank and information about its records, see Washington, "The Freedmen's Savings and Trust Company," 170–81.

28. Huldah Gordon pension claim, Huldah Gordon affidavit, Dec. 1, 1874. Huldah's former owner's name was originally recorded as "Cahoon" but was also recorded as "Calhoun" in several affidavits.

29. Huldah Gordon pension claim, William Cahoon affidavit, 1876. Herbert Gutman's records also indicate that Robert's father, Tom, had been purchased from George Godwin (*Black Family in Slavery and Freedom*, 130).

30. Wm. McKinley, Midgeville, to E. M. Stanton, secretary of war, May 29, 1867, Letters Received, BRFAL. As Anderson Twine's case suggests, though the former master could provide other information about Albert such as his description and the approximate time and place of his enlistment and death, without knowledge of Albert's surname the Pension Office would have great difficulty finding his records.

31. Pension claim of Benjamin B. Manson, father of John White, Co. I, 14th USCT, Benjamin B. Manson affidavit, 1909.

32. Ibid.

33. Ibid.

34. Frankel, *Freedom's Women*, 20.

35. Cited in Rawick, *American Slave*, vol. 16, *Kansas Narratives*, 5. See also ibid., *Ohio Narratives*, 10, 26, 97; ibid., *Tennessee Narratives*, 37, 40, 60; ibid., vol. 15, *North Carolina Narratives*, pt. 2, pp. 38, 360. Throughout the many volumes of narratives, it is common to find interviewees with the same names as their former owners, though many do not offer any explanation for having taken the master's surname.

36. Cited in ibid., Supplement, ser. 1, vol. 6, *Mississippi Narratives*, pt. 1, 255.

37. Litwack, *Been in the Storm*, 249.

38. Huldah Gordon pension claim, Huldah Gordon affidavit, March 29, 1883.

39. Eugene Genovese makes a similar point in *Roll, Jordan, Roll*, 446. As Herbert Gutman is careful to point out about Cahoon, a master's choices were made for his own benefit but affected his slaves' lives, mostly by creating problems for them (*Black Family in Slavery and Freedom*, 143).

40. Benjamin B. Manson pension claim, Benjamin B. Manson affidavit, 1909.

41. Rena Eason pension claim, Rena Eason, Gates County, N.C., to D. A. Carpenter, U.S. pension agent, Knoxville, Tenn., Sept. 29, 1888.

42. Ibid., Miles Eason affidavit, Nov. 14, 1888, Catherine Eason affidavit, Aug. 5, 1880.

43. Magdol, *A Right to the Land*, 175; Litwack, *Been in the Storm*, 327–32.

44. Joseph Reidy argues that in the 1870s and 1880s white planters generally wanted to maintain in former slaves a dependent, available workforce (*From Slavery to Agrarian Capitalism*, esp. chap. 9).

45. Ibid., 221–22; Rena Eason pension claim, [illegible], special examiner, to Green B. Raum, commissioner of pensions, Aug. 6, 1890.

46. On freed people's desire for landownership, see Oubre, *Forty Acres and a Mule*. Edward Magdol offers an overview of the relatively small number of black landowners in the South during the last half of the nineteenth century (*A Right to the Land*, 209–13, 217–18).

47. Rena Eason pension claim, [illegible], special examiner, to Green B. Raum, commissioner of pensions, Aug. 6, 1890.

48. Edwards, *Gendered Strife and Confusion*, 91–92.

49. Rena Eason pension claim, Rena Eason, Gates County, N.C., to D. A. Carpenter, U.S. pension agent, Knoxville, Tenn., Sept. 28, 1888.

50. Ibid.

51. Brown, "Narrative of William Wells Brown," 46.

52. Spender, "The Male Line," 24–28.

53. On married women's property rights in early America, see Salmon, *Women and the Law of Property in Early America*. Norma Basch addresses property rights for married women in the nineteenth century in *In the Eyes of the Law*.

54. On married women's legal status, see Kerber, *Women of the Republic*, 119–20, 139–55; for the nineteenth century, see Hartog, *Man and Wife in America*, 93–135. Suzanne Lebsock discusses married women's legal status in the South in *Free Women of Petersburg*, 22–35; see also Bardaglio, *Reconstructing the Household*, 31–34.

55. By 1865 some twenty-nine states had created laws that granted property rights to married women. Michael Grossberg explains that the concern for the "best interests of the child" and the belief in the mother's inherent ability to nurture played significant roles in restricting paternal custody rights in the nineteenth century (Grossberg,

Governing the Hearth, 237–54); for variations in southern law, see Bardaglio, *Reconstructing the Household,* 137–57.

56. Cited in Rawick, *American Slave,* vol. 15, *North Carolina Narratives,* pt. 2, p. 277, see also p. 271; ibid., Supplement, ser. 1, vol. 6, *Mississippi Narratives,* pt. 1, 3; ibid., vol. 6, *Alabama Narratives,* 92.

57. Cited in ibid., vol. 8, *Arkansas Narratives,* pt. 1, p. 24, see also p. 122 and pt. 2, p. 84.

58. Cited in ibid., vol. 15, *North Carolina Narratives,* pt. 2, p. 360, see also p. 310.

59. Nancy White pension claim, Mary Scott affidavit, Nov. 3, 1885.

60. Ibid., Henry Addison affidavit, Nov. 2, 1885.

61. White, *Ar'n't I a Woman?* 153.

62. Jones, *Labor of Love, Labor of Sorrow,* 41. It is important to note that Jones takes Eugene Genovese to task for arguing that slave men and women shared a "healthy sexual equality." Jones cites Deborah White as well but fails to make a distinction between Genovese's "healthy sexual equality" and White's notion that slave women had "more autonomy" in their marriages than white women did.

63. Frankel, *Freedom's Women,* 125–35.

64. Edwards, *Gendered Strife and Confusion,* 147, 180–82; Schwalm, *A Hard Fight for We,* 260–66.

THREE According to the Custom of Slaves: Widows' Pension Claims and the Bounds of Marriage

1. J. M. Tracy to Bvt. Major William Fowler, Rutherford Co., Tenn., July 18, 1866, Claim Division, Letters Received, BRFAL.

2. McClintock, "Civil War Pensions and the Reconstruction of Union Families," 472; see also Edwards, *Gendered Strife and Confusion,* 61.

3. Grossberg, *Governing the Hearth,* 79.

4. Ibid., 69–102; Stein, "Common Law Marriage," 278–82.

5. An exception to the policy of nonintervention in marriage was the prohibition of interracial marriages in the South. See Bardaglio, *Reconstructing the Household,* 59.

6. Fisk, *Plain Counsels for Freedmen,* 31.

7. *Preliminary and Final Reports of the American Freedman's Inquiry Commission,* 38th Cong., 1st sess., 1863–64, S. Exdoc. 53, 3. This attitude was typical of the abolitionists who believed that the environment of slavery and racial segregation affected slaves' morality, intelligence,

and industry. See Schwalm, *A Hard Fight for We*, 240; McPherson, "The Negro: Innately Inferior or Equal?" 79–94.

8. Report from Middlesex County (agent's name illegible) to O. Brown, Feb. 28, 1866, Records of the Assistant Commissioner of the State of Virginia, BRFAL.

9. On the Freedmen's Bureau's position on the value of legalizing the marriages of freed people, see Schwalm, *A Hard Fight for We*, 239. Laura Edwards demonstrates that the same ideas about the socializing function of marriage operated in the construction of laws concerning marriage and the family under the Black Codes in North Carolina (*Gendered Strife and Confusion*, 28). Michael Grossberg has also argued more generally that popular belief in the nineteenth century held that "stable marriages performed critical roles in the society by producing healthy children, curbing sexual passions, and protecting private accumulation" (Grossberg, *Governing the Hearth*, 18).

10. One could make the same argument for the cases that appeared before southern courts in which former slaves sued each other for custody of their children. See Bardaglio, *Reconstructing the Household*, 145.

11. *Congressional Globe*, 38th Cong., 1st sess., 1863–64, 34:3233.

12. *Statutes at Large of USA* 13 (1863–64): 389. The act also provided that if the couple had resided in a state that would allow them to marry, the usual proof would be required to substantiate the marriage.

13. Many held the belief that a couple could substantiate their "commitment to matrimony" by "acknowledgment, cohabitation, and reputation of marriage." See Grossberg, *Governing the Hearth*, 69–90.

14. *Congressional Globe*, 39th Cong., 1st sess., 1865–66, 36:2667–70.

15. *Statutes at Large of USA* 14 (1865–67): 58. The act of July 4, 1864, also was amended to include the widows and children of sailors and to provide not only pension but bounty and back pay as well. See also McClintock, "Civil War Pensions and the Reconstruction of Union Families," 473–79; Frankel, *Freedom's Women*, 88.

16. *Statutes at Large of USA* 17 (1871–73): 570. This provision became sec. 4705 of the *Revised Statutes of U.S.* (1873–74). On Aug. 7, 1882, legislation was passed that provided that marriages should be proved according to the law of the place where the couple resided when they were married, or where the right to pension was accrued. However, the law exempted marriages that fell under sec. 4705 of the *Revised Statutes of U.S.* See *U.S. Statutes at Large* 22 (1881–83): 345.

17. On the issue of former slaves who chose not to legalize their marriages, Laura Edwards argues that some "saw no advantage in

changing their ways" (*Gendered Strife and Confusion*, 54–59). In his dissertation Donald Shaffer argued that pension records offer strong evidence that former slaves continued to marry according to slave customs ("Marching On," 127–31). Noralee Frankel also points to the practice of continuing community-sanctioned marriages, but she clarifies that these cases tended to be older former slaves who did not feel it necessary to legalize preexisting slave marriages. Frankel argues, "Many marriages that were reported to the Freedmen's Bureau after the war were first-time marriages rather than remarriages of slave couples" (*Freedom's Women*, 80–84).

18. Jones, *Labor of Love, Labor of Sorrow*, 46.

19. Edwards, *Gendered Strife and Confusion*, 147–48. Leslie Schwalm argues that the misperception that black women in South Carolina's low country fully withdrew from field or domestic labor in the first years after emancipation grew out of freedwomen's efforts to make their families a priority over their employment (*A Hard Fight for We*, 204–11). Tera Hunter describes how domestic workers in Atlanta avoided "living in" and regularly quit their jobs to address their families' and communities' needs (*To 'Joy My Freedom*, 58–60).

20. Edwards, *Gendered Strife and Confusion*, 161.

21. On single women relying upon extended kin, see Frankel, *Freedom's Women*, 150–54.

22. Jones, *Labor of Love, Labor of Sorrow*, 73.

23. Pension claim of Sarah Bundick Pitts, widow of Riley Pitts, Co. K, 7th USCI (includes claim of Sallie Cropper Pitts, widow). Sarah was free at the time she married Riley, and the evidence from her claim suggests she may have been born free.

24. Ibid., Sarah Pitts affidavit, May 19, 1868.

25. Ibid., Edmund Bayly and Harry Bayly affidavit, May 14, 1869.

26. Ibid., Sarah Pitts affidavit, March 17, 1892.

27. Ibid., completed application form, Oct. 1872.

28. Pension claim of Sallie Cropper Pitts, widow of Riley Pitts, Co. K, 7th USCI, claim form, April 1872.

29. Ibid., Abraham Heath and Betsy Cropper affidavit, April 4, 1872.

30. Ibid., commissioner of pensions, Washington D.C., to Mrs. N. W. Parramore, postmistress, Accomack County, Va., Sept. 14, 1872, Margaret Ayres, postmistress, Drummondtown, Va., to commissioner of pensions, Washington, D.C., Sept. 21, 1872.

31. Ibid., Sarah L. Cropper, Accomack County, Va., to Charles C. Brown, Norfolk, Va., July 18, 1872.

32. Ibid., Charles Brown, pension attorney, Norfolk, Va., to J. H. Baker, commissioner of pensions, July 23, 1872.

33. Sarah Bundick Pitts pension claim, E. Carver, special examiner, Accomack County, Va., to commissioner of pensions, Washington, D.C., May 24, 1899.

34. Ibid., Sarah Pitts affidavit, May 19, 1868.

35. Pearson, *Letters from Port Royal,* 144. Harriet Ware was a missionary in the South Carolina Sea Islands during the "rehearsal for Reconstruction." For more on Ware and the missionary effort in the South Carolina Islands, see Rose, *Rehearsal for Reconstruction.*

36. Herbert Gutman described many incidents of multiple marriages and the difficulty that arose for both former slaves and government agents trying to resolve them in *The Black Family in Slavery and Freedom,* 419–25.

37. Litwack, *Been in the Storm,* 241.

38. *Congressional Globe,* 39th Cong., 1st sess., 1865–66, 36:2669. In spite of the fact that no legislation was passed to deal specifically with the problem of two widows, the fact that it had been a topic of discussion in Congress and later was addressed by the Pension Office suggests that cases in which two women claimed the same pension were somewhat common. For similar cases, see pension claim of Susan Wright, widow of Presley Wright, Co. B, 1st USCT (Polly Douglass, contesting widow); pension claim of Daffney Bowder (or Bowden), widow of Stephen Bowder, Co. B, 59th USCT (Lizzie Bowden, contesting widow).

39. *General Instructions to Special Examiners* (1882), 18.

40. For a discussion of the differences between slave and free marriage, see Everly, "Marriage Registers of Freedmen," 150–54; Burnham, "An Impossible Marriage." On the legal bounds of marriage in nineteenth-century American society, see Grossberg, *Governing the Hearth,* esp. chaps. 3 and 4.

41. Pension claim of Margaret Fields, widow of John Fields, Co. B, 118th USCT; Rachel Walters pension claim. Less frequently, slaves were married in a ceremony performed by a white preacher; see Genovese, *Roll, Jordan, Roll,* 475–76.

42. Cited in Rawick, *American Slave,* vol. 14, *North Carolina Narratives,* pt. 1, p. 84.

43. Harriet Berry pension claim; Isabella Cherry pension claim; Hagar Washington pension claim.

44. Frankel, *Freedom's Women,* 12. On the issue of slave women and

divorce, see White, *Ar'n't I a Woman?* 156–57. Laura Edwards offers examples of how practices of marrying and separating under slavery proved difficult to reconcile in the courts after emancipation (*Gendered Strife and Confusion,* 57–58).

45. Sarah B. Pitts pension claim, Edmund Pitts deposition, May 24, 1899, George Pruitt deposition, May 24, 1899.

46. Ibid., Sarah Pitts affidavit, May 24, 1899.

47. Ibid.

48. Ibid.

49. White, *Ar'n't I a Woman?* 76. Herbert Gutman refers to these marriages as "broad" marriages (*Black Family in Slavery and Freedom,* 131, 135–38).

50. Sarah B. Pitts pension claim, Sarah Pitts affidavit, May 24, 1899.

51. Ibid.

52. Though uncommon, Gutman argues, some slave husbands had more than one wife (*Black Family in Slavery and Freedom,* 418).

53. Sarah B. Pitts pension claim, E. Carver, special examiner, Accomack County, Va., to commissioner of pensions, May 24, 1899.

54. Pension claim of Rosetta Crandall, contesting widow of Ephraim Crandall, Co. B, 35th USCT.

55. Pension claim of Sally Timmons, widow of Abraham Timmons, Co. G, 33d USCT. Sally applied for a widow's pension as the wife of Abraham Timmons in 1865. She offered as proof a marriage certificate witnessed and officiated by Rufus Saxton, Union army general and Freedmen's Bureau official, and by Mansfield French, a prominent missionary. Sally and Abraham were able to marry by legal ceremony when Abraham joined the Union army.

56. William and Alice Timmons pension claim.

57. Ibid., Webster Davis, assistant secretary, Department of the Interior, Washington, D.C., to commissioner of pensions, Feb. 27, 1898.

58. Ibid., Lucinda Williams affidavit, Nov. 27, 1894.

59. Ibid. In an 1895 affidavit Priscilla testified that she had been present at the wedding ceremony. A year later she testified that "there was no marriage ceremony."

60. Ibid., Walter Ayres, special examiner, Buffalo, N.Y., to D. J. Murphy, commissioner of pensions, Washington, D.C., July 15, 1896.

61. Ibid., Priscilla Gary affidavit, Nov. 27, 1894. Priscilla was one of Jane's children by Holland.

62. Ibid., Sarah Williams affidavit, May 2, 1896.

63. Ibid., James Penny alias James Rawles affidavit, May 2, 1896.

64. White, *Ar'n't I a Woman?* 105–7; Genovese, *Roll, Jordan, Roll,* 457–75; Gutman, *Black Family in Slavery and Freedom,* 60.

65. On freed people's attitudes, see Frankel, *Freedom's Women,* 98.

66. William and Alice Timmons pension claim, Webster Davis, assistant secretary, Department of the Interior, Washington, D.C., to commissioner of pensions, Washington, D.C., Feb. 27, 1898 [or 1899].

67. Ibid. Davis cited the case of Annie Hughes: "There can be no question but that slaves, in their quasi matrimonial status, could be guilty of an illicit relation and that an illicit connection between a male and female slave could exist as the same relation could exist between a free male and female."

68. Ibid., William and Alice Timmons, Clarcona, Fla., to [commissioner of pensions], Washington, D.C., April 12, 1897.

69. Noralee Frankel offers this definition of the term as it applied to slave marriages (*Freedom's Women,* 90).

70. Ibid., 90–92. Noralee Frankel points to the existence of many such "took-ups" in her work on Mississippi freedwomen, though she is careful to point out that the policy of terminating the pensions of widows who remarried might account for a larger number of took-ups in the pension records than existed in the African-American population in general. A notable exception to the acceptance of this practice was found among black church leaders, who advocated the formalization of intimate relationships (ibid., 83–86; see also Schwalm, *A Hard Fight for We,* 244–45). The concept of "taking up" appears in claims of some poor whites as well (Edwards, *Gendered Strife and Confusion,* 60–61).

71. In her 1866 Mother's Application for Pension, Catherine's age was recorded as sixty-six, but in her 1880 affidavit from special examination, Catherine's age was recorded as ninety, rather than eighty.

72. According to section 3 of the act of July 14, 1862, if a soldier or sailor died of wound or disease contracted in the line of duty "and has not left or shall not leave a widow nor legitimate child, but has left or shall leave a mother who was dependent upon him for support . . . the mother shall be entitled to receive the same pension." See also Glasson, *Federal Military Pensions,* 139–42.

73. Catherine Camphor pension claim, Catherine Camphor, 1866 Application for Pension, 1867 Proof of Dependence, and Cyrus M. Diggs affidavit, March 18, 1868.

74. Ibid., Sarah A. Bounds affidavit, July 10, 1880.

75. Ibid., Sarah Bounds affidavit, Aug. 15, 1881.

76. Ibid., Sarah Jarrett Camphor affidavit, July 10, 1880.

77. Ibid., testimony from Patrick Murray, postmaster, Pikesville County, Baltimore, Md., April 21, 1881, and Henrietta Mann affidavit, July 10, 1880.

78. *Statutes at Large of USA* 15 (1867–69). The act of July 27, 1868, established the order of succession for relatives eligible to receive pension: widow, child, mother, father, and orphan brothers or sisters under sixteen years of age; for discussion of this act, see Glasson, *Federal Military Pensions,* 139.

79. White, *Ar'n't I a Woman?* 105–6; Gutman, *Black Family in Slavery and Freedom,* 75–76; Jones, *Labor of Love, Labor of Sorrow,* 35.

80. Catherine Camphor pension claim, Catherine Camphor affidavit, July 13, 1880.

81. Ibid.

82. Ibid.

83. Pension claim of Lucy Allen, widow of Charles Allen, Co. A, 107th USCI, William Hughes, special examiner, Lexington, Ky., to commissioner of pensions, Washington, D.C., Jan. 21, 1893. Lucy's pension file also contains an earlier attempt to gain a pension.

84. Ibid., Lucy Allen affidavit, Jan. 16, 1893.

85. Ibid.

86. Ibid., Elizabeth Holly affidavit, Jan. 23, 1893.

87. The Aug. 7, 1882, act provided that a widow pensioner who engaged in "open and notorious adulterous cohabitation" would lose her pension (*U.S. Statutes at Large* 22 [1881–83]: 345). On this piece of legislation and other efforts by the government to regulate marriage in general and widows' private lives specifically, see McClintock, "Civil War Pensions and the Regulation of Union Families," 476–79.

88. Pension claim of Mathilda Hubbard, widow of Richard Kearny, Co. I, 52d USCT, Mathilda Hubbard affidavit, Sept. 3, 1877.

89. Ibid., J. K. Kearny affidavit, May 4, 1876, July 7, 1883.

90. Pension claim of Betsy Booker, widow of Adam Booker, Co. A, 53d USCT, Lizzie Crutchen affidavit, Dec. 11, 1874.

91. Pension claim of Amanda Van Buren, widow of Martin Van Buren, Co. B, 87th USCT, Amanda Van Buren affidavit, Jan. 27, 1879.

92. Ibid.

93. Ibid.

94. Ibid., John H. Benton, special examiner, New Orleans, La., to commissioner of pensions, Washington, D.C., Jan. 31, 1879.

FOUR "The Order of Civilization": Minors' Pensions, Legitimacy, and the Father-Centered Familiy

1. Vernier, *American Family Laws*, 148–49.

2. Douglass, *My Bondage and My Freedom*, 51–52.

3. Ibid.

4. On slaves' informal or "social" claims to property, see Penningroth, "Slavery, Freedom, and Social Claims to Property," 405–35.

5. Douglass, *My Bondage and My Freedom*, 34.

6. Ibid., 153; Jones, *Labor of Love, Labor of Sorrow*, 41.

7. For the common-law notion of the parent-child relation and its application in America up until 1935, see Vernier, *American Family Laws*.

8. Stevenson, "Distress and Discord in Virginia Slave Families," 110. Margaret Burnham outlines the legal background of slaves' parenting experience in "An Impossible Marriage," 203–5.

9. Burnham, "An Impossible Marriage," 198 and nn. 44–48.

10. Brenda Stevenson offers a comprehensive enumeration of the ways antebellum Virginia slave owners encouraged "matrifocal and matrilocal families among their slaves" ("Distress and Discord in Virginia Slave Families," 107–8; Stevenson, *Life in Black and White*, 206–25). For more on the mother's social and reproductive role in slavery, see White, *Ar'n't I a Woman?* 68–71, 112–14; Dill, "Our Mother's Grief," 419.

11. White, *Ar'n't I a Woman*, 159. White argues that this was the case in slavery despite the fact that slave families were "unusually egalitarian," that men and women's roles within the family complemented each other and were thus equally important.

12. McDaniel, "The Power of Culture," 225–38; White, *Ar'n't I a Woman?* 65–66, 106–7.

13. On popular views of a woman's role in the nineteenth century, see Welter, "The Cult of True Womanhood," 131–75; Cott, *Bonds of Womanhood*. On the reciprocal duties of the marriage contract, see Wietzman, *Marriage Contract*, xxii.

14. Malone, *Sweet Chariot*, 259. Malone argues that this attitude was at the root of the myth of the matriarchal slave family.

15. Ibid., 35–49.

16. Flaherty, "Law and the Enforcement of Morals in Early America," 203–53; Smith and Hindus, "Premarital Pregnancy in America," 530–70.

17. Wells, "Illegitimacy and Bridal Pregnancy in Colonial America," 355–56; Grossberg, *Governing the Hearth,* 198, 215–18; Abramovitz, *Regulating the Lives of Women,* 95–96.

18. Mintz, "Regulating the American Family," 389; Grossberg, *Governing the Hearth,* 196–97.

19. Grossberg, *Governing the Hearth,* 201–7; see also Vernier, *American Family Laws,* 148–49, 156.

20. Grossberg, *Governing the Hearth,* 222.

21. Ibid., 197, 207–15; see also Vernier, *American Family Laws,* 189–90. Michael Grossberg, as well as Steven Mintz, points out that by the middle decades of the nineteenth century, judges began limiting fathers' custody rights and leaning more toward "maternal preference" (Grossberg, 253; Mintz, "Regulating the American Family," 394).

22. *Statutes at Large of USA* 14 (1865–67): 58, 17 (1871–73): 570.

23. Wells, "Illegitimacy and Bridal Pregnancy in Colonial America," 351; Burnham, "An Impossible Marriage," 218 n. 134; Hodes, *White Women, Black Men,* 48.

24. Davis, *Return of Martin Guerre.*

25. At the time John applied for the pension, a minor would receive $8 a month from the date of his or her father's death until he or she turned sixteen. The sum total of $8 per month from Elias's death in December 1865 to John's sixteenth birthday in August 1876 would have been either $1,024 or $1,032.

26. Pension claim of John Robinson, minor child of Elias Robinson, Co. F, 13th USCI, Emily Hornlett affidavit, March 13, 1889.

27. Ibid., John Robinson, Nashville, Tenn., to William W. Dudley, commissioner of pensions, Sept. 27, 1884.

28. Ibid., John Robinson affidavit, April 12, 1883.

29. Ibid., Henry Douglass affidavit, Dec. 1, 1880.

30. Ibid., William B. Robinson affidavit, July 31, 1884.

31. Ibid., Paul Rucker affidavit, April 8, 1889, Jane Stokes affidavit, April 29, 1890, John Stokes affidavit, April 29, 1890.

32. Pension claim of James Frazier, minor child of Simon Frazier, Co. F, 54th USCT, James Frazier affidavit, Feb. 16, 1901.

33. Ibid., James Frazier affidavit, March 31, 1897, Walker Frazier affidavit, March 1, 1901, Heuston Blackburn affidavit, June 22, 1901, Write Allen affidavit, March 8, 1901.

34. Ibid., E. F. Ware, commissioner of pensions, Washington, D.C., to Mr. Dalton, chief of board of review, Dec. 22, 1902.

35. Ibid., Brum Harrison affidavit, Aug. 21, 1901.

36. *Revised Statutes of U.S.,* sec. 4704, states: "In the administration of the pension-laws, children born before the marriage of their parents, if acknowledged by the father before or after the marriage, shall be deemed legitimate."

37. James Frazier pension claim, James Frazier affidavit, Feb. 16, 1901.

38. Ibid., Henry Blackman affidavit, Nov. 2, 1897, and May 2, 1901.

39. Berlin et al., "Afro-American Families in the Transition from Slavery to Freedom," 89.

40. David A. Martin et al. pension claim, Thomas Harris affidavit, July 18, 1883, Charles M. Lawrence affidavit, July 1884.

41. Ibid., Thomas Harris affidavit, May 22, 1888.

42. Ibid.

43. Berlin et al., *Destruction of Slavery,* 395–412.

44. David A. Martin et al. pension claim, Lida Jamison affidavit, May 21, 1888. Most likely Lida was responding to a question about her father's appearance. Pension officials often compared the description that claimants gave then with those recorded when the soldier enlisted.

45. Ibid., Hannah Jackson affidavit, May 21, 1888.

46. Ibid., Elder J. W. Young affidavit, April 12, 1889.

47. Foner, *Reconstruction,* 201; see also Scott, "The Battle Over the Child," 101–13.

48. Bardaglio, *Reconstructing the Household,* 162.

49. Cited in Rawick, *American Slave,* vol. 12, *Georgia Narratives,* pt. 1, p. 24.

50. Ibid., Supplement, ser. 1, vol. 10, *Mississippi Narratives,* pt. 5, p. 2230. Leon Litwack also points out that many former slaves left their owners' farms and plantations as a means of testing or exercising their freedom (*Been in the Storm,* 296–301).

51. Cited in Rawick, *American Slave,* Supplement, ser. 1, vol. 10, *Mississippi Narratives,* pt. 5, 2316–17.

52. Cited in ibid., vol. 12, *Georgia Narratives,* pt. 1, p. 21.

53. Ibid., vol. 2, *South Carolina Narratives,* pt. 1, p. 5.

54. Jacobs, *Incidents in the Life of a Slave Girl,* 9.

55. Schwartz, *Born in Bondage,* 76. In her chap. 3 Schwartz examines the insinuation of owners into the lives of slave children and owners' interference in slaves' parenting.

56. David A. Martin et al. pension claim, Lida Jamison affidavit, May 21, 1888.

57. Ibid., B. P. McDaniel, special examiner, Bowling Green, Mo., to John C. Black, commissioner of pensions, Washington, D.C., May 23, 1888.

58. Ibid., Kitty Rice affidavit, April 12, 1889. Several other witnesses made similar claims; see ibid., Joseph Bell affidavit, May 22, 1888, Amanda Kibby affidavit, May 22, 1888.

59. Toney Sharp pension claim.

60. Ibid., Toney Sharp affidavit, June 4, 1888.

61. Ibid., Violet Dunbar affidavit, Sept. 27, 1889; Harriet Sharp affidavit, Sept. 27, 1889; Preston Sharp affidavit, Sept. 26, 1889.

62. Ibid., Leon Turner, special examiner, Harellsville, N.C., to Hiram Smith, commissioner of pensions, Washington D.C., Sept. 30, 1889. These were the conditions, in addition to determining the date of Violet's second marriage, that the special examiner outlined in his report to the commissioner of pensions.

63. Ibid., Violet Dunbar affidavit, Sept. 27, 1889.

64. Ibid., Toney Sharp affidavit, June 4, 1888.

65. Ibid., Harriet Sharp affidavit, Sept. 27, 1889.

66. Ibid., Benjamin Pruden affidavit, Sept. 28, 1889.

67. White makes this argument in response to Herbert Gutman's assertion that since slave children were named for their fathers—keeping fathers present in their lives even in their absence—fathers were central figures in slave families. White, *Ar'n't I a Woman?* 109.

68. My ideas about a collaborative concept of identity were generated in part by McClintock, "The Very House of Difference."

69. Toney Sharp pension claim, Henry Clay Sharp affidavit, Sept. 27, 1889.

70. Laney Jane Joiner pension claim (also includes claim of minor children), Mary Batchellor affidavit, May 9, 1887. The Joiner children made a claim in conjunction with their mother's claim; the testimony in her claim was used for both.

71. Stevenson, *Life in Black and White*, 222.

72. Laney Jane Joiner pension claim, Mary Batchellor affidavit, May 9, 1887.

73. Within the pension record is a copy of the original Batchellor family record. Jack and George, the two youngest children, appear in the copy as "Jack Joiner" and "George Joiner," but in both entries "Joiner" was crossed out, indicating, according to the pension official who made the record, either an erasure or a cancellation (ibid., "Age Paper," June 1886).

74. Ibid., Lewis Joiner affidavit, June 23, 1886.

75. Ibid., John H. Joiner affidavit, June 24, 1886.

76. Ibid., Ann Eliza Joiner affidavit, June 23, 1886.

77. Ibid., Jack Joiner affidavit, June 24, 1886.

78. Ibid., A. B. Casselman, special examiner, North Carolina, to commissioner of pensions, Washington, D.C., June 28, 1886.

79. Pension claim of Ned Barnard, father of Zachariah Barnard alias Gregory, Co. F, 36th USCT, case review, May 20, 1892.

80. Pension claim of Rachel Holden, mother of Peter Holden, Co. B, 79th USCT, Rachel Holden affidavit, July 19, 1879.

81. Pension claim of Priscilla Hagan, mother of Oliver Hagan, Co. A, 5th USCT, Priscilla Hagan affidavit, Nov. 5, 1889.

82. Ibid.

83. Cited in Rawick, *American Slave*, vol. 11, *Arkansas Narratives*, pt. 7, pp. 110, 138, and vol. 2, *South Carolina Narratives*, pt. 1, p. 224.

84. Cited in ibid., vol. 2, *South Carolina Narratives*, pt. 1, pp. 127–28.

FIVE "My Master . . . Supported Me": Parents' Claims and the Role of the Provider

1. *U.S. Statutes at Large* 15 (1867–69): 235–37.

2. For more on the principle of reciprocity in family law, see Clark, *Law of Domestic Relations*, 250–51; Weitzman, *Marriage Contract*, xxii; on the responsibility of the male provider, see ibid., 23–26.

3. Davis and Schwartz, *Children's Rights and the Law*, 7, 19–21; Houlgate, *Child and the State*, 23; Vernier, *American Family Laws*, 109; Mintz, "Regulating the American Family," 390.

4. *Benton's Abridgment of the Debates of Congress*, Dec. 9, 1818, 219.

5. Vernier, *American Family Laws*, 93; for a discussion of Blackstone's work on this subject, see Davis and Schwartz, *Children's Rights and the Law*, 19–21.

6. For an overview of the concept of family as changing within the lifetime of its members and the need to study the "life-course" of the family, see Tamara Hareven, "The History of Family and the Complexity of Social Change," 95–124.

7. On "fictive" kinship networks, see Gutman, *Black Family in Slavery and Freedom*, 185–229. On the flexibility of slave family and household structure, see Malone, *Sweet Chariot*. Jacqueline Jones describes the elastic nature of former slaves' families in the decades after the war (*Labor of Love, Labor of Sorrow*, 84–85).

8. Berlin and Morgan, "Introduction," in *Slaves' Economy*, 2–4,

10–11; Joyner, *Down by the Riverside*, 129–30; White, *Ar'n't I a Woman?* 155–56.

9. Berlin and Morgan, "Introduction," in *Slaves' Economy*, 15.

10. White, *Ar'n't I a Woman?*, 155–56; Rose, "Childhood in Bondage," 41.

11. Jacobs, *Incidents in the Life of a Slave Girl*, 6.

12. Ibid., 10–11.

13. Pension claim of Nancy Woods, mother of Price Woods, Co. I, 56th USCT, Nathan McDowell and Paulina Johnson affidavit, April 12, 1869. In his work on property relations among slaves on the Georgia coast, Dylan Penningroth describes slave parents' use of their children's labor toward the creation of family wealth and the accumulation of property ("Slavery, Freedom, and Social Claims to Property," 415–16).

14. Jones, *Labor of Love, Labor of Sorrow*, 60–65; Jones, "The Political Economy of Sharecropping Families," 86, 124–25. Laura Edwards notes the necessity of women's contributions to the household economy because of economic insecurity in *Gendered Strife and Confusion*, 148.

15. Jones, *Labor of Love, Labor of Sorrow*, 65, 85; Schwalm, *A Hard Fight for We*, 246–47. On the continuation of the "ethos of mutuality" as a response to economic and social hardship in the twentieth century, see Lemann, *Promised Land;* Stack, *All Our Kin.*

16. Schwalm, *A Hard Fight for We*, 250. Noralee Frankel makes a similar point about the misapplication of the title "patriarch" to freedmen (*Freedom's Women*, 124–25).

17. Brinckerhoff, *Advice to Freedmen*, 28–30 (excerpt from an advice tract printed in 1864 or 1865, used to instruct former slaves in freedmen's schools).

18. On the social and economic changes that created a new rhetoric of male and female "spheres" in the nineteenth century, see Ryan, *Cradle of the Middle Class.* On the white, northern, middle-class nineteenth-century ideal of family and male and female roles, see Degler, *At Odds*, especially chap. 2; Cott, *Bonds of Womanhood;* Welter, "The Cult of True Womanhood."

19. Edwards, *Gendered Strife and Confusion*, 145–83.

20. On northerners' assumptions about slaves' attitudes toward ownership of property, see Penningroth, "Slavery, Freedom, and Property among African Americans," 408.

21. Martha Taylor pension claim, Martha Taylor affidavit, June 2, 1876, Spencer Crawley and Samuel Crosby affidavit, Nov. 21, 1866.

22. Ibid., William Gordon and Phillip Brookins affidavit, Oct. 24, 1870.

23. Ibid.

24. *RCP,* 48th Cong., 1st sess., 1883, H. Exdoc. 1, 315.

25. For an explanation and examples of the difficulties that white parents faced, see McClintock, "Civil War Pensions and the Reconstruction of Union Families," 466–71.

26. Ibid., 469.

27. Pension claim of Patsey Sneed, mother of John Sneed, Co. G, 12th USCI, Alfred Vaughn and Carlo Frazier affidavit, Nov. 25, 1868.

28. For an example of a father's claim, see pension claim of Edward Jackson, father of Jefferson Jackson, Co. D, 53d USCT.

29. *RCP,* 51st Cong., 1st sess., 1889, H. Exdoc. 1, 419.

30. Nancy Woods pension claim, Alonzo T. Taylor affidavit, Oct. 25, 1872, Eli W. Southworth affidavit, Jan. 7, 1873. Although Nancy originally applied for a pension on behalf of the service of both sons, after 1870 Henry's name disappears from the claim. Nancy's pension was awarded on behalf of Price's service.

31. Pension claim of Eliza Williams, mother of Theodore Williams, Co. I, 4th USCI, Hugh L. Hambleton affidavit, Aug. 18, 1869, Mary Jane Williams affidavit, Oct. 2, 1869, Frisby Sprouts affidavit, Dec. 11, 1869.

32. Pension claim of Juda Gray, mother of Alfred Gray, Co. K, 42d USCT, Juda Gray affidavit, April 21, 1886.

33. Ibid., Margaret Wood affidavit, nd.

34. Ibid., Juda Gray affidavit, n.d.

35. Ibid., Henry Gray affidavit, Aug. 20, 1885.

36. *U.S. Statutes at Large* 17 (1871–73): 571. The conditions for dependence also applied to fathers' and minor siblings' pensions. See also McClintock, "Civil War Pensions and the Reconstruction of Union Families," 468–69.

37. Huldah Gordon pension claim, J. H. Clements, special examiner, Portsmouth, Va., to commissioner of pensions, Washington, D.C., July 10, 1876.

38. Juda Gray pension claim, Harvey Gray affidavit, April 21, 1886.

39. Ibid., Harriet Gray affidavit, April 22, 1886.

40. Ibid., Juda Gray affidavit, April 21, 1886.

41. Ibid., John Gray affidavit, April 22, 1886.

42. Ibid., George Albertson, legal reviewer, claim rejection notice, May 5, 1886.

43. Edward Jackson pension claim, J. Stein affidavit, Nov. 19, 1885, Edward Jackson affidavit, Jan. 23, 1884.

44. Ibid., [illegible] Hames and Marshall Sarten affidavit, Feb. 10, 1885.

45. Ibid., E. M. [illegible], M.D., to John C. Black, commissioner of pensions, May 22, 1885.

46. Hannah Gregory pension claim. A similar case involving a step-father is cited in chap. 1 above.

47. Ned Barnard pension claim, Ned Barnard affidavit, June 20, 1884, Ned Barnard affidavit, n.d.

48. Ibid., Ned Barnard affidavit, Jan. 18, 1892.

49. Ibid., Thomas Barnard affidavit, April 5, 1886.

50. Ibid., Ned Barnard affidavit, n.d.

51. Lebsock, *Free Women of Petersburg*, 104–5.

52. Ned Barnard pension claim, Ned Barnard affidavit, Jan. 18, 1892, and April 16, 1886.

53. Ibid., James H. Feribee and Charles J. Feribee affidavit, Jan. 31, 1887. These two friends described Ned this way.

54. White, *Ar'n't I a Woman?* 117.

55. Margaret Fields pension claim, Margaret Fields affidavit, Feb. 12, 1889.

56. Pension claim of Miles Cartwright, Co. D, 8th USCHA, Alpin Davis affidavit, Nov. 3, 1887.

57. Huldah Gordon pension claim; Benjamin B. Manson pension claim; see also pension claim of Harriet Gray, mother of Harvey alias Abner Gray, Co. F, 88th USCT, Harriet Gray affidavit, Jan. 29, 1894; Rachel Walters pension claim.

58. Rena Eason pension claim; Rachel Holden pension claim, C. B. [illegible], postmistress, Albany, Kans., to H. M. Atkinson, commissioner of pensions, Washington, D.C., June 11, 1875; Tennessee Lissia pension claim, Lucy Nichols affidavit, June 8, 1880.

59. Edwards, *Gendered Strife and Confusion*, 89–92. Edwards argues that the traditional metaphor for mobility in the South's postemancipation labor system, the "ladder" that had at its top landownership and, in descending order, renting, sharecropping, and waged labor, is problematic, in part, precisely because many laborers made use of more than one "rung" at a time.

60. On the change in pension legislation under the 1890 act, see Weber, *Bureau of Pensions*, 15–17; Glasson, *Federal Military Pensions*, 232–42. Theda Skocpol traces the "liberalization" of the Civil War

pension system, including the 1879 Arrears Act, to political party competition in the postbellum era (*Protecting Soldiers and Mothers*, 102–51). The act of June 27, 1890, can be found in *U.S. Statutes at Large* 26 (1890): 182–83.

61. Pension claim of Evans Haynes, father of Anthony Land, Co. H, 81st USCI, letter from Second Auditor's Office to commissioner of pensions, Washington, D.C., Feb. 14, 1882, and Thomas Haynes and Isaac Haynes affidavit, April 23, 1882.

62. Ibid., statement by chancery clerk J. W. Chisholm, April 27, 1883.

63. Ibid., W. W. Dickson and Jack Barrow affidavit, April 30, 1883.

64. *U.S. Statutes at Large* 26 (1890): 182.

65. *RCP,* 47th Cong., 2d sess., 1882, H. Exdoc. 1, 713. See also ibid., 50th Cong., 1st sess., 1887, H. Exdoc. 1, 1068; ibid., 51st Cong., 1st sess., 1889, H. Exdoc. 1, 419.

66. *Congressional Record,* 51st Cong., 1st Sess., 1890, 21:912–13.

67. Haynes pension claim, Dr. Haynes affidavit, April 23, 1883.

68. Pension claim of Joseph Payne, father of Samuel Payne alias Everett, Co. B, 18th USCT, Joe Payne affidavit, Aug. 22, 1893.

69. Ibid.

70. Ibid., Joe Payne, Chillicothe, Mo., to Green B. Raum, commissioner of pensions, Washington, D.C., Dec. 16, 1892.

71. Ibid., Victor L. Dodge, special examiner, Leavenworth, Kans., to commissioner of pensions, Washington, D.C., Oct. 30, 1894.

72. Ibid., Christopher Patterson deposition, July 17, 1894.

73. Harriet Gray pension claim.

74. Ibid., F. L. Campbell, assistant secretary, Department of the Interior, to commissioner of pensions, March 26, 1901.

75. Ibid., George Johnson affidavit, Sept. 24, 1899.

76. Ibid., Harvey Gray affidavit, Nov. 26, 1894.

77. Ibid., F. L. Campbell, assistant commissioner of pensions, to commissioners of pensions, n.d. Campbell paraphrased the wording of the appeal.

78. Ibid.

EPILOGUE The Storytellers

1. DuBois, *Souls of Black Folk,* 3.

2. "Speech by Martin Luther King, Jr., at Holt Street Baptist Church," in Carson et al., *Eyes on the Prize Civil Rights Reader,* 48.

Sources Cited

ARCHIVE COLLECTIONS

National Archives, Washington, D.C. Records of the Bureau of Refugees, Freedmen, and Abandoned Lands. Record Group 105.
——. Records of the Veterans Administration. Record Group 15.

GOVERNMENT PUBLICATIONS AND DOCUMENTS

Annual Report of Commissioner of Pensions, 39th Cong., 1st sess., 1865, H. Exdoc. 1; 40th Cong., 2d sess., 1868, H. Exdoc. 1; 41st Cong., 3d sess., 1870, H. Exdoc. 1; 42d Cong., 3d sess., 1872, H. Exdoc. 1; 44th Cong., 1st sess., 1875, H. Exdoc. 1; 45th Cong., 3d sess., 1878, H. Exdoc. 1; 47th Cong., 1st sess., 1881, H. Exdoc. 1; 47th Cong., 2d sess., 1882, H. Exdoc. 1; 48th Cong., 1st sess., 1883, H. Exdoc. 1; 50th Cong., 1st sess., 1887, H. Exdoc. 1; 51st Cong., 1st sess., 1889, H. Exdoc. 1.
Congressional Globe. 46 vols. Washington, D.C., 1834–73.
Congressional Record. Washington, D.C., 1873–.
Freedmen's Affairs: Laws in Relation to Freedmen, 39th Cong., 2d sess., 1866–67, S. Exdoc. 6.
General Instructions to Special Examiners of the United States Pension Office. Washington, D.C., 1882.
"General Orders No. 8: Marriage Rules." In *Report of Commissioners of Freedmen's Bureau.* 39th Cong., 1st sess., 1865–66, H. Exdoc. 70.
Letter from Commissioner of Pensions, 43d Cong., 1st sess., 1873, H. Misdoc. 221.
Preliminary and Final Reports of the American Freedmen's Inquiry Commission, 38th Cong., 1st sess., 1864, S. Exdoc. 53.

Reports of Assistant Commissioners of the Freedmen's Bureau, 39th Cong., 1st sess., 1865–66, S. Exdoc. 27.

Revised Statutes of the United States, 1873–1874. Washington, D.C., 1873–74.

Statutes at Large of the United States of America, 1789–1873. 17 vols. Washington, D.C., 1850–73.

United States Statutes at Large. Washington, D.C., 1874–.

PUBLISHED PRIMARY SOURCES

Baker, T. Lindsay, and Julie Baker, eds. *The WPA Oklahoma Slave Narratives.* Norman, Okla., 1996.

Benton's Abridgment of the Debates of Congress. Vol. 6. 1958; rept. New York, 1970.

Berlin, Ira, Barbara J. Fields, Thavolia Glymph, Joseph P. Reidy, and Leslie S. Rowland, eds. *Freedom: A Documentary History of Emancipation, 1861–1867*, ser. 1, vol. 1, *The Destruction of Slavery.* New York, 1985.

Berlin, Ira, Joseph P. Reidy, and Leslie S. Rowland, eds. *Freedom: A Documentary History of Emancipation, 1861–1867*, ser. 2, *The Black Military Experience.* Cambridge, 1982.

Berlin, Ira, et al., eds. *Free at Last: A Documentary History of Slavery, Freedom, and the Civil War.* New York, 1992.

Botume, Elizabeth Hyde. *First Days amongst the Contrabands.* 1893; rept. New York, 1963.

Brinckerhoff, Isaac W. *Advice to Freedmen* (1864–65?). In *Freedmen's Schools and Textbooks*, vol. 4, ed. Robert C. Morris. New York, 1980.

Brown, Helen E. *John Freeman and His Family* (1864). In *Freedmen's Schools and Textbooks*, vol. 5, ed. Robert C. Morris. New York, 1980.

Brown, William Wells. "Narrative of William Wells Brown, a Fugitive Slave." In *Four Fugitive Slave Narratives*, ed. Robin Winks. Reading, Mass., 1969.

Douglass, Frederick. *My Bondage and My Freedom.* 1855; rept. New York, 1969.

DuBois, W. E. B. *The Souls of Black Folk.* New York, 1989.

Fisk, Clinton B. *Plain Counsels for Freedmen* (1866). In *Freedmen's Schools and Textbooks*, vol. 5, ed. Robert C. Morris. New York, 1980.

Jacobs, Harriet. *Incidents in the Life of a Slave Girl Written by Herself.* 1866; rept., ed. Jean Fagan Yellin, Cambridge, Mass., 1987.

Pearson, Elizabeth Ware, ed. *Letters from Port Royal, 1862–1868.* 1906; rept. New York, 1969.

Rawick, George, ed. *The American Slave: A Composite Autobiography.* 41 vols., ser. 1, Supplement, ser. 1 and 2. Westport, Conn., 1972, 1978, 1979.

Towne, Laura M. *The Letters and Diary of Laura M. Towne.* 1912; rept., ed. Rupert S. Holland, New York, 1968.

Waterbury, Jared Bell. *Friendly Counsels for Freedmen* (1864–65?). In *Freedmen's Schools and Textbooks*, vol. 4, ed. Robert C. Morris. New York, 1980.

Wright, Richard. *Black Boy.* 1937; rept. New York, 1966.

SECONDARY SOURCES

Abramovitz, Mimi. *Regulating the Lives of Women: Welfare Policy from Colonial Times to the Present.* Boston, 1988.

Bardaglio, Peter W. *Reconstructing the Household: Families, Sex, and the Law in the Nineteenth-Century South.* Chapel Hill, N.C., 1995.

Bardaglio, Peter W., and Eileen Boris. "The Transformation of Patriarchy: The Historic Role of the State." In *Families, Politics, and Public Policy: A Feminist Dialogue on Women and the State,* ed. Irene Diamond, 70–93. New York, 1983.

Basch, Norma. *In the Eyes of the Law: Women, Marriage, and Property in Nineteenth-Century New York.* Ithaca, N.Y., 1982.

Benston, Kimberly W. "I Yam What I Am: Naming and Unnaming in Afro-American Literature." *Black American Literature Forum* 16 (Spring 1982): 3–11.

Berlin, Ira. *Slaves without Masters: The Free Negro of the Antebellum South.* Oxford, 1994.

Berlin, Ira, and Philip D. Morgan, eds. *The Slaves' Economy: Independent Production by Slaves in the Americas.* Portland, Oreg., 1991.

Berlin, Ira, Steven F. Miller, and Leslie Rowland. "Afro-American Families in the Transition from Slavery to Freedom." *Radical History Review* 42 (1988): 89–121.

Blankenhorn, David, and Mary Ann Glendon, eds. *Seedbeds of Virtue: Sources of Competence, Character, and Citizenship in American Society.* New York, 1995.

Blassingame, John. *The Slave Community: Plantation Life in the Antebellum South.* New York, 1972.

Bloch, Ruth. "The Gendered Meanings of Virtue in Revolutionary America." *Signs: Journal of Women in Culture and Society* 13:1 (Autumn 1987): 37–60.

Burnham, Margaret. "An Impossible Marriage: Slave Law and Family Law." *Law and Inequality* 5 (July 1987): 187–225.

Carson, Clayborne, et al. *The Eyes on the Prize Civil Rights Reader: Documents, Speeches, and Firsthand Accounts from the Black Freedom Struggle.* New York, 1991.

Clark, Homer J. *The Law of Domestic Relations in the United States.* St. Paul, 1988.

Clinton, Catherine. "Reconstructing Freedwomen." In *Divided Houses: Gender and the Civil War,* ed. Catherine Clinton and Nina Silber, 306–19. New York, 1992.

Cody, Cheryll Ann. "There Was No 'Absalom' on the Ball Plantations: Slave Naming Practices in the South Carolina Low Country, 1720–1865." *American Historical Review* 92:3 (June 1987): 563–96.

Cott, Nancy. *The Bonds of Womanhood: "Woman's Sphere" in New England, 1780–1835.* New Haven, 1977.

Davis, Natalie Zemon. *The Return of Martin Guerre.* Cambridge, Mass., 1983.

Davis, Samuel M., and Mortimer Schwartz. *Children's Rights and the Law.* Lexington, Mass., 1987.

Degler, Carl. *At Odds: Women and the Family in America from the Revolution to the Present.* New York, 1980.

Dill, Bonnie Thornton. "Our Mother's Grief: Racial and Ethnic Women and the Maintenance of Families." *Journal of Family History* 13:4 (1988): 415–31.

Edwards, Laura F. *Gendered Strife and Confusion: The Political Culture of Reconstruction.* Urbana, Ill., 1997.

Engs, Robert. *Freedom's First Generation: Black Hampton, Virginia, 1861–1890.* Philadelphia, 1979.

Everly, Elaine. "Marriage Registers of Freedmen." *Prologue* 5 (Fall 1973): 150–54.

Flaherty, David. "Law and the Enforcement of Morals in Early America." *Perspectives in American History* 5 (1971): 203–53.

Foner, Eric. *Reconstruction: America's Unfinished Revolution, 1863–1877.* New York, 1988.

Frankel, Noralee. *Freedom's Women: Black Women and Families in Civil War Era Mississippi.* Bloomington, Ind., 1999.

Genovese, Eugene. *Roll, Jordan, Roll: The World the Slaves Made.* New York, 1972.

Gettys, Luella. *The Law of Citizenship in the United States.* Chicago, 1934.

Glasson, William. *Federal Military Pensions in the United States.* New York, 1918.

Grossberg, Michael. *Governing the Hearth: Law and Family in Nineteenth-Century America.* Chapel Hill, N.C., 1985.

Gutman, Herbert. *The Black Family in Slavery and Freedom, 1750–1925.* New York, 1976.

Hareven, Tamara. "The History of Family and the Complexity of Social Change." *American Historical Review* 96 (Feb. 1991): 95–124.

Hartog, Hendrik. *Man and Wife in America: A History.* Cambridge, Mass., 2000.

Hodes, Martha. *White Women, Black Men: Illicit Sex in the Nineteenth-Century South.* New Haven, 1997.

Holmes, Amy E. "'Such Is the Price We Pay': American Widows and the Civil War Pension System." In *Towards a Social History of the Civil War: Exploratory Essays,* ed. Maris A. Vinovskis, 171–95. Cambridge, 1990.

Houlgate, Laurence. *The Child and the State: A Normative Theory of Juvenile Rights.* Baltimore, 1980.

Hunter, Tera W. *To 'Joy My Freedom: Southern Black Women's Lives and Labors after the Civil War.* Cambridge, Mass., 1997.

Inscoe, John C. "Generation and Gender as Reflected in Carolina Slave Naming Practices: A Challenge to the Gutman Thesis." *South Carolina Historical Magazine* 94 (Oct. 1993): 252–63.

James, Joseph B. *The Framing of the Fourteenth Amendment.* Urbana, Ill., 1956.

Jones, Jacqueline. *Labor of Love, Labor of Sorrow: Black Women, Work, and the Family from Slavery to the Present.* New York, 1985.

——. "The Political Economy of Sharecropping Families: Blacks and Poor Whites in the Rural South, 1865–1915." In *In Joy and In Sorrow,* ed. Carol Bleser, 196–214. New York, 1991.

——. *Soldiers of Light and Love: Northern Teachers and Georgia Blacks.* Chapel Hill, N.C., 1980.

Jordan, Winthrop. *White over Black: American Attitudes toward the Negro, 1550–1812.* Chapel Hill, N.C., 1968.

Kaczorowski, Robert J. "To Begin the Nation Anew: Congress, Citizenship, and Civil Rights after the Civil War." *American Historical Review* 92:1 (Feb. 1987): 45–68.

Kerber, Linda. *Women of the Republic: Intellect and Ideology in Revolutionary America.* Chapel Hill, N.C., 1980.

Lebsock, Suzanne. *The Free Women of Petersburg: Status and Culture in a Southern Town, 1784–1860.* New York, 1984.

Lemann, Nicholas. *The Promised Land: The Great Black Migration and How It Changed America.* New York, 1991.

Litwack, Leon. *Been in the Storm So Long: The Aftermath of Slavery.* New York, 1979.

———. *North of Slavery: The Negro in the Free States, 1790–1860.* Chicago, 1961.

Lively, Donald E. *The Constitution and Race.* New York, 1992.

Lyons, John D. *Exemplum: The Rhetoric of Example in Early Modern France and Italy.* Princeton, N.J., 1989.

Magdol, Edward. *A Right to the Land: Essays on the Freedmen's Community.* Westport, Conn., 1977.

Malone, Ann Patton. *Sweet Chariot: Slave Family and Household Structure in Nineteenth-Century Louisiana.* Chapel Hill, N.C., 1992.

McClintock, Anne. "'The Very House of Difference': Race, Gender, and the Politics of South African Women's Narrative in *Poppie Nongena.*" In *The Bounds of Race: Perspectives on Hegemony and Resistance,* ed. Dominick LaCapra, 196–230. Ithaca, N.Y., 1991.

McClintock, Megan J. "Civil War Pensions and the Reconstruction of Union Families." *Journal of American History* 83 (Sept. 1996): 456–80.

McDaniel, Antonio. "The Power of Culture: A Review of the Idea of Africa's Influence on Family Structure in Antebellum America." *Journal of Family History* 15:2 (1990): 225–38.

McFeely, William. *Yankee Stepfather: General O. O. Howard and the Freedmen.* New Haven, 1968.

McPherson, James. "The Negro: Innately Inferior or Equal?" In *Blacks in the Abolitionist Movement,* ed. John H. Bracey, August Meier, and Elliot Rudwick, 79–94. Belmont, Calif., 1971.

Mintz, Steven. "Regulating the American Family." *Journal of Family History* 14:4 (1989): 387–408.

Morgan, Edmund S. *American Slavery, American Freedom: The Ordeal of Colonial Virginia*. New York, 1975.

Nieman, Donald G. *To Set the Law in Motion: The Freedmen's Bureau and the Legal Rights of Blacks, 1865–1868*. New York, 1979.

Oubre, Claude. *Forty Acres and a Mule: The Freedmen's Bureau and Black Land Ownership*. Baton Rouge, La., 1978.

Penningroth Dylan. "Slavery, Freedom, and Social Claims to Property among African Americans in Liberty County, Georgia, 1850–1880." *Journal of American History* 84:2 (Sept. 1997): 405–35.

Reidy, Joseph. *From Slavery to Agrarian Capitalism in the Cotton Plantation South: Central Georgia, 1800–1880*. Chapel Hill, N.C., 1992.

Rose, Willie Lee. *Rehearsal for Reconstruction: The Port Royal Experiment*. New York, 1964.

Ryan, Mary. *Cradle of the Middle Class: The Family in Oneida County, New York*. New York, 1980.

Salmon, Marylynn. *Women and the Law of Property in Early America*. Chapel Hill, N.C., 1986.

Schwalm, Leslie A. *A Hard Fight for We: Women's Transition from Slavery to Freedom in South Carolina*. Urbana, Ill., 1997.

Schwartz, Marie Jenkins. *Born in Bondage: Growing Up Enslaved in the Antebellum South*. Cambridge, Mass., 2000.

Scott, Rebecca. "The Battle over the Child: Child Apprenticeship and the Freedmen's Bureau in North Carolina." *Prologue* 10 (Summer 1978): 101–13.

Shaffer, Donald R. "'I Do Not Suppose That Uncle Sam Looks at the Skin': African Americans and the Civil War Pension System, 1865–1934." *Civil War History* 46 (June 2000): 132–47.

——. "Marching On: African-American Civil War Veterans in Postbellum America, 1865–1951." Ph.D. diss., University of Maryland, 1996.

Shklar, Judith. *American Citizenship: The Quest for Inclusion*. Cambridge, Mass., 1991.

Skocpol, Theda. *Protecting Soldiers and Mothers: The Political Origins of Social Policy in the United States*. Cambridge, Mass., 1992.

Smith, Daniel Scott, and Michael Hindus. "Premarital Pregnancy in

America, 1640–1971: An Overview and Interpretation." *Journal of Interdisciplinary History* 4 (Spring 1975): 530–70.

Sobel, Mechal. *The World They Made Together: Black and White Values in Eighteenth-Century Virginia.* Princeton, N.J., 1987.

Spender, Dale. *Man Made Language.* London, 1980.

Stack, Carol. *All Our Kin: Strategies for Survival in a Black Community.* New York, 1974.

Stanley, Amy Dru. "Conjugal Bonds and Wage Labor: Rights of Contract in the Age of Emancipation." *Journal of American History* 75 (Sept. 1988): 471–500.

Stein, Stuart J. "Common-Law Marriage: Its History and Certain Contemporary Problems." *Journal of Family Law* 9 (1969): 271–99.

Stevenson, Brenda E. "Distress and Discord in Virginia Slave Families, 1830–1860." In *In Joy and In Sorrow: Women, Family, and Marriage in the Victorian South, 1830–1900,* ed. Carol Bleser, 103–24. New York, 1991.

———. *Life in Black and White: Family and Community in the Slave South.* New York, 1996.

Thornton, John. "Central African Names and African-American Naming Patterns." *William and Mary Quarterly,* 3d ser., 50:4 (Oct. 1993): 727–42.

Tushnet, Mark. *The American Law of Slavery, 1810–1860: Considerations of Humanity and Interest.* Princeton, N.J., 1981.

Vernier, Chester. *American Family Laws: A Comparative Study of the Forty-Eight American States, Alaska, the District of Columbia, and Hawaii (to January 1, 1935),* vol. 4, *Parent and Child.* Stanford, Calif., 1936.

Vinovskis, Maris A. "Have Social Historians Lost the Civil War? Some Preliminary Demographic Speculations." In *Towards a Social History of the American Civil War: Exploratory Essays,* ed. Maris A. Vinovskis, 1–30. Cambridge, 1990.

Washington, Reginald. "The Freedmen's Savings and Trust Company and African American Genealogical Research." *Prologue* 29:2 (Summer 1997): 170–81.

Weber, Gustavus A. *The Bureau of Pensions: Its History, Activities, and Organizations.* Baltimore, 1923.

Wells, Robert V. "Illegitimacy and Bridal Pregnancy in Colonial America." In *Bastardy and Its Comparative History,* ed. Peter

Laslett, Karla Oversteen, and Richard M. Smith, 349–61. Cambridge, Mass., 1980.

Welter, Barbara. "The Cult of True Womanhood." *American Quarterly* 18 (Summer 1966): 131–75.

White, Deborah Gray. *Ar'n't I a Woman? Female Slaves in the Plantation South.* New York, 1985.

Williamson, Joel. *After Slavery: The Negro in South Carolina during Reconstruction, 1861–1877.* Chapel Hill, N.C., 1965.

Wood, Gordon. *The Creation of the American Republic, 1776–1787.* New York, 1969.

Wood, Peter H. *Black Majority: Negroes in Colonial South Carolina from 1670 through the Stono Rebellion.* New York, 1974.

Index

Index

Index

Taylor, Martha, 157–58

Taylor, Walter, 158

Testimony: assessing credibility of, 47–51; fraudulent, 34, 35–36; oral type of, 39–40; preference for whites', 40, 41, 42–44, 46, 88–89, 110, 195n.55; self-interest in, 32–33

Thirteenth Amendment, 4–6

Three-fifths compromise, 5–6

Tilh, Arnaud Du (character), 123–24, 126–27

Timmons, Abraham, 97–100, 205n.55

Timmons, Alice: age book of, 46; claim denied for, 96, 99–100, 114; familial support for, 171; identity of, 101; testimony for, 97–98

Timmons, Jane, 97–101

Timmons, Priscilla, 46, 97, 98, 205n.59

Timmons, Sally, 205n.55

Timmons, William: age book of, 46; claim denied for, 96, 99–100, 114; familial support for, 171; identity of, 101; testimony for, 97–98

Tracy, J. M., 79, 80

Trell, Ellen, 75

Turner, L., 48–49

Twine, Anderson, 60–62, 66

Twine, Lucinda, 60–62

Tyler, Eliza, 171

Uniforms, as symbols of citizenship, 8

Union army: assistance from, 26, 191n.10; black soldiers in, 19, 190nn.37–38; impact on slaves, 24–26; notifications of death from, 30–31. *See also* United States Colored Troops (USCT)

United States Colored Troops (USCT): bounty for enlisting in, 27–28; citi-

zenship based on service in, 7–8; members of, 23, 26; names used in, 179–80; pension claims based on service in, 3; recruiters for, 25; southern units of, 20–21

Van Buren, Amanda, 111–13

Van Buren, Martin, 111

Virginia: marriages between slave and free people in, 169; proslavery republicans in, 2–3

Virtue: family as source of, 9; marriage as source of, 82; in republicanism, 1, 187n.3

Voting rights, 5–7

Walston, Samuel I., 87

Walters, Rachel, 50, 91

Ware, Harriet, 89–90, 204n.35

Washington, George, 91, 101

Washington, Hagar, 30–31, 49, 91, 101

Wells, Robert V., 122

West Africa: childrearing in, 118; kinship traditions in, 130

White, Deborah Gray: on mother-child bond, 117, 118, 208n.11; on mother's role, 140; on sexuality, 99, 201n.62; on subsistence, 153

White, John, 66–67, 75

White, Julia, 146–47

White, L. B., 70

White, Nancy: character of, 45–46; events dated by, 41–42; family name of, 75–76

White, Starkey, 42

Whites: attitudes toward African-American families, 10–11, 118–19; attitudes toward slaves and slavery, 30, 41–47, 201–2n.7; establishing de-

DATE DUE